Edexcel A2 English Literature

Mike Royston   Jackie Moore

STUDENT BOOK

Consultants: Jen Greatrex   Peter Druée   Richard Hoyes

D0543186

Skills Coverage Map

Skill/specification coverage	UNIT 3	UNIT 4
Analysing unprepared poetry	6-21, 41-54	
Identifying and comparing themes	8-9, 67-86, 101-104	
Understanding choice of vocabulary (diction)	10-11	
Understanding imagery	12-13	
Understanding structure	14-17, 36-37	
Understanding and comparing form and genre	17-19, 67-86, 104-106	
Identifying voice and register	19-20, 35-36, 43-45	
Analysing unprepared prose	21-40, 41-54	
Responding to setting	26-29	
Analysing characterisation	30-32	
Identifying point of view	33-34	
Understanding irony	38-40	
Using comparison	47-49	
Writing creatively to aid reading skills	50-51	
Practising writing exam answers	54-65, 113-125	
Choosing combinations of texts	65-66	
Writing a comparative analysis of texts	84-86	
Understanding and comparing historical, social, literary, cultural contexts of texts	88-100, 107-109	150
Comparing interpretations and evaluations of texts	101-112	
Choosing your texts, topic and approach		128-137, 147-155
Planning your coursework		138-139, 156-157
Developing research skills		140-145
Understanding critical approaches to texts		150-152
Writing your study or studies		156-164
Writing your creative response		165-171
Writing your commentary		172-174
Revising and editing		175-179

Contents

GCE A2 English Literature: Introduction

Welcome to English Literature at Advanced level. In your AS year, you will have studied a variety of poetry, prose and drama texts.

Now you will explore new poetry and prose fiction, including post-1990, reacting to them in new ways and approaching them from different literary perspectives and you will be able to develop a study of texts that interest and engage you. These can be poetry, prose or drama.

How can I make English Literature most rewarding ?

- Enjoy reading – even when the text may seem unfamiliar and strange. The more you stick with it, the more you will learn and be able to say about it.
- Try to read more widely than just the texts for the course – if you find a poet or a playwright or a writer whose work interests you then search out something else written by that person. Look them up on websites or in sound archives too.
- Find out what other people, including the writers themselves, have said about the texts you are studying.
- Practise writing about your texts. During the course you will need to do this sometimes concisely by providing short answer responses, sometimes in essays and sometimes creatively.

What texts will I explore?

Unit 3 – Interpretations of prose and poetry In Section A, you will sample unprepared poetry or prose fiction from any period in preparation for the exam. You will learn to show how structure, form and language create meaning, and to articulate a personal evaluation of the text.

In Section B, you will study up to three prescribed texts from one of four topic groups: 'Relationships', 'Identifying Self', 'Journeys' and 'War'. You will learn to compare texts, both poetry and prose fiction (including post-1990 texts), and explore links in genre, period, context and in literary interpretation.

Unit 4 – Reflections in literary studies Unit 4 is the coursework unit and builds on and extends your studies and reading from AS units. In this unit you will carry out your own independent research and reading around your chosen three texts, leading to one or two literary studies or a creative response with commentary.

How will I be assessed?

Unit 3 is assessed by an external exam. Unit 4 is assessed by coursework.

Unit 3:

In Unit 3 you will be assessed by a 2 hour and 45 minute exam. You will be asked to:

- analyse an unprepared poetry or prose fiction text
- write a comparative analysis of your chosen texts/topic group.

Unit 4:

In Unit 4 you will complete one or two literary studies, or a creative response with commentary, of 2500-3000 words.

How to use this book

This **Student Book** is divided into **Unit 3** and **Unit 4**:

- Unit 3 supports your work for the A2 exam.
- Unit 4 supports your work for the A2 coursework.

The **Teaching and Assessment CD-ROM** provides additional support for both units. It can be used alongside this book.

Unit 3 Interpretations of prose and poetry: an outline

Unit 3 in this **Student Book** is divided into two sections, reflecting the two sections of the exam. They are:

Section A: Unprepared poetry or prose (pages 6-64).

Section A covers the skills and knowledge required for Section A of the exam, preparing you to write an analysis of one unprepared poem OR piece of prose fiction.

Section B: Paired texts (pages 65-125).

Section B covers the skills and knowledge required for Section B of the exam, preparing you to write an essay comparing two or three prescribed texts from the genres of poetry and prose fiction, at least one of which has been published after 1990.

Unit 4 Reflections in literary studies: an outline

Unit 4 in this Student Book focuses on your coursework. It is divided into five main sections.

Sections A and B (pages 128-155). These sections will help you to choose your topic based on your central text, to make connections with other texts and to decide on your approach, and to start planning and researching your writing.

Sections C and D (pages 156-174). These sections will help you to prepare for either the literary studies (Section C) or the creative response and commentary (Section D), guiding you through from the planning stage to producing your first draft.

Section E (pages175-179). This section will help you to edit and revise your first draft and to present the final piece with an accurate use of technical detail.

- The Unit 3 exam is 2 hours and 45 minutes.
- In **Section A** of the exam you will choose to answer an essay question on EITHER an unprepared poem OR an unprepared prose extract.
- In **Section B** of the exam you will write a sustained essay on at least two of the texts you have studied.

You will hand in EITHER one extended study OR two shorter studies OR one piece of creative writing plus your commentary on it: a 'creative response.' The coursework folder must be 2500-3000 words.

Unit 3: Interpretations of prose and poetry

What you will do in the course

In Unit 3 of Edexcel A2 English Literature, you will:

- read a selection of poetry and prose fiction from the fourteenth century to the present day
- analyse previously unseen poetry and/or prose
- compare three texts chosen from a range of poetry collections and novels, at least one of which will be published after 1990
- relate texts to the contexts in which they were produced or to which they refer
- interpret texts in the light of other readers' interpretations.

How you will be examined

There is one exam of 2 hours 45 minutes. There are two questions. You will be asked to:

- analyse an unprepared (unseen) poem OR prose fiction passage in Section A
- write an essay comparing at least two prescribed texts in Section B.

Examiners use four Assessment objectives (AOs) to mark your answers.

	Assessment objective	What this means in practice
AO1	Articulate creative, informed and relevant responses to literary texts, using appropriate terminology and concepts, and coherent, accurate written expression	You should use: • ideas from literary study • suitable literary terms • a clear and fluent style.
AO2	Demonstrate detailed critical understanding in analysing the ways in which structure, form and language shape meanings in literary texts	You should show understanding of: • how language conveys meaning • how form and structure convey meaning • how language, form and structure combine to convey meaning.
AO3	Explore connections and comparisons between different literary texts, informed by interpretations of other readers	You should show awareness of: • how texts compare and contrast • how texts can be interpreted differently.
AO4	Demonstrate understanding of the significance and influence of the contexts in which texts are written and received	You should show awareness of: • the historical, social and literary background of texts • how context shapes meaning in texts • how readers find meaning in texts.

You will also need to show that you have developed the skills you acquired at AS. The evidence of this will be:

- your ability to choose your own focus for unprepared analysis
- your ability to compare texts in a variety of ways
- your ability to interpret texts as a modern reader, in an independent way
- the use you make of wide reading.

Section A: Unprepared poetry or prose

In Section A you will read and analyse a range of poetry and prose fiction. There are no prescribed texts. You need to look at writing from different periods.

For the Section A exam, you will use the same skills of literary analysis as you did at AS to comment on unprepared poetry or prose. However, at A2 you are expected to take this further by:

- making your own decisions about what to comment on in the text
- evaluating the writer's techniques, and giving your opinion about their effectiveness
- writing your response in essay form.

Section B: Paired texts

In Section B you will study three texts chosen from a topic group: 'Relationships' OR 'Identifying Self' OR 'Journeys' OR 'War'. These texts will be a combination of novels and poetry. The choice is wide, allowing you to compare texts written in different periods.

For the Section B exam, you need to:

- respond to texts in the light of a reader's comment or 'proposition'
- find suitable ways of comparing at least two of your chosen texts
- show how the context of your chosen texts influences the way they are written
- show how other readers interpret, or might interpret, your chosen texts
- give a personal interpretation of your chosen texts as a modern reader in a modern context.

How this book will help you

The activities for Section A of this unit are designed to help you in three main ways. They will:

- develop further what you learned at AS about how to analyse unprepared poetry and prose
- build up your skills in a step-by-step way, so that you can return to some aspects of literary analysis you may feel less confident about, and move on to others when you are ready
- support you in taking an independent approach to analysing unprepared texts.

The activities for Section B of this unit are designed to help you in three main ways. They will:

- develop further what you learned at AS about how to make comparisons between texts
- show you how to understand context, and explain how it influences writers
- support you in making a personal interpretation of texts as a twenty-first-century reader.

How to succeed in Unit 3

You can achieve a high mark for this unit by:

- developing the confidence to interpret texts yourself
- developing the confidence to judge the effectiveness of texts yourself
- reading a wide range of prose fiction, poetry, and literary criticism; the more you read and research, the better your exam performance is likely to be.

A Unprepared poetry or prose

This section covers the skills you need to analyse unprepared poetry or prose. It builds up these skills in a systematic way, using poems and prose fiction extracts from different periods. You will benefit from working through the activities in Part 1 (poetry) and Part 2 (prose) in order, though they are also self-contained so that you can dip in and practise aspects of analysis you may need to improve.

Assessment objectives

Examiners use two assessment objectives for Section A. They are:

A01: (10 marks) Articulate creative, informed and relevant responses to literary texts, using appropriate terminology and concepts, and coherent, accurate written expression

A02: (30 marks) Demonstrate detailed critical understanding in analysing the ways in which structure, form and language shape meaning in literary texts.

1 Analysing unprepared poetry

Part 1 shows you how to:

- respond to a poem that is new to you
- distinguish between a poem's **subject matter** and **theme**
- comment on a poem's **diction** and **imagery**
- comment on a poem's **form** and **structure**.

This part reinforces and develops what you learned in Section A of Unit 1. At A2, you will need to apply your analytical skills in more detail and respond at greater length. You will also be expected to give personal interpretations of poems and a judgement about their effectiveness.

Giving a first response: What meaning can I find here?

When faced with a poem that is new to you, your first step is to decide on the meaning being made. This sounds obvious, but remember that 'meaning' is not something that belongs only to the poet. It depends on your own *interpretation* of the words on the page as well as how the poet presents them. As a reader, you help to create the meaning of a poem by the way you read and respond to it. Activity 1 demonstrates this process at work.

Activity 1

1 Read the two poems below aloud. Work with a partner. Partner A should read 'Intimates'. Partner B should read 'Les Grands Seigneurs'.

Intimates

Don't you care for my love? she said bitterly.

I handed her the mirror, and said:
Please address these questions to the proper person!
Please make all requests to head-quarters!
5 In all matters of emotional importance
please approach the supreme authority direct! –
So I handed her the mirror.

And she would have broken it over my head,
but she caught sight of her own reflection
10 and that held her spellbound for two seconds
while I fled.

D.H. Lawrence

Les Grands Seigneurs

Men were my buttresses, my castellated towers,
the bowers where I took my rest. The best and worst
of times were men: the peacocks and the cockatoos,
the nightingales, the strutting pink flamingoes.

5 Men were my dolphins, my performing seals; my sailing-ships,
the ballast in my hold. They were the rocking-horses
prancing down the promenade, the bandstand
where the music played. My hurdy-gurdy monkey-men.

I was their queen. I sat enthroned before them.
10 out of reach. We played at courtly love:
the troubadour, the damsel and the peach.

But after I was wedded, bedded, I became
(yes, overnight) a toy, a plaything, little woman,
wife, a bit of fluff. My husband clicked
15 his fingers, called my bluff.

Dorothy Molloy

Key terms

- subject matter
- theme
- diction
- imagery
- form
- structure
- direct speech
- tone
- metaphor

2 Partner A should take on the role of the speaker in 'Intimates'. Explain what you are saying about (a) women and (b) relations between the sexes. Partner B should take on the role of the speaker in 'Les Grands Seigneurs'. Explain what you are saying about (a) men and (b) courtship and marriage. Your partner can prompt you with questions.

3 Come out of role. Consider as a class the views about male–female relationships expressed in these poems. Explain and justify any differences of interpretation by referring to:

- D.H. Lawrence's use of **direct speech** and the **tone** of the male speaker
- the title and the last stanza of 'Intimates'
- Dorothy Molloy's use of **metaphor**, and the tone of the speaker
- the title and the last stanza of 'Les Grands Seigneurs'.

4 Did you find one of these poems easier to interpret than the other? If so, talk about why. Then say which of them you prefer. How do *you* judge the success of a poem?

Writing in the exam

You will be given one unprepared poem to analyse. Your focus will be on how the poet uses structure, form and language to shape meaning.
You will not be given the short 'prompt' questions that were provided in the exam for Section A of Unit 1. You need, therefore, to make your own decisions about what to comment on.

Key terms

- perspective (point of view)
- persona

Giving a considered response: How do the style and language work?

Once you feel familiar with a new poem and comfortable with your interpretation of it, build on your first response by considering its style and language. Style is not an aspect of poetry that is separate from meaning. Poets create meaning by the choices they make of language, form and structure.

Activity 2 asks you to demonstrate this process at work. It acts as an introduction to commenting on style in poetry.

Activity 2

Across AS and A2

The work you did on poetry analysis in Unit 1 provides an essential platform for Section A. The relevant parts of the AS Student Book are 'Exploring Poetry', pages 7–48, and 'Unseen Poetry', pages 80–85. Remind yourself of the basic concepts involved in analysing poems, and the literary terms used. The activities in this part assume that your understanding of these terms is secure. Whenever you find this is not the case, check your work at AS.

1 Read the poem opposite aloud. It was written during the First World War.

2 Make a first response to this poem in a small group. Discuss what you think Sassoon is saying about the part played in war by (a) commanding officers, and (b) ordinary soldiers.

3 Share your ideas in a class discussion. Then explore how Sassoon's choices of language shape your response to the 'Majors at the Base'.

Consider:
- the adjectives and verbs used to describe them: 'fierce', 'scarlet', 'puffy', 'petulant', 'Guzzling', 'gulping', 'toddle'
- the tone of voice given to the Major in lines 6 to 8
- the shift in **perspective** (or **point of view**) in lines 9 and 10.

The poem conveys strong feeling. Say how effectively you think it does so, and why.

4 Write a short analysis of the way Sassoon's choices of language create meaning in 'Base Details'. Use the ideas you discussed in question 3 above.

Base Details

If I were fierce, and bald, and short of breath,
   I'd live with scarlet Majors at the Base,
And speed glum heroes up the line to death.
   You'd see me with my puffy petulant face,
Guzzling and gulping in the best hotel,
   Reading the Roll of Honour. 'Poor young chap,'
I'd say – 'I used to know his father well;
   Yes, we've lost heavily in this last scrap.'
And when the war is done and youth stone dead,
I'd toddle safely home and die – in bed.

Siegfried Sassoon

Identifying themes in a poem: What ideas is the poet exploring?

In making an analysis of a poem that is new to you, you need to be clear about its theme or themes. Bear in mind that theme is not the same as subject matter. A poem's *subject matter* is what it describes. Its *themes* are the ideas that are explored through the subject matter. Activities 3 and 4 demonstrate the difference.

Activity 3

Complete a copy of the table below. It distinguishes between subject matter and themes in Sassoon's 'Base Details'.

Subject matter	Themes
Describes officers behind the lines in the First World War enjoying a comfortable lifestyle.	Shows how officers in the First World War are shamefully out of touch with the reality of fighting at the front.

Make two further entries. Then compare your table with a partner's.

Activity 4

1 Read the poem below aloud. In it, the poet creates a **persona** (an imagined person), Mrs Aesop. She is describing life with her husband, a famous author from ancient Greece who wrote fables and proverbs. The poem refers to several of these – for example, 'A bird in the hand is worth two in the bush', 'Look before you leap', 'The Tortoise and the Hare'.

2 Give a first response to this poem in a small group. Discuss what issues you think Duffy is raising through the persona of Mrs Aesop about (a) men, (b) marriage and (c) literature and life.

3 Identify as many references to proverbs and fables in the poem as you can. Then explain how Duffy builds them into Mrs Aesop's narrative. Can you see a serious point to them, or do you think Duffy is just showing off her ingenuity for comic effect?

4 Working with a partner, create a table like the one in Activity 3 to identify the subject matter and themes.

5 Compare your tables in a class discussion. If there are disagreements, try to resolve them by looking back to the definitions of theme and subject matter above. Then write your own definitions to refer to in future work on poetry. Include examples from 'Base Details' and 'Mrs Aesop'.

Mrs Aesop

By Christ, he could bore for Purgatory. He was small,
didn't prepossess. So he tried to impress. *Dead men,
Mrs Aesop*, he'd say, *tell no tales*. Well, let me tell you now
that the bird in his hand shat on his sleeve,
never mind the two worth less in the bush. Tedious.

Going out was worst. He'd stand at our gate, look, then leap;
scour the hedgerows for a shy mouse, the fields
for a sly fox, the sky for one particular swallow
that couldn't make a summer. The jackdaw, according to him,
envied the eagle. Donkeys would, on the whole, prefer to be lions.

On one appalling evening stroll, we passed an old hare
snoozing in a ditch – he stopped and made a note –
and then, about a mile further on, a tortoise, somebody's pet,
creeping, slow as marriage, up the road. *Slow
but certain, Mrs Aesop, wins the race*. Asshole.

What race? What sour grapes? What silk purse,
sow's ear, dog in a manger, what big fish? Some days
I could barely keep awake as the story droned on
towards the moral of itself. *Action, Mrs A., speaks louder
than words*. And that's another thing, the sex

was diabolical. I gave him a fable one night
about a little cock that wouldn't crow, a razor-sharp axe
with a heart blacker than the pot that called the kettle.
I'll cut off your tail, all right, I said, *to save my face*.
That shut him up. I laughed last, longest.

Carol Ann Duffy

Writing in the exam

Begin your analysis by giving your initial response to the poem's meaning. You could begin by writing: 'The main theme seems to be…', or 'The poet focuses on X, which suggests that…'. This part of your analysis may sound exploratory, which is fine. Remember the crucial difference between theme and subject matter: you get no credit for giving only a paraphrase.

Vocabulary or diction in poems: Why this word rather than that?

A poet starts with a blank page. Before the poem is finished, large numbers of potential words will have been tried out, rejected and replaced by others that say, as exactly as possible, what the poet wants to say. Activity 5 asks you to explore this process at work.

Activity 5

1 Read the extract below aloud. It is from a poem by Ted Hughes.

> ### The Horses
>
> I climbed through woods in the hour-before-dawn dark.
> Evil air, a frost-making stillness,
>
> Not a leaf, not a bird, –
> A world cast in frost. I came out above the wood
>
> 5 Where my breath left tortuous statues in the iron light.
> But the valleys were draining the darkness
>
> Till the moorline – blackening dregs of the brightening grey –
> Halved the sky ahead. And I saw the horses:
>
> Huge in the dense grey – ten together –
> 10 Megalith-still. They breathed, making no move,
>
> With draped manes and tilted hind-hooves,
> Making no sound.
>
> I passed: not one snorted or jerked its head.
> Grey silent fragments
>
> 15 Of a grey silent world.

2 Look closely at lines 1 to 5 with a partner. Use words from the list below to replace Ted Hughes' choices at appropriate points:
   • end-of-night   • clammy   • wrapped   • vaporous   • zinc-coloured.

3 What differences to meaning have you made? Be precise about this; for example, if you replaced 'iron' with 'zinc-coloured', compare and contrast the sense impressions created by the two adjectives.

4 Now do a similar exercise on lines 6 to 15. Choose five of Hughes' words to replace with ones of your own. Then join up with another pair. Compare your choices and explain the difference to meaning you have made.

5 Draw on your work in questions 2 to 4 above to consider as a class Hughes' choices of diction in this extract. What impressions do they give of his climb through the woods and his first sight of the horses? Which of the descriptions do you find most effective in creating atmosphere?

6 Read the rest of 'The Horses', below.

> I listened in emptiness on the moor-ridge.
> The curlew's tear turned its edge on the silence.
>
> Slowly detail leafed from the darkness. Then the sun
> Orange, red, red erupted
>
> 20 Silently, and splitting to its core tore and flung cloud,
> Shook the gulf open, showed blue,
>
> And the big planets hanging –
> I turned
>
> Stumbling in the fever of a dream, down towards
> 25 The dark woods, from the kindling tops,
>
> And came to the horses.
>   There, still, they stood,
> But now steaming and glistening under the flow of light,
>
> Their draped stone manes, their tilted hind-hooves
> 30 Stirring under a thaw while all around them
>
> The frost showed its fires. But still they made no sound.
> Not one snorted or stamped,
>
> Their hung heads patient as the horizons,
> High over valleys, in the red levelling rays –
>
> 35 In din of the crowded streets, going among the years, the faces,
> May I still meet my memory in so lonely a place
>
> Between the streams and the red clouds, hearing curlews,
> Hearing the horizons endure.
>
> *Ted Hughes*

Key terms

- **rhythms**
- **consonance**
- **assonance**
- **connotation**

Take it further

Extend your analysis of 'The Horses' to include comment on Hughes' use of line length, stanza forms, varied **rhythms**, **consonance** and **assonance** to create and convey meaning. Then evaluate the effectiveness of these stylistic devices in the poem as a whole.

a Explore as a class Hughes's themes in this poem.
Remind yourself, if necessary, of the difference between theme and subject matter by looking back to Activity 4.

b Look carefully at the following parts of the poem:
- 'Shook the gulf open, showed blue, / And the big planets hanging' (lines 21–22)
- 'Their hung heads patient as the horizons, / High over valleys' (lines 33–34)
- 'May I still meet my memory in so lonely a place / Between the streams and the red clouds, hearing curlews / Hearing the horizons endure' (lines 36–38)
Relate Hughes's diction here to his themes as you now understand them.

c Write a short analysis of the way in which Hughes's choices of diction create meaning in 'The Horses'. Include comments on how the **connotations** and the sounds of words help to convey the poem's themes.

Imagery in poems: How does it work?

Imagery is the use of descriptive language to compare one thing with another. Metaphor, *simile* and *personification* are stylistic devices that poets use freely to create and convey their themes. It is sometimes said that imagery simply decorates or adds colour to a poet's ideas, but this is too narrow. At advanced level you need to think of imagery as a fundamental part of meaning because it expresses the way the poet sees the world. Activities 6 and 7 ask you to explore how poets use imagery.

Key terms

- simile
- personification
- extended metaphor
- rhyming couplets
- sibilance
- enjambement

Activity 6

1 Read the poem opposite aloud. It was first printed in 1612.

2 Working in a small group, copy and complete the table below to trace Raleigh's **extended metaphor** comparing human life with an Elizabethan play. Aim for five or six entries.

On the Life of Man

WHAT is our life? a play of passion,
Our mirth the music of division*,
Our mothers' wombs the tiring houses* be,
Where we are dressed for this short comedy.
Heaven the judicious sharp* spectator is
That sits and marks who still doth act amiss,
Our graves that hide us from the searching sun,
Are like drawn curtains when the play is done,
Thus march we playing to our latest rest,
Only we die in earnest, that's no jest.

Walter Raleigh

* division: a brief interval between the acts
  of a play, with musical entertainment
* tiring houses: dressing rooms
* sharp: discerning

Aspect of the 'play' metaphor	Raleigh's 'Life of Man' theme
'this short comedy'	Human life is fleeting – and a 'comedy' because (perhaps) it ends happily in heaven

3 Compare your finished tables in a class discussion. How effective do you find Raleigh's use of imagery? Are there some aspects of his extended metaphor that you think work better than others? Explain your judgements.

4 Choose your own extended metaphor for a poem entitled 'On the Life of Twenty-First Century Man'. In a small group or with a partner, develop this along the lines of Raleigh's poem and to a similar length. Decide whether to use **rhyming couplets** or a different form.

5 Read some of the completed poems aloud in class. Comment on their effectiveness, making sure you give clear reasons for your judgements.

Across AS and A2

As you work through these activities, refer back to your work in Unit 1 on how poets use imagery. The AS Student Book has relevant material on pages 34–37 and 81–83 about the use of simile, metaphor and personification. It reminds you that the effect of these can be very different from poem to poem, and that you need to comment on these features beyond the level of merely pointing them out.

Activity 7

1 Read the poem opposite aloud.

2 Consider as a class the way Sylvia Plath creates and conveys her ideas about words by using images related to:
   - tree-felling
   - horses
   - water
   - a skull
   - stars.

3 The imagery in this poem is highly compressed: one image merges into another and expands the meaning. Look for two examples of this. Then discuss whether you find this technique effective in a poem about language – or whether you find the imagery *too* rich and elaborate.

4 Read the extract below aloud. Its title refers to a farm where the poet spent happy times as a child.

a Identify and comment on Thomas' use of imagery to describe:
   - the farmhouse
   - time
   - himself
   - dusk

   Some of these images are highly original. Choose three that you think fall into this category. Explain to a partner why you find them effective or ineffective.

b Imagery in a poem does not do its work alone. Its effects are supported by the poet's use of other devices, in this case principally the *sound* and the *rhythm* of the verse. With your partner, find examples of Thomas' use of
   - assonance
   - a lively, energetic rhythm
   - *sibilance*
   - *enjambement* to create a fluid, fast-moving rhythm.

   Relate these to the meaning and effect of the stanza.

5 Write a short analysis of the use of imagery in EITHER 'Words' OR the extract from 'Fern Hill'. Make sure that you relate your comments to the themes of the poem as you understand them.

Words

Axes
After whose stroke the wood rings,
And the echoes!
Echoes traveling
Off from the centre like horses.   5

The sap
Wells like tears, like the
Water striving
To re-establish its mirror
Over the rock   10

That drops and turns,
A white skull,
Eaten by weedy greens.
Years later I
Encounter them on the road –   15

Words dry and riderless,
The indefatigable hoof-taps.
While
From the bottom of the pool, fixed stars
Govern a life.   20

Sylvia Plath

From 'Fern Hill'

Now as I was young and easy under the apple boughs
About the lilting house and happy as the grass was green,
    The night above the dingle* starry,
        Time let me hail and climb
    Golden in the heydays of his eyes,   5
And honoured among wagons I was prince of the apple towns
And once below a time I lordly had the trees and leaves
        Trail with daisies and barley
Down the rivers of the windfall light.

Dylan Thomas

* dingle: a wooded hollow

Independent research

Sample poems from the following volumes: Selected Poems of *D.H. Lawrence* (Penguin), *Selected Poems of Carol Ann Duffy* (Penguin), *Collected Poems of Ted Hughes* (Faber), *Collected Poems of Sylvia Path* (Faber), *Collected Poems of Philip Larkin* (Faber). Choose poems that relate to your chosen topic area for Section B of this unit. Compile a personal anthology and use the poems to illuminate your study of your prescribed poetry and/or prose texts.

Take it further

Write an analysis of Raleigh's poem 'On the Life of Man' (page 12). Comment on the way the poem's form and structure help to convey themes created through the imagery.

Writing in the exam

When commenting on imagery, take care not only to explain what it means but also to relate its use to the poet's treatment of the subject matter. Look for dominant images in the poem, patterns of imagery, and the use of extended metaphor. Explain their *effect* on you as a reader, and say whether you find them effective.

The structure of poems:
Why is the poem built in this way?

The structure of a poem is the way it is built. A poet chooses to arrange the words in a certain order, and decides how (or whether) to form them into stanzas. Taken together, the word patterns, line arrangement and stanzas make up the poem's structure. The poet's craft lies in using this structure to give shape to the ideas he or she wants to convey.

In Activities 8 and 9 you will explore ways in which the structure of a poem is an integral part of its meaning. Bear in mind that the structural elements of a poem will be closely related to its form, or genre: see pages 17–18 below.

Activity 8

1 Read the poem opposite aloud.

2 Discuss with a partner the way Williams constructs this poem. It does not rhyme. It has two full stops. It has two commas. Can you see any reason why he has arranged the poem into five stanzas, each with four lines?

3 Write out the words as if they were a paragraph of prose from a short story or a novel. Read this aloud. Does it sound different from the poem? If so, why? Share your ideas in a class discussion. Decide whether the structure Williams has chosen makes 'The Horse' into a poem, or whether it is just chopped-up prose.

4 Read the poem below aloud. The poet is reflecting on the materialism of modern society.

The Horse

The horse moves
independently
without reference
to his load

5 He has eyes
like a woman and
turns them
about, throws

back his ears
10 and is generally
conscious of
the world. Yet

he pulls when
he must and
15 pulls well, blowing
fog from

his nostrils
like fumes from
the twin
20 exhausts of a car.

William Carlos Williams

Jigsaws II

Property! Property! Let us extend
Soul and body without end:
A box to live in, with airs and graces,
A box on wheels that shows its paces,
5 A box that talks or that makes faces,
And curtains and fences as good as the neighbours'
To keep out the neighbours and keep us immured*
Enjoying the cold canned fruit of our labours
In a sterilised cell, unshared, insured.

10 Property! Property! When will it end?
When will the Poltergeist ascend
Out of the sewer with chopper and squib*
To burn the mink and the baby's bib
And cut the tattling wire* to town
15 And smash all the plastics, clowning and clouting,
And stop all the boxes shouting and pouting
And wreck the house from the aerial down
And give these ingrown souls an outing?

Louis MacNeice

* immured: walled in, fortified
* squib: firework
* tattling wire: phone line, for idle gossip

a Give a first response to this poem in a small group. Discuss what you think the speaker is saying about (a) society's obsession with 'property', (b) material values, and (c) the future of consumerism.

b Look at the speaker's choices of diction and imagery. Comment on the way he describes:
• houses and cars • work
• the telephone • people's souls.

What do you think the poet uses 'the Poltergeist' to represent?

c Now relate your interpretation of the poem to its structure. Find textual evidence to support the following statements about how it is built up and shaped.

A The two stanzas are meant to contrast: this is the controlling structural feature of the poem.

B The poet arranges the lines in stanza 1 in a list: this reflects his view that materialism is purposeless and sterile.

C The verbs in stanza 2 are carefully placed to form a pattern: they suggest violence, reflecting the poet's wish to see materialism destroyed.

D The poem's structure reflects its title: in stanza 1 the poet assembles the pieces of a jigsaw depicting modern life; in stanza 2 he looks forward to this jigsaw being dismantled.

5 Consider as a class the *pace* and *rhythm* of the poem. Re-read its two stanzas aloud. Do you find that the way they are constructed makes you read them rapidly, with a flat rhythm in stanza 1 and an aggressive rhythm in stanza 2? Why do you think this is? How does this match what MacNeice is saying in the poem?

Across AS and A2

Look back to your work on the structure of poems in Unit 1. The AS Student Book has relevant material on pages 11–30 about a poet's use of rhyme, line arrangement and word order. You should also refer back to the way you commented on structure in your prescribed poems for Section B of Unit 1: the AS Student Book has guidance on this on pages 91–103.

Activity 9

1 Read the poem opposite aloud. It was first published in 1794.

2 This poem can be seen to be about the destructive effect that repressed anger has on relationships. Talk with a partner about how Blake develops this theme through his metaphor of a 'poison tree'.

3 Turn your attention to the poem's structure. There are four stanzas in the poem. Explore with your partner how each stanza forms part of the poem's overall shape. Make a table like this:

A Poison Tree

I was angry with my friend,
I told my wrath*, my wrath did end.
I was angry with my foe:
I told it not, my wrath did grow:

5
And I water'd it in fears,
Night and morning with my tears;
And I sunned it with smiles,
And with soft deceitful wiles.

And it grew both day and night,
10 Till it bore an apple bright,
And my foe beheld it shine,
And he knew that it was mine,

And into the garden stole,
When the night had veil'd the pole*:
15 In the morning glad I see
My foe outstretch'd beneath the tree.

William Blake

* told my wrath: let my anger out
* veil'd the pole: covered the earth

Stanza number	Structural features	Effects created
1	The four lines are divided into two rhyming couplets	Establishes the basic pattern of the poem – the contrast between 'I told my wrath' and 'I told it not'
	Strong rhymes in lines 1 & 2 and lines 3 & 4, emphasised by end-stopping	Reinforces the antithesis between 'friend' and 'foe' and between 'end' and 'grow' – these are picked out by rhyme as the key words in the poem
	All the structural elements of this stanza are balanced and symmetrical – the rhyme, the regular rhythm, the repetition of 'I' and 'my'	Reflects the poem's theme – on the one hand, anger 'told' will end; on the other hand, anger 'not told' will grow into hate – the poem is a fable or parable and the balanced structure works to point up its moral

Key terms

• structural pattern

• alliteration

Writing in the exam

Remember that the term 'structure' applies both to the way in which a poem is built overall and to specific details of its construction such as word order, line arrangement and stanza forms. Commenting on the effect of these is essential for marks in the higher bands of AO2. Never generalise about structure: always comment on specific details, like those listed in the table about Blake's 'The Poison Tree'.

4 Compare your completed tables in a class discussion. This is a poem with a strong *structural pattern*. How does its shape reflect what Blake is saying about the consequences of anger that is allowed to fester? Do you think this structure is effective?

5 Write a short analysis of Blake's use of structure to help convey his central theme in this poem. Make sure you comment on specific details: avoid generalisation.

6 Look back as a class at what you have learned from Activities 8 and 9 about how poets use structure to create and convey their themes. Make a list of things to look out for when you are next asked to comment on the structure of a poem.

Aspects of structure:
How do poets use rhyme, rhythm and sound?

Poets use rhyme (or the absence of rhyme), rhythm and sound to create and convey meaning. Bear in mind that the use of rhyme and rhythm in a poem will be closely related to its form, or genre: see pages 17–18 below.

Writing in the exam

Commenting on rhyme, rhythm and sound is difficult, particularly in exam conditions. Remember to:
• *listen* to the poem – read it 'aloud' inside your head
• use technical terms to describe rhyme, rhythm and sound and, most importantly, describe the *effect* of these in the poem; you get no credit for writing only 'This poem is written in rhyming couplets' or 'The rhythm is uneven'
• relate your comments on rhyme, rhythm and sound to your understanding of the poem's theme; always explain, never just observe.

Activity 10

1 The opening lines of the poem below were written by Gerard Manley Hopkins, a priest who saw in nature evidence of God as creator of the world.

God's Grandeur

The world is charged with the grandeur of God.
    It will flame out, like shining from shook foil;
    It gathers to a greatness, like the ooze of oil
Crushed. Why do men then now not reck his rod*?

* reck his rod: show
concern for his power

2 Read lines 1 to 3 aloud to a partner. Try saying them in various ways: slowly, rapidly, enthusiastically, reverently, and so on. Decide between you which tone of voice suits the poem best.

3 Find examples of *alliteration* (repetition of the same initial sound) in lines 1, 2 and 3. Try to explain the effect they have when spoken aloud. Is the effect appropriate to what these words are describing?

4 Lines 1 and 4, and lines 2 and 3, are linked by rhyme. Can you think of any reason why Hopkins has chosen to do this?

5 Share your ideas in class discussion. Then read the rest of the poem, opposite.

6 Discuss in a small group what Hopkins is saying here about (a) how God's grandeur is to be found in nature, despite man's negative impact on the world, and (b) how God continues to care for his creation like a loving parent.

7 Devise four questions to ask another group about Hopkins' use of rhyme, rhythm and sound *at particular points in the poem*. Make sure that you discuss and decide on your own answers first.

8 Put your questions to another group, and answer their questions. If you find alternative interpretations or points about style, you might agree to differ – as long as you can justify your ideas from the text.

9 Review as a class the work you have done in this Activity. Do you think it has helped you understand the poem better? How far has it helped you to appreciate Hopkins' craft as a poet? Make a list of things to look out for when you are next asked to comment on the use of rhyme, rhythm and sound in an unprepared poem

Generations have trod, have trod, have trod; 5
   And all is seared with trade*; bleared, smeared with toil;
   And wears man's smudge and shares man's smell: the soil
Is bare now, nor can foot feel, being shod.

And for all this, nature is never spent*; 10
   There lives the dearest freshness deep down things;
And though the last lights off the black West went
   Oh, morning, at the brown brink eastward, springs –
Because the Holy Ghost over the bent
   World broods* with warm breast and with ah! bright wings.

Gerard Manley Hopkins

* trade: man's handiwork
* spent: exhausted
* broods: nurtures

Use of form in poems: Why choose this genre?

The form of a poem indicates its genre. A poem could be written as **_free verse_**, a sonnet, a **_ballad_**, in rhyming couplets, and so on. In the poem in Activity 9, for example, Blake uses **_quatrains_**; Gerard Manley Hopkins' poem in Activity 10 uses the Miltonic sonnet form.

Whereas *structure* can be described as the bricks from which the poem is built, *form* is the architecture of the building. In Activities 11 and 12 you will explore the form of two poems and relate this to the poets' themes.

Take it further

Write a detailed analysis of Hopkins' 'God's Grandeur' OR Hardy's 'In Time of "The Breaking of Nations"'. Show how the poet uses a range of stylistic techniques, including choice of form, to create and convey his themes.

Activity 11

1 Read the poem opposite aloud. It was written in 1915 and its title refers to the First World War.

2 Give a first response to this poem in a small group. Discuss what you think Hardy is saying about (a) love, (b) war, and (c) life in the English countryside.

3 In this poem, Hardy uses formal features that are characteristic of **_lyrical_** poetry. Decide whether these are well-matched to its theme, given that lyrical poetry is:
- one of the oldest forms of English verse
- song-like, with a regular, steady **_metre_**
- normally about love and lovers
- associated with the countryside.

4 Share your ideas in class discussion. Then look carefully at Hardy's choice of diction. Contrast it with Hopkins' in 'God's Grandeur' (Activity 10). How do their different choices of diction reflect their different intentions?

   * harrowing: ploughing
   * maid and her wight: young girl and her young man

In Time of 'The Breaking of Nations'

I

ONLY a man harrowing* clods
   In a slow silent walk
With an old horse that stumbles and nods
   Half asleep as they stalk.

II

Only thin smoke without flame
   From the heaps of couch-grass;
Yet this will go onward the same
   Though Dynasties pass.

III

Yonder a maid and her wight*
   Come whispering by:
War's annals will cloud into night
   Ere their story die.

Thomas Hardy

Key terms

- **free verse**
- **ballad**
- **quatrain**
- **lyric**
- **metre**

Key terms

- villanelle
- Shakespearean sonnet
- iambic pentameter

Activity 12

1 Read the poem opposite aloud. It is in the form of a **villanelle**: a 19-line poem with an aba rhyme scheme. It has five three-line stanzas followed by one four-line stanza. Lines 1 and 3 from the first stanza are picked up and repeated in the rest of the poem.

2 Give a first response to this poem with a partner. Discuss what you think the speaker is saying about (a) her relationship as it is now, (b) how her relationship has changed, and (c) what first love is like.

3 Look closely at the form of the poem. Talk about these aspects of it:
- Two particular lines are repeated from stanza to stanza. What is the effect of this repetition on you as a reader?
- There are only two rhymes in the poem, which has a strong rhyme scheme. Remind yourself what these rhymes are. Do you find this technique effective for what is being described – or do you think it becomes monotonous?
- The form of the last stanza differs from that of the other stanzas. How? Do you find this effective as a way of concluding the poem?

4 Share your ideas in a class discussion. Decide how well the form of the poem is matched to its themes. Give your honest opinion, making sure you justify it from the text.

5 Read the poem opposite aloud. It is Mick Gowar's companion piece to the villanelle you have been working on. It has the same title. Decide how the two poems combine to form a whole.

6 This poem is in the form of a sonnet. Work with a partner to show that:
- it has three quatrains and a couplet, as in **Shakespearean sonnets**
- its rhyme scheme is ababcdcdefefgg, as in Shakespearean sonnets
- its basic metre is **iambic pentameter**, as in Shakespearean sonnets.

First Love

She:

I don't know why, but something's going wrong –
I felt the point of no return slip by.
Though we're still happy, we still get along

my heart beats like a toneless leaden gong
where once it leapt and raced as if to fly.
I don't know why. But something's going wrong

in me: the spark, the naturalness, has gone –
each day it's getting harder to deny;
though we're still happy, we still get along

I'm out of step. He hasn't changed. How long
each kiss feels with deceit; each touch a lie.
I don't know why, but something's going wrong.

I'd never felt such love – so fierce and strong:
each sight of him, each parting made me cry.
Though we're still happy, we still get along

the love that was to last a whole life long
is coming to an end. No second try,
though we're still happy, we still get along.
I don't know why, but something's going wrong.

Mick Gowar

First Love

He:

I knew it had to come. I couldn't bear
It then; can't take it now. I'll make amends.
I'm willing to agree, now. So – be fair,
there's no need to split up. We'll just be friends.
Like you suggested. Not see quite so much
of each other. Please! I agree. You're right.
I made too much of what we had. Been such
a fool. I'll take the blame. We'll start tonight
– The New Improved Regime. We'll both be free
to do just what we want – the adult way.
I'll do just as you want me to. You'll see.
I'm willing to do anything you say.
I promise. I won't make a scene. Won't cry.
If you'll do just one thing. Don't say goodbye.

Mick Gowar

7 Discuss why Mick Gowar may have chosen this particular form for the '*He*' poem of the pair about first love. Is the voice of the poem a recognisably male voice, in your opinion, and do the feelings expressed seem 'typically male'? How well is the form of the poem matched to its themes?

8 Compare in a class discussion the use of the sonnet form by Mick Gowar with the use Gerard Manley Hopkins makes of the sonnet form in 'God's Grandeur' (Activity 10). The two poems are on very different subjects and use different types of sonnet. Discuss which of them works more successfully.

The voice of a poem: How do I comment on register and tone?

All poems have their own voice. This can be:

- the voice of the poet himself or herself speaking directly
- the voice of a persona the poet creates to express a particular viewpoint.

In responding to the voice of a poem, you need to be alert to **register**, that is the choice of diction appropriate to a particular situation or context, and the way the *tone* conveys the speaker's feelings and attitudes. (Bear in mind that the 'I' of a poem is not always the same as the writer. It is best to refer to the 'speaker' of a poem.)

In Activity 13 you will explore the use of voice in poems and relate it to the poets' themes.

Activity 13

1 The poem opposite was written by a group of female performers. Read it aloud around the class; you could take one line each.

Men Are…

men are strong, men are tough
men are surly, men are rough
men have mates, men drink beer
man are brave and don't show fear
men slap backs, men sing songs   5
men are men and men are strong
men don't touch, men aren't drips
men shake hands with vice-like grips.

men like fighting, men like cars
men like shouting with men in bars   10
men like football and now and then
men like men like men like men
no they don't, men beat up queers
men live with their mums for years and years
men have beards and hairy chests   15
men walk through blizzards in string vests.

men can embrace and bare their soul
but only if they've scored a goal
men leap tall buildings, men are tough
men don't know when they've had enough   20
men drive fast cars with wide wheels
men like fur-lined steering-wheels
men have muscles, men have sweat
men haven't learned to grow up yet.

men climb mountains in the snow   25
men don't cook and men don't sew
men are bosses, men are chums
men build office blocks and slums
men make bombs, men make wars
men are stupid, men are bores   30
men ignore what women see
and call our story **his**tory.

The Raving Beauties

Independent research

'Men Are…' is a performance poem. Listening to poets reading and performing their poems is the best way to tune in to voice. Visit www.poetryarchive.org to listen to a range of poetry presentations. A DVD produced by Bloodaxe, called *In Person: 30 Poets*, has contemporary poets reading their work. Try to listen to recordings of John Agard, Jean 'Binta' Breeze, Carol Ann Duffy, Liz Lochhead, Adrian Mitchell and Benjamin Zephaniah, all of whom are outstanding readers/performers.

2 Discuss your response to this poem in a small group. Do you think its register and tone are successful in conveying its theme, as you understand it?

3 Now consider the poem's form and structure, and how this is closely linked to the use of voice. Try reading the stanzas in a different order. Are they interchangeable – or have they been constructed so that they develop meaning as the poem goes on? Would the poem work effectively without its strong rhyme and its repetitive rhythm?

4 Work together to write a stanza for a companion poem entitled 'Women Are…'. Then perform your stanzas as a class. How well do they work compared with 'Men Are…'?

5 Read the poem below aloud. Its speaker reveals his identity in the opening line.

Executive

I am a young executive. No cuffs than mine are cleaner;
I have a Slimline brief-case and I use the firm's Cortina.
In every roadside hostelry from here to Burgess Hill
The *maitres d'hotel* all know me well and let me sign the bill.

5 You ask me what it is I do. Well actually, you know,
I'm partly a liaison man and partly P.R.O.*
Essentially I integrate the current export drive
And basically I'm viable from ten o'clock till five.

For vital off-the-record work – that's talking transport-wise –
10 I've a scarlet Aston-Martin – and does she go? She flies!
Pedestrians and dogs and cats – we mark them down for slaughter.
I also own a speed-boat which has never touched the water.

She's built of fibre-glass, of course. I call her 'Mandy Jane',
After a bird I used to know – No soda, please, just plain –
15 And how did I acquire her? Well to tell you about that
And to put you in the picture I must wear my other hat.

I do some mild developing. The sort of place I need
Is a quiet country market town that's rather run to seed.
A luncheon and a drink or two, a little *savoir faire* –
20 I fix the Planning Officer, the Town Clerk and the Mayor.

And if some preservationist attempts to interfere
A 'dangerous structure' notice from the Borough Engineer
Will settle any buildings that are standing in our way –
The modern style, sir, with respect, has really come to stay.

John Betjeman

*P.R.O.: Public Relations Officer

Key terms

• **dramatic monologue**

• **slang**

• **jargon**

• **satire**

6 Explore in a small group the speaker's attitude to (a) business, (b) himself, and (c) the English heritage. What view of him do you think Betjeman wants you to take?

7 Examine the way Betjeman creates a distinctive voice for the speaker in this *dramatic monologue*. Focus on:
  • his tone of voice
  • his use of contemporary *slang* and business *jargon*
  • his liking for the names of things.

8 In this poem, Betjeman attempts to *satirise* the young executive by presenting us with his view of himself in his own voice. How successful do you think the satire is?

Summary of your learning in Part 1

In this part you have developed your skills of analysing unprepared poetry in the following areas:

- making your own interpretation of meaning rather than waiting to be told
- identifying a poem's theme(s) and differentiating between theme and subject matter
- appreciating how poets make precise choices of diction to create the meaning they want
- appreciating how poets use imagery to express their view of the world
- identifying aspects of a poem's form and structure
- appreciating that poets choose particular genres and structures to match their purposes
- relating a poet's use of form and structure to the presentation of themes
- commenting on the way poets use voice and viewpoint to shape a reader's response.

Copy this list of skills. Use a tick system to show how confident you are now of being able to apply each of them: 3 ticks = 'very confident', 2 ticks = 'gaining more confidence', 1 tick = 'lacking confidence'. This self-evaluation should lead, if necessary, to a programme of skill revision before you move on to further work on poetry analysis in Part 3.

2   Analysing unprepared prose

Part 2 provides a practical basis for your work on prose analysis in Section A. It shows you how to:

- identify the focus of a passage and what the writer is doing in it
- comment on how writers create *setting* and character
- comment on how writers use *narrative point of view* and *voice*
- comment on how writers use *syntax* (sentence construction).

This part reinforces and develops your learning in Section A of Unit 1. At A2 you will need to apply your analytical skills in fuller detail and respond at greater length. You will also be expected to give a personal interpretation of the passage and a judgement about its effectiveness.

> ### Independent research
>
> Sample the following volumes: *Selected Poems of Louis MacNeice.*(Faber), *Selected Poems of Gerard Manley Hopkins* (Palgrave Macmillan), *Selected Poems of Thomas Hardy* (Penguin), and *The Best of John Betjeman* (Penguin). Choose poems that relate to your chosen topic area in Section B of this unit. Compile a personal anthology and use the poems to illuminate your study of your prescribed poetry and/or prose texts.

> ### Key terms
>
> - setting
> - narrative point of view
> - voice
> - syntax

> ### Writing in the exam
>
> You will be given one unprepared prose text to analyse. Your focus will be on how the writer uses structure, form and language to shape meaning.
>
> You will not be given the short 'prompt' questions that were provided in the exam for Unit 1. You need, therefore, to make your own decisions about what to comment on. The highest marks in the exam are awarded for 'evaluative' responses: that is, for showing what meaning *you* find in the poem and how your understanding of it has been shaped. Do not be afraid to commit yourself to making your own interpretation and evaluation: the meaning of poems is not fixed before you read them, and their effectiveness is a matter for you to decide.

Giving a first response:
How do I find my way in?

When faced with a prose passage that is new to you, your first step is to decide what kind of response to make to it. Ask yourself two basic questions about the writing: 'What is the writer *doing* in this text?' and '*How* is he or she doing it?'

Activity 14 shows you how to find your way in to a new text by applying these questions to two openings of novels.

Activity 14

1 Read the texts below.

Text A:

From *Persuasion* by Jane Austen

Sir Walter Elliott, of Kellynch-hall, in Somersetshire, was a man who, for his own amusement, never took up any book but the Baronetage; there he found occupation for an idle hour, and consolation in a distressed one; there his faculties were roused into admiration and respect, by contemplating the limited remnants of the earliest
5 patents*; there any unwelcome sensations, arising from domestic affairs, changed naturally into pity and contempt, as he turned over the almost endless creations of the last century – and there, if every other leaf were powerless, he could read his own history with an interest which never failed – this was the page at which the favourite volume always opened:

10   'ELLIOTT OF KELLYNCH-HALL.

    'Walter Elliott, born March 1, 1760, married, July 15, 1784, Elizabeth, daughter of James Stevenson, Esq. of South Park, in the county of Gloucester; by which lady (who died 1800) he has issue Elizabeth, born June 1, 1785; Anne, born August 9, 1787; a still-born son, Nov. 5, 1789; Mary, born
15 Nov. 20, 1791.'

Precisely such had the paragraph originally stood from the printer's hands; but Sir Walter had improved it by adding, for the information of himself and his family, these words, after the date of Mary's birth – 'married, Dec. 16, 1810, Charles, son and heir of Charles Musgrove, Esq. of Uppercross, in the county of Somerset,' – and
20 by inserting most accurately the day of the month on which he had lost his wife.

* limited remnants of the earliest patents: the few survivors of the oldest aristocratic families

---

Text B:

From *A History of the World in 10½ Chapters* by Julian Barnes

They put the behemoths in the hold along with the rhinos, the hippos and the elephants. It was a sensible decision to use them as ballast; but you can imagine the stench. And there was no-one to muck them out. The men were overburdened with the feeding rota, and their women, who beneath those leaping fire-tongues of scent
5 no doubt reeked as badly as we did, were far too delicate. So if any mucking-out was to happen, we had to do it ourselves. Every few months they would winch back the thick hatch on the aft deck and let the cleaner-birds in. Well, first they had to let the smell out (and there weren't too many volunteers for winch-work); then six or eight of the less fastidious birds would flutter cautiously around the hatch for a minute or
10 so before diving in. I can't remember what they were called – indeed, one of those pairs no longer exists – but you know the sort I mean. You've seen hippos with their mouths open and bright little birds pecking away between their teeth like distraught dental hygienists? Picture that on a larger, messier scale. I am hardly squeamish, but even I used to shudder at the scene below decks: a row of squinting monsters being
15 manicured in a sewer.

There was strict discipline on the Ark: that's the first point to make.

2 Give a first response to these texts with a partner. What clues are there that they each come from the *start* of a narrative, where the writers are establishing a particular relationship between the reader and the text? In each case, consider:
  • what you are being shown about the setting – where and when?
  • what you are being shown about the characters – who, and in what relation to each other?
  • what you can say about the **narrator** and the narrative style – who is telling the story, and how is it being told?

3 As well as being written in different periods, these passages are from quite different types of novel. Discuss and note down the ways in which you think they contrast.

4 Share your ideas in a class discussion. Then consider how the writers try to draw you into the story. Say how effectively you think each writer:
  • presents events/character
  • creates a distinctive voice for the narrator
  • builds up your curiosity.

5 Did you find that one of the texts engaged your interest more than the other? If so, talk about why. Then say which of these novels you would prefer to continue reading. What do you expect the novel would be about?

Across AS and A2

Your work on prose analysis in Unit 1 provides an essential platform for Section A. The relevant parts of the AS Student Book are 'Exploring Prose', pages 49–78, and 'Unseen Prose', pages 86–90. Remind yourself of the basic concepts involved in analysing prose fiction and the literary terms used. The activities in this part assume that your understanding of these terms is secure. Whenever this is not the case, check back to your work at AS.

Giving a considered response:
How do the style and language work?

Once you feel familiar with a new prose text and confident that you understand it, build on your first response by considering its style and language. Style is not an aspect of prose that is separate from meaning. Writers create meaning by the choices they make of language, form and structure.

Activity 15 (below) shows you this process at work: it acts as an introduction to analysing prose style.

Key term

• narrator

Activity 15

1 Read the text below. It is from a novel set in the 1970s.

From *The History Man* by Malcolm Bradbury

It is four in the morning when the party comes to its end. The last guests stand in the hall, some of them needing the support of the wall; they say their goodbyes; they venture through the door into the quietness of early-morning Watermouth. The Kirks, that hospitable couple, usher them forth, and then they go upstairs to
5 their disorderly bedroom, which smells sharply of pot, and push the bed back into position, and take the ashtrays off it, and undress, and get under the duvet. They say nothing, being tired people; they do not touch each other, having no need; Barbara, in her black nightdress, folds her body into Howard's, her buttocks on his knees, and they are quickly asleep. And then it is the morning, and the Habitat alarm clock
10 rings on the bedside table, and they wake again, back into the life of ordinary things. Consciousness returns, and feels heavy with use; Howard presses his eyelids open, jerks towards being, regresses, tries again. Traffic thumps on the creases of the urban motorway; a diesel commuter train hoots on the viaduct; the graders are revving on the construction sites. The bed vibrates and bounces; Barbara is getting up. The
15 Habitat alarm clock says it is v to viii. Barbara pads across to the door, and takes her housecoat from the hook; she goes across to the window and pulls back the curtain to admit dull wet daylight. The room appears in its unmitigated thinginess, flavoured with the dusty smell of cigarette smoke, the sweet aftersmell of pot. A thrown-off dress, gutted by its long zip, hangs askew on the door. On the junkshop chest of
20 drawers, its grain surface rough, one handle gone, two handles broken, are some plates, three full ashtrays, and many empty wine glasses from the supermarket. The lavatory flushes along the landing.

Key terms

- **third-person narration**
- **dialogue**

2 Give a first response to this text in a small group. What do you think Malcolm Bradbury is showing you about (a) the lifestyle of the Kirks, (b) their relationship as a married couple, and (c) their values? You will need to read inferentially as well as literally; for example, what might Bradbury be implying about the Kirks by writing that 'they do not touch, having no need'?

3 Explore further Bradbury's use of language to present the Kirks to you. Comment on:
- the extensive detail he gives about their home and their possessions – use as a reference-point his phrase 'The room appears in its unmitigated thinginess'
- the effect of the adjectives in the phrases 'that hospitable couple', 'their disorderly bedroom', 'the dusty smell of cigarette smoke', 'the junkshop chest of drawers'
- the connotations of words in 'usher them forth', 'the creases of the urban motorway', 'A thrown-off dress, gutted by its long zip, hangs askew'.

4 Share your ideas in a class discussion. Then consider how the following aspects of style help to guide your response to the Kirks:
- the use of **third-person narration**
- the use of the present tense
- the focus on description and the absence of **dialogue**.

Remember that the Kirks are not real people: they are Bradbury's inventions who exist only through the language he uses to create them.

5 Write a short analysis of the way in which Bradbury's choices of language create meaning in this text. Base this on the bullet points in questions 3 and 4 above.

Identifying the writer's focus:
What am I being asked to respond to?

In commenting on an extract rather than a whole novel, you need to be clear about its specific focus before you proceed to analyse its structure, form and language. The writer could, for instance, be chiefly concerned to create character, to reveal a relationship between characters, to develop the plot, to describe setting, and so on. The key question to ask yourself is 'What is the writer asking me to respond to here?' You may find several answers, but there will be one that predominates.

In Activity 16 you will identify the focus of a text as a basis for commenting on its style and language.

Activity 16

1 Read the text opposite. It is from a novel in which two middle-aged men, Jimmy Sr and Bimbo, set up a mobile fast-food business in Dublin. In this extract they are road-testing the van they have converted for the job. They use Irish **idioms**.

2 Discuss with a partner what you think Roddy Doyle is asking you to respond to in this text. How does he present the situation and try to engage your interest in it? In your discussion, include comments on:
- the small amount of description relative to the large amount of dialogue
- the use of **colloquial** and **idiomatic language**
- the absence of **authorial comment**.

3 Share your ideas in a class discussion. Give your opinion about the effectiveness of Roddy Doyle's narrative techniques here.

From *The Van* by Roddy Doyle

They got in. Bimbo put in the key.

The van had a new engine.

– Here we go.

It went first time.

5 – Yeow!

They went to Howth.

– Maybe we should get music for it, said Jimmy Sr when they were going through Sutton. They'd stalled at the lights, but they were grand now, picking up a head of
10 steam.

– Like a Mister Whippy van.

– Would that not confuse people?

– How d'yeh mean?

– Well, said Bimbo. – They might run out of their houses
15 lookin' for ice-creams an' all we'll be able to give them is chips.

Jimmy Sr thought about this.

– Is there no chip music? he said. – Mind that oul' bitch there. She's going to open the door there, look it.

20 – What d'yeh mean? said Bimbo.

He stopped Jimmy Sr from getting to the horn.

– Yeh should've just taken the door off its fuckin' hinges an' kept on goin', said Jimmy Sr.

– The music, said Bimbo.

25 – Yeah, said Jimmy Sr. – The Teddy Bears' Picnic is the ice-cream song, righ'. Is there no chipper song?

– No, said Bimbo. – I – No, I don't think –

– Your man, look it; don't let him get past yeh! – Ah, Jaysis. – I'm drivin' back, righ'.

4 Read the text below. It is from the start of a novel written in 1993.

From *The Shipping News* by Annie Proulx

Here is an account of a few years in the life of Quoyle, born in Brooklyn and raised in a shuffle of dreary upstate towns.

Hive-spangled, gut roaring with gas and cramp, he survived childhood; at the state university, hand clapped over his chin, he camouflaged torment with smiles and silence. Stumbled through his twenties and into his
5   thirties learning to separate his feelings from his life, counting on nothing. He ate prodigiously, liked a ham knuckle, buttered spuds.

His jobs: distributor of vending machine candy, all-night clerk in a convenience store, a third-rate newspaperman. At thirty-six, bereft, brimming with grief and thwarted love, Quoyle steered away to Newfoundland, the rock that had generated his ancestors, a place he had never been nor thought to go.

10   A watery place. And Quoyle feared water, could not swim. Again and again the father had broken his clenched grip and thrown him into pools, brooks, lakes and surf. Quoyle knew the flavour of brack and waterweed.

From this youngest son's failure to dog-paddle the father saw other failures multiply like an explosion of virulent cells – failure to speak clearly; failure to sit up straight; failure to get up in the morning; failure in
15   attitude; failure in ambition and ability; indeed, in everything. His own failure.

Key terms

- figurative language

5 Discuss what you think Annie Proulx is asking you to respond to in this text. What narrative techniques does she use to engage your interest in it? In your discussion, include comments on:
- the highly compressed style
- the use of *figurative language*
- the extent of authorial comment.

6 Compare, in a class discussion, the narrative techniques in this text with those used by Roddy Doyle. What are the main differences? How do these reflect the writer's different purposes, as you understand them?

Take it further

Write an analysis of the passage from *A History of the World in 10½ Chapters* in Activity 14 OR the passage from *The Shipping News* above as the opening to a novel. Relate the narrative techniques you find to the writers' purposes, and evaluate their effectiveness.

Writing in the exam

Begin your analysis by giving your initial response to the meaning of the passage: 'The writer's main purpose seems to be…', 'The writer focuses on X, which suggests that…'. This part of your analysis may sound exploratory, which is fine. Remember the crucial difference between summarising what the text is about and describing a writer's intentions: you get no credit for just showing you can 'comprehend' by paraphrasing.

Creating setting: How do writers evoke place and time, and why?

All prose fiction writers create for the reader particular settings and locations, a context within which the plot and characters develop. In an extract, your response to setting should take account of these other factors. In Activities 17 and 18 you will explore the way writers use their descriptions of setting to help them present character and theme.

Activity 17

1 Read the text below. It is the opening of a short story written in 1917.

> ### From *Carnation* by Katherine Mansfield
>
> On those hot days Eve – curious Eve – always carried a flower. She snuffed it and snuffed it, twirled it in her fingers, laid it against her cheek, held it to her lips, tickled Katie's neck with it, and ended, finally, by pulling it to pieces and eating it, petal by petal.
>
> 5 'Roses are delicious, my dear Katie,' she would say, standing in the dim cloak-room, with a strange decoration of flowery hats on the hat pegs behind her – 'but carnations are simply divine! They taste like – like – ah well!' And away her little thin laugh flew, fluttering among those huge, strange flower heads on the wall behind her. (But how cruel her little thin laugh was! It had a long sharp beak and claws and two bead eyes, thought fanciful Katie.)
>
> To-day it was a carnation. She brought a carnation to the French class, a deep, deep red one, that looked as though it 10 had been dipped in wine and left in the dark to dry. She held it on the desk before her, half shut her eyes and smiled.
>
> 'Isn't it a darling?' she said. But –
>
> '*Un peu de silence, s'il vous plaît,*' came from M. Hugo. Oh, bother! It was too hot! Frightfully hot! Grilling simply!
>
> The two square windows of the French Room were open at the bottom and the dark blinds drawn half-way down. Although no air came in, the blind cord swung out and back and the blind lifted. But really there was not a breath 15 from the dazzle outside.
>
> Even the girls, in the dusky room, in their pale blouses, with stiff butterfly-bow hair ribbons perched on their hair, seemed to give off a warm, weak light, and M. Hugo's white waistcoat gleamed like the belly of a shark.

2 Give a first response to this text in a small group. What impressions does Katherine Mansfield give you of (a) Eve's character, (b) her relationship with Katie, and (c) the atmosphere in the French Room? How do you think the story will develop?

3 Work in your group to explore how Katherine Mansfield uses the setting of the school to create mood and atmosphere. Do this by completing a copy of the table below.

Detail of setting	Effect on reader
'those hot days'… 'Grilling simply'	Establishes a feeling of lethargy, which seems to affect everyone except Eve
'the dim cloak-room, with a strange decoration of flowery hats on the hat pegs'	
'no air came in… there was not a breath from the dazzle outside'	
'the dusky room … a warm, weak light'	

Writing in the exam

In commenting on setting in your analysis, you need to show how it is created and how it is used by the writer. Setting evokes mood and atmosphere. Mood and atmosphere are used for such purposes as conveying character and feeling, creating narrative tension and developing themes. Try to be precise about this.

4 Now read the end of the story. M. Hugo has been reciting French love poetry to the girls. Eve and Katie apart, they have all become enervated by the heat. Eve shows her flower to Katie…

> She made a warm, white cup of her fingers – the carnation inside. Oh, the scent! It floated across to Katie. It was too much. Katie turned away to the dazzling light outside the window.
>
> 5 Down below, she knew, there was a cobbled courtyard with stable buildings around it. That was why the French Room always smelled faintly of ammonia. It wasn't unpleasant; it was even part of the French language for Katie – something sharp and vivid and – and – biting!
>
> Now she could hear a man clatter over the cobbles and the jing-jang of the pails he carried. And now *Hoo-hor-her*! *Hoo-hor-her*! as he worked at the pump and a
> 10 great gush of water followed. Now he was flinging the water over something, over the wheels of a carriage perhaps. And she saw the wheel, propped up, clear of the ground, spinning round, flashing scarlet and black, with great drops glancing off it…
>
> She saw him simply – in a faded shirt, his sleeves rolled up, his chest bare, all splashed with water – and as he whistled, loud and free, and as he moved, swooping
> 15 and bending, Hugo-Wugo's voice began to warm, to deepen, to gather together, to swing, to rise – somehow or other to keep time with the man outside (Oh, the scent of Eve's carnation!) until they became one rushing, rising, triumphant thing, bursting into light, and then –
>
> The whole room broke into pieces.
>
> 20 'Thank you, ladies,' cried M. Hugo, bobbing at his high desk, over the wreckage.
>
> And, 'Keep it, dearest,' said Eve. '*Souvenir tendre*,' and she popped the carnation down the front of Katie's blouse.

5 Discuss in your group the way you interpret this story. Remember that you create meaning by the way you respond: it is not fixed in advance. Include comments about:
- how the scene outside the French Room contrasts with the scene inside it
- what kind of experience you think Katie has at the end of the story
- how the settings in *Carnation* could be seen as symbolic.

6 Share your responses in class discussion. Then judge the extent to which the story's effect depends upon Katherine Mansfield's use of setting.

Activity 18

Independent research

Build up your own collection of modern short stories and use them to write critical analyses in preparation for the Section A exam, as well as to enjoy them for their own sake. Writers you might try include: Kate Chopin, D.H. Lawrence, Ernest Hemingway, John Steinbeck, David Storey, Alice Walker, Ruth Rendell, Fay Weldon, Michèle Roberts, Martin Amis, Maeve Binchy, Joyce Carol Oates and Beryl Bainbridge.

1 Read the text below. It is from a novel written in 1964 and set in medieval times. The central character is a priest who is supervising the building of a cathedral. He sees this as a test of his faith in God. In the extract below, bad weather arrives and slows down the work.

From *The Spire* by William Golding

… the rain came for three days, with only half a day to follow it of low cloud and soaked air; so that housewives hung what linen there was to wash before smouldering fires that dirtied more linen than they dried; and then there was wind and rain for a week. When he came out of this deanery, cloaked for the hurried
5 passage to the cathedral, he would see the clouds at roof level so that even the battlements of the roof were blurred by them. As for the building itself, the bible in stone, it sank from glorification to homilectics*. It was slimy with water streaming down over moss and lichen and flaking stones. When the rain drizzled, then time was a drizzle, slow and to be endured. When the rain lashed down, then the thousand
10 gargoyles – and now men thought how their models mouldered in the graveyards of the Close or the parish churches – gave vent. They uttered water as if this were yet another penalty of damnation; and what they uttered joined with what streamed down glass and lead and moulding, down members and pinnacles, down faces and squared headlands to run bubbling and clucking at the foot of the wall. When the wind came,
15 it did not clear the sky, but cuffed the air this way and that, a bucketful of water with every cuff, so that even a dean must stagger, pushed from behind; or leaning against a gust like a blow, find his cloak whipped out like wings. When the wind fell, the clouds fell too and he could no longer see the top half of the building; and because of the drizzle he lost the sense of the size of it. Therefore the approaching eye had
20 to deal with a nearer thing, some corner of wet stone, huge in detail and full of imperfections, like a skin seen too close. The reentrants* on the north side – but there was no direction of light to show which was north and which south – stank with the memories of urination. The flood waters by the river, spread over the causeway, took no account of the guards at the city gate, but invaded the greasy streets. Men and
25 women and children crouched by what fire they had and the smoke from damp logs or peat formed a haze under every roof. Only the alehouses prospered.

* from glorification to homilectics: from the divine to the human
* reentrants: alcoves

2 Look carefully in a small group at Golding's choices of language in this text. What impressions do they give you of (a) the extent of the bad weather, (b) the effect of the weather on the cathedral, and (c) the effect of the weather on the priest?

Select three phrases which you consider effective in describing how the weather makes an impact on the surroundings. Explain why you find them striking.

3 Share your responses in a class discussion. Then explore Golding's narrative technique in this text. Comment on:
- the effect of the figurative language in (a) 'the bible in stone', (b) 'then time was a drizzle', (c) 'cuffed the air this way and that, a bucketful of water with every cuff', and (d) 'full of imperfections, like a skin seen too close'
- the way in which the sound of words echoes their meaning
- the length and rhythm of sentences: how does their construction reflect what they describe?

4 *The Spire* explores how the priest's faith is tried in the course of building the cathedral. Discuss Golding's use of setting to convey this theme in the extract. How is the severe weather made to seem like a personal assault on the priest? How does his view of the building ('the bible in stone') change as the extract develops?

Key term

- characterisation

Characterisation: How do writers create and convey character?

Characters in prose fiction are objects of the writer's craft. They do not exist outside the text. In making your analysis, therefore, you need to write about **characterisation**: the techniques writers use to create and convey their imagined characters. This is quite different from making a 'character study,' as if they were real people. In Activities 19 and 20 you will explore writers' techniques of characterisation.

Activity 19

1 Read the text below. It is taken from a novel written in 1853. The narrator, Esther, and an acquaintance, Richard, are visiting Mrs Jellyby. She is a Christian philanthropist who devotes her time to her 'African project', bringing aid and enlightenment to the people of Nigeria.

From *Bleak House* by Charles Dickens

We passed several more children on the way up [to Mrs Jellyby's room], whom it was difficult to avoid treading on in the dark; and as we came into Mrs Jellyby's presence, one of the poor little things fell downstairs – down a whole flight (as it sounded to me), with a great noise.

5 Mrs Jellyby, whose face reflected none of the uneasiness which we could not help showing in our own faces as the dear child's head recorded its passage with a bump on every stair – Richard afterwards said he counted seven, besides one for the landing – received us with perfect equanimity. She was a pretty, very diminutive, plump woman of from forty to fifty, with handsome eyes, though they had a curious habit of seeming to look a long way off. As if – I am quoting Richard again – they could see nothing nearer than Africa!

10 'I am very glad indeed,' said Mrs Jellyby in an agreeable voice, 'to have the pleasure of receiving you. I have a great respect for Mr Jarndyce, and no one in whom he is interested can be an object of indifference to me.'

We expressed our acknowledgements and sat down behind the door, where there was a lame invalid of a sofa. Mrs Jellyby had very good hair but was too much occupied with her African duties to brush it.
15 The shawl in which she had been loosely muffled dropped onto her chair when she advanced to us; and as she turned to resume her seat, we could not help noticing that her dress didn't nearly meet up the back and that the open space was railed across with a lattice-work of stay-lace – like a summer-house.

The room, which was strewn with papers and nearly filled by a great writing-table covered with similar litter, was, I must say, not only very untidy but very dirty. We were obliged to take notice of that with
20 our sense of sight, even while, with our sense of hearing, we followed the poor child who had tumbled downstairs: I think into the back kitchen, where somebody seemed to stifle him...

'You find me, my dears,' said Mrs Jellyby, snuffing the two great office candles in tin candlesticks, which made the room taste strongly of hot tallow (the fire had gone out, and there was nothing in the grate but ashes, a bundle of wood, and a poker), 'you find me, my dears, as usual, very busy;
25 but that you will excuse. The African project at present employs my whole time. It involves me in correspondence with public bodies and private individuals anxious for the welfare of their species all over the country. I am happy to say it is advancing. We hope by this time next year to have from a hundred and fifty to two hundred healthy families cultivating coffee and educating the natives of Borrioboola-Gha, on the left bank of the Niger.'

2 Give a first response to this text with a partner. What do you think Dickens is showing you about Mrs Jellyby by the details he chooses to present? (Remember that he is *inventing* Mrs Jellyby for the reader.) Copy and complete the table on the following page to record your responses.

Details about Mrs Jellyby	Textual evidence	What this shows about her
1 Lives in semi-darkness	The visitors ascend 'in the dark'; Mrs J greets them by snuffing out 'two great office candles' by whose light she was working	
2 Has a large family but is unconcerned when one child tumbles dangerously down the stairs	Her 'face reflected none of the uneasiness which we could not help showing'	

Make three or four further entries. Then use your completed table to discuss why this can be seen as an ironic portrayal of character, given that Mrs Jellyby devotes herself to charitable causes.

3 Share your responses in a class discussion. Focus on Dickens' techniques of characterisation here, bearing in mind that good writers do nothing by accident and use a range of narrative devices to guide the reader's response. Talk about the effects Dickens creates by choosing to present Mrs Jellyby in the following ways:
   - through the eyes and in the language of Esther, a young woman
   - through giving particular details of Mrs Jellyby's appearance and the appearance of her room
   - through her direct speech and by drawing attention to (a) her tone, (b) her use of the phrase, which is typical of her, 'have the pleasure of receiving you', and (c) the strong emphasis she puts on 'correspondence with public bodies and private individuals'
   - through a developing portrait of Mrs Jellyby so that the reader's impressions of her build up in the course of the text.

4 Write a short analysis of the way Dickens uses varied techniques of characterisation to present Mrs Jellyby to the reader. Base this on the bullet points in question 3 above. Judge the effectiveness of each technique you describe.

Writing in the exam

Remember that in writing about character you will gain credit for showing how character is *created* and *presented* by the writer, rather than for giving your opinion about what the character is like. Use phrases like 'The writer characterises X by…' and 'The characterisation is achieved by the way in which the writer…'

Across AS and A2

As you work through this sub-section, refer back to your work in Unit 1 on how writers create and convey character. The AS Student Book has relevant material on pages 75–76 and 88–90. It reminds you that techniques of characterisation can be very different from text to text, and that you need to comment on them beyond the level of merely describing what the character is like.

Activity 20

1 Read the text below. It is the opening of a short story written in 1991.

From *Down the Clinical Disco* by Fay Weldon

You never know where you'll meet your own true love. I met mine down the clinical disco. That's him over there, the thin guy with the jeans, the navy jumper and the red woolly cap. He looks pretty much like anyone else, don't you think? That's hard work on his part, not to mention mine, but we got there in the end. Do you want a drink? Gin? Tonic? Fine. I'll just have an orange juice. I don't drink. Got to be careful. You never know

5   who's watching. They're everywhere. Sorry, forget I said that. Even a joke can be paranoia. Do you like my hair? That's a golden gloss rinse. Not my style really: I have this scar down my cheek: see, if I turn to the light? A good short crop is what suits me best, always has been: I suppose I've got what you call a strong face. Oops, sorry, dear, didn't mean to spill your gin; it's the heels. I do my best but I can never manage stilletos. But it's an ill wind; anyone watching would think I'm ever so slightly tipsy, and that's normal, isn't it. It is not absolutely

10   A-okay not to drink alcohol. On the obsessive side. *Darling, of course there are people watching.*

Let me tell you about the clinical disco while Eddie finishes his game of darts. He hates darts but darts are what men do in pubs, okay? The clinical disco is what they have once a month at Broadmoor. (Yes, that place. Broadmoor. The secure hospital for the criminally insane.) You didn't know they had women there? They do. One woman to every nine men. They often don't look all that like women when they go in but they sure as hell look like them when (and if,

15   if, if, if, if, if) they go out.

How did I get to be in there? You really want to know? I'd been having this crummy time at home and this crummy time at work. I was pregnant and married to this guy I loved, God knows why in retrospect, but I did, only he fancied my mother, and he got her pregnant too – while I was out at work – did you know women can get pregnant at fifty? He didn't, she didn't, I didn't – but she was! My mum said he only married me to be

20   near her anyway and I was the one who ought to have an abortion. So I did. It went wrong and messed me up inside, so I couldn't have babies, and my mum said what did it matter, I was a lesbian anyway, just look at me. I got the scar in a road accident, in case you're wondering. And I thought what the hell, who wants a man, who wants a mother, and walked out on them… No, I'm not crying. What do you think I am, a depressive? I'm as normal as the next person.

Take it further

Choose a text from Activities 14–20 which you think presents character in a striking way. Make an analysis of the writer's techniques of characterisation and give your opinion about their effectiveness.

Key term

• idiolect

2 Give a first response to this text in a small group. Establish the basic elements of the narrative. What is the setting? Who is the narrator and who do you think she is addressing? What does the writer show you about her life at present and in the past?

3 Explore Fay Weldon's technique of characterisation here. Agree on three or four clear statements you can make about how it differs from Dickens' in *Bleak House*. Relate these to what Fay Weldon is trying to do in her text compared with what Dickens is trying to do in his.

4 Compare your ideas with another group's. Then re-read aloud the three paragraphs from *Down the Clinical Disco*. Listen carefully to the **idiolect** (that is, the individual way of speaking) of the narrator. Comment on the way she uses language, focusing on:
- her colloquial register and use of idioms
- the way her narrative meanders, particularly in paragraph 1
- any changes of tone you can identify as the text goes on
- the way her syntax becomes more disjointed in paragraph 3.

Do you think Fay Weldon is presenting her character in a sympathetic or an unsympathetic light – or does she withhold judgement and leave it to the reader to decide?

5 Draw on your work in Activities 19 and 20, and in earlier activities, to make a class list of things you might comment on when writing about characterisation. As you do this, remember that characterisation can work in many ways. Your task is to identify and comment on the techniques used in a particular text, not to assume they will always be the same.

Point of view: How is the narrative presented, and the reader positioned?

Key terms

- **omniscient point of view**

- **first-person**

- **free indirect style**

All prose fiction writers present their narratives from a particular point of view. The point of view gives shape, and therefore structure, to a text, whether it is a whole novel or the kind of extract you will be given in the exam. The narrator's point of view positions you as a reader in a certain way and guides your response.

Remember that narrative point of view is the stance the writer chooses to take up in order to tell the story. The story may, for instance, be told in the third person from an **omniscient point of view**, where the writer assumes a god-like knowledge of the events and characters and shares this with the reader. On the other hand, it may be told in the **first person** from the subjective, restricted point of view of a character in the story: in this case, the reader sees only through the eyes and mind of that character. It may combine third- and first-person narration through the use of **free indirect style**, where the writer adopts the point of view (though not the voice) of a character.

The use of narrative point of view is never a simple matter, and it will call for explanation and comment in any text. Bear in mind that point of view in narrative refers to the stance of the writer in presenting the story: it is not the view held by a character towards other characters or events.

In Activities 21 and 22 you will explore how writers use narrative point of view to position readers and guide their response.

Activity 21

1 Look back as a class at these three texts:
- *A History of the World in 10½ Chapters* (Activity 14)
- *Persuasion* (Activity 14)
- *The Spire* (Activity 18).

Identify the narrative point of view in each text and discuss how it is established by the writer.

2 Find examples from the texts used in Activities 14–20 of (a) a third-person omniscient point of view, (b) a first-person point of view, and (c) free indirect style. Show how these different points of view are used to guide your response in each case.

Activity 22

1 Read the text on page 34. It is from a novel written in 1993 and set partly in Flanders during the First World War. In this extract, Jack Firebrace, a private, is on sentry duty during a battle. He has recently received a letter from his wife in London telling him that their son John is seriously ill in hospital.

Writing in the exam

Commenting on the writer's point of view and then showing how it shapes the reader's response is fundamental to successful analysis. Try to establish what the point of view is early on in your answer. This will help to keep you focused on technique, and relevant comments on style and language will develop out of it. Be alert to the possibility that the point of view may shift in the course of an extract.

From *Birdsong* by Sebastian Faulks

Jack was so tired that he had passed the stage where sleep was possible. His body had found some automatic course, powered by what source of wakefulness he couldn't say, that kept him awake if not alert while other men nodded and dozed on the ground, some slumped as though dead on the floor of the trench, some leaning
5 with their backs to the wooden boards. From further down the line he could hear trench repair parties at work.

John's face was now in his mind quite brightly: the wan, solitary boy at the tail of the street gang, the stumbling baby with his troublesome steps. He could hear his piping London voice with its parrot greetings and unfounded optimism. His pictured his boy
10 in the high-ceilinged hospital ward with its yellow smudge of gas lamps, the starched headdresses of the nurses and the smell of soap and disinfectant.

Sleep came to him like an unseen assailant. It was not the sinister light of the ward but the lamps of a huge bar in a pub on Lea Bridge Road: the men in suits and flat caps, smoke rising, ale glasses held aloft. There were other pictures, end to end: the
15 kitchen of his parents house in Stepney; a park, a dog; the lit pub again, thronged with people; John's face, the dear boy. He was aware of a great temptation being offered, some ease of mind, some sleep for which he would sell the lives of his comrades, and he embraced the offer, not aware that he was already slumbering, head slumped forward, cradled between the aching shoulders that had dug out French
20 earth for hours without respite.

He did not know he was asleep until he was awake again, feeling himself slump forward as a boot cracked into his ankle.

'What's your name?' It was an officer's voice.

'Firebrace, sir.'

25 'Oh, it's you, Firebrace'. He recognized Captain Weir's surprised tone.

'Were you asleep?' The first officer's voice was cold.

'I don't know, sir. I was just listening and –'

'You were asleep on duty. It's a court martial offence. See me tomorrow at six. Your sergeant will bring you. You know the punishment.'

30 'Yes, sir.'

Jack watched the two men walk on and swing left at the end of the firebay, the red ends of their cigarettes glowing.

2 Discuss with a partner the use of narrative point of view in this text. The point of view does not remain the same throughout. Explore how Sebastian Faulks presents Jack's experiences to you in (a) the first paragraph, down to 'repair parties at work', (b) the next two paragraphs, down to 'for hours without respite', and (c) the remaining paragraphs, beginning 'He did not know he was asleep'.

3 Share your responses in a class discussion. Then relate your conclusions to Faulks' purposes in this text, as you understand them. What attitude do you take towards Jack by seeing him partly from an external and partly from an internal point of view? What attitude do you take to the two officers at the end of the text, which is written in a detached third-person style?

4 Write a short analysis of the use and *effect* of narrative point of view in this text. Explain how the variations in point of view present Jack to the reader in a strongly sympathetic light.

Narrative voice and the voices of characters

Narrative voice is the voice of the person from whose point of view the events of a narrative are seen. Sometimes this will be the third-person voice of a detached observer. Sometimes it will be the voice of a character addressing the reader directly. Sometimes it will be the first-person voice of a character who seems to be speaking to an unidentified listener (as in *Down the Clinical Disco* in Activity 20). Narrative voice is closely related to narrative point of view: your comments on one will normally lead to comments on the other.

You need to distinguish in your analysis between the narrative voice and the voices of characters in the story. They speak in direct speech or dialogue. In Activity 23 you will explore a writer's voice that also presents voices in dialogue.

Activity 23

1 Read the text below. It was written in 2005 and is set in the First World War. In this extract, Viscount Abercrombie, a celebrated war poet, has just taken up his commission as a captain at the front line in Flanders. His first duty is to deal with a private found guilty of refusing to obey an order.

From *The First Casualty* by Ben Elton

A cold drizzle was falling and it seemed that what summer there had been in Flanders that year was already over. Abercrombie stepped up to address the prisoner.

'I do not know you, Private Hopkins,' he said, 'and I had not taken up my post when the offence of which you have been found guilty was committed. I therefore take no pleasure in what is now required of me. However, the army
5 code leaves me no choice.'

Hopkins attempted to hold his head up and stare Abercrombie down but his whole body was shaking with fear.

'We all have a choice,' he mumbled. 'Don't assuage your conscience with me.'

If Abercrombie had heard the man, he ignored his comment.

'You have been found guilty of disobeying a direct order.'

10 'I didn't refuse to fight! I refused to put on a lice-ridden jacket! Would you have put it on, *Viscount*?'

'You disobeyed an order. Repeatedly. You could by rights have been shot. Do you have anything to say?'

'Yes.'

'Speak then.'

'Your poetry's shit, Captain. "Forever England"? What a lot of lying shit. I've heard *boys* quote it, Captain. Sixteen-
15 year-old *boys* parroting that shit as they marched off to their deaths. Forever England? Forever shit. Shit, shit, shit.'

Abercrombie stood for a moment as if he had been struck. The colour drained from his face. It seemed to the policeman watching that the captain had to make some effort to collect himself.

'Is that all, Private?' he asked finally.

'Yes, and more than enough.'

20 'Field Punishment Number One!'

Two of the military policemen removed Hopkins's handcuffs and dragged him towards the gun limber. Then they lashed him across one of its wheels, spreading his limbs wide like the male figure in Da Vinci's famous sketch, a copy of which Abercrombie had had pinned upon his wall at school.

Hopkins hung upon the wheel all day.

Take it further

Use your own private reading of novels to practise commenting on writers' use of voice in narrative. Pick passages at random, read them twice, and then write brief notes on (a) the narrative voice and how it presents events/ situations in the novel, and (b) the voices of characters and how their idiolects reflect their personalities/ feelings.

2 Give a first response to the text with a partner. With which character do you feel more sympathy, and why?

3 Look closely at the dialogue between Abercrombie and Hopkins. Consider the textual evidence for making the following statements, and say whether you agree with them.

   A Ben Elton presents Abercrombie as an officer to whom Hopkins is just a criminal rather than a human being.

   B Ben Elton presents Hopkins as wild and out of control.

   C Hopkins's outburst seems to be directed at propaganda poetry in general rather than at Abercrombie's poems in particular.

   D The severe punishment Abercrombie gives is personally motivated rather than an imposition of 'the army code'.

E Ben Elton allows the reader to interpret this dialogue in different ways.

4 Share your ideas in small group discussion. Take particular account of the narrative voice here. Consider the effect of the narrator's comments in:
   • the first sentence of the text
   • 'If Abercrombie had heard the man, he ignored his comment'
   • 'It seemed to the policeman watching that the captain had to make some effort to collect himself'
   • the description of Hopkins being lashed to the wheel and the information that Abercrombie had Da Vinci's 'famous sketch' on display in his public school study
   • the last sentence of the text, with its emphasis on the verb 'hung' (as opposed to, say, 'remained').

5 Compare in a class discussion the way Sebastian Faulks in *Birdsong* (Activity 22) and Ben Elton in *The First Casualty* use narrative voice to present a view of war. What impressions does each writer give of ordinary soldiers, on the one hand, and of officers, on the other? Do they evoke these impressions in similar or in different ways?

Syntax: How does sentence structure contribute to meaning?

In constructing a narrative voice, writers use a range of syntactical forms and devices to make the voice distinctive and to create particular effects. They craft words into patterns as carefully as poets do. Your analysis, therefore, needs to take account of:

• the length and structure of sentences
• the rhythm of sentences
• the pattern of sentences in a section of text
• the use of grammar to create representations of thought or speech.

The sounds of words in a sentence or a group of sentences will also contribute to the making of meaning. In Activity 24 you will explore the ways in which writers use syntax, grammar and sound to construct voice in their narratives.

Activity 24

1 Read the text below. It is from a novel written in 2006, set in America in the future. A father and his young son are among the few survivors of a global catastrophe. In this extract they are trying to reach the coast.

From *The Road* by Cormac McCarthy

They bore on south in the days and weeks to follow. Solitary and dogged. A raw hill country. Aluminium houses. At times they could see stretches of the interstate highway below them through the bare stands of second-growth timber. Cold and growing colder. Just beyond the high gap in the mountains they stood and looked over the great gulf to the south where the country as far as they could see was burned away, the blackened shapes of rock rising out of the shoals of ash and billows of ash rising up and blowing downcountry through the waste. The track of the dull sun moving unseen beyond the murk.

They were days fording that cauterized terrain. The boy had found some crayons and painted his facemask with fangs and he trudged on uncomplaining. One of the front wheels of the cart had gone wonky. What to do about it? Nothing. Where all was burnt to ash before them no fires were to be had and the nights were long and dark and cold beyond anything they'd yet encountered. Cold to crack the stones. To take your life. He held the boy shivering against him and counted each frail breath in the blackness.

2 Explore as a class the way Cormac McCarthy has structured these two paragraphs. Focus on:
- the use and effect of short phrases rather than sentences in parts of the text
- the effect of the long sentence with several **subordinate clauses** beginning 'Just beyond the high gap'
- the effect of representing thought by 'What to do about it? Nothing' (as opposed to, say, 'There was nothing they could do about it')
- the pace and rhythm of sentences: how would you describe this and its effect on you as you read?

Make sure you relate these aspects of structure to McCarthy's purposes as you understand them.

3 Read the text below. It is the opening of a short story first published in 1843. The narrator has resolved to commit a murder.

From *The Tell-Tale Heart* by Edgar Allan Poe

True! – nervous – very, very dreadfully nervous I had been and am; but why will you say I am mad? The disease had sharpened my senses – not destroyed – not dulled them. Above all was the sense of hearing acute. I heard all things in the heaven and in the earth. I heard many things in hell. How, then, am I mad? Hearken! And observe how healthily – how calmly I can tell you the whole story.

It is impossible to say how first the idea entered my brain; but, once conceived, it haunted me day and night. Object there was none. Passion there was none. I loved the old man. He had never wronged me. He had never given me insult. For his gold I had no desire. I think it was his eye! yes it was this! He had the eye of a vulture – a pale blue eye, with a film over it. Whenever it fell upon me, my blood ran cold; and so by degrees – very gradually – I made up my mind to take the life of the old man, and thus rid myself of the eye forever.

4 Discuss as a class the following aspects of structure and the effects they create:
- Poe's use of the first-person voice in a passage that addresses the reader, or an implied listener, directly
- the use of a conversational tone and an informal register
- the heavy use of punctuation and the varied syntax.

What impression of the narrator's character emerges from Poe's use of these devices?

> **Key term**
> - subordinate clause

How writers guide readers' judgements

The explicit purpose of some prose fiction is to make the reader share the attitude a writer has towards his or her subject matter. This will often involve judgements about a character. Look back briefly to the extract from *Bleak House* in Activity 19 to remind yourself how Dickens shapes your view of Mrs Jellyby. In analysing the style of an extract, you need to be alert to a writer's possible use of ***irony*** to guide the reader's response. In Activity 25 you will explore the way irony works in two satirical novels.

Activity 25

1 Read the text below, which is from a nineteenth-century novel. In this extract the narrator, an aspiring author, pays a visit to the headmaster of a minor public school.

From *The Way of All Flesh* by Samuel Butler

When Dr Skinner was a very young man, hardly more than five-and-twenty, the headmastership of Roughborough Grammar School had fallen vacant, and he had been unhesitatingly appointed. The result justified the selection. Dr Skinner's pupils distinguished themselves at whichever University they went to. He moulded their
5   minds after the manner of his own, and stamped an impression on them which was indelible in after-life. Some boys, of course, were incapable of appreciating the beauty and loftiness of Dr Skinner's nature. Some such boys, alas! there will be in every school: upon them Dr Skinner's hand was very properly a heavy one.

I once had the honour of playing a game of chess with this great man. It was during
10   the Christmas holidays, and I had come down to Roughborough for a few days on business. It was very gracious of him to take notice of me, for if I was a light of literature at all it was of the very lightest kind.

The game had been a long one, and at half-past nine, when supper came in, we had each of us a few pieces remaining. 'What will you take for supper, Dr Skinner?' said
15   Mrs Skinner in a silvery voice.

He made no answer for some time, but at last, in a tone of almost superhuman solemnity, he said, first, 'Nothing,' and then, 'Nothing whatever'.

By and by, however, I had the sense come over me as though I were nearer to the consummation of all things* than I had ever yet been. The room seemed to grow
20   dark, as an expression came over Dr Skinner's face which showed that he was about to speak. The expression gathered force, the room grew darker and darker. 'Stay,' he at length added, and I felt that here at any rate was an end to a suspense which was rapidly becoming unbearable. 'Stay – I may presently take a glass of cold water – and a small piece of bread and butter'.

25   As he said the word 'butter' his voice sank to a hardly audible whisper; then there was a sigh as though of relief when the sentence was concluded, and the universe this time was safe.

---

* the consummation of all things: the end of the world

2 Discuss with a partner the attitude you take towards Dr Skinner. As a starting-point, consider what textual evidence there is for seeing him as:
- an excellent role model for his pupils
- kind
- condescending
- happily married
- intellectually distinguished
- conceited.

Then turn your attention to particular words and phrases Butler uses to present Dr Skinner to the reader. Say how you interpret the following:
- 'stamped an impression on them which was indelible in after-life'
- 'upon them Dr Skinner's hand was very properly a heavy one'
- 'in a tone of almost superhuman solemnity'.

3 Find other words and phrases that suggest that Butler is using his narrator to give a surface impression of Dr Skinner at odds with the view he holds himself. 'Saying one thing and meaning the opposite' is a partial definition of irony, which will take you some of the way to appreciating Butler's narrative technique. Look also for examples of **hyperbole** (deliberate exaggeration for comic effect), **bathos** (a sense of anti-climax for comic effect) and **incongruity** (a comic mismatch between two things).

4 Read the text below. It is from a novel written in 1932 satirising (that is, making fun of through ridicule) prose fiction that owes too much to Freudian psychology and ideas about the passionate harmony between man and nature. Adam, an old farm servant, is in love with the image of a teenage girl, Elfine, who is having a relationship with Richard Hawk-Monitor from 'the Hall'. It is spring.

From *Cold Comfort Farm* by Stella Gibbons

By the time the buggy reached Beershorn, which was a good seven miles from Howling, Adam had forgotten what he was going there for. The reins lay between his knotted fingers, and his face, unseeing, was lifted to the dark sky.

From the stubborn interwoven strata of his subconscious, thought seeped up into his
5 dim conscious; not as an integral part of that consciousness, but as an impalpable emanation, a crepuscular addition, from the unsleeping life in the restless trees and fields surrounding him. The country for miles, under the blanket of the dark which brought no peace, was in its annual ferment of spring growth; worm jarred with worm and seed with seed. Frond leapt on root and hare on hare. Beetle and finch-fly
10 were not spared. The trout-sperm in the muddy hollow under Nettle Flitch Weir were agitated, as well they might be. The long screams of hunting owls tore across the night, scarlet lines on black. In the pauses, every ten minutes, they mated. It seemed chaotic, but it was more methodically arranged than you might think. But Adam's deafness and blindness came from within, as well as without; earthly calm seeped up
15 from his subconscious and met descending calm in his conscious. Twice the buggy was pulled out of hedges by a passing farm-hand, and once narrowly shaved the vicar, driving home from tea at the Hall.

'Where are you, my birdling?' Adam's blind lips asked the unanswering darkness and the loutish shapes of the unbudded trees. 'Did I cowdle thee as a mommet for
20 this?'

He knew that Elfine was out on the Downs, striding on her unsteady colt's legs towards the Hall and the bright, sardonic hands of Richard Hawk-Monitor.

Key terms
- **hyperbole**
- **bathos**
- **incongruity**

Key term

• parody

5 Explore as a class how Stella Gibbons' satire works in this text. Include in your discussion some consideration of:
  • the writer's use of an apparently serious narrative voice
  • phrases that give the reader hints that she is not really serious but making fun of a fictional genre
  • the meaning of 'impalpable emanation', 'crepuscular', 'cowdle' and 'mommet' (look them up in a dictionary)
  • *parody* – that is, imitation for comic effect
  • exaggerated imagery.

  Do you think the satire is effective – or is it unsubtle and overdone?

6 Write a short analysis of the writer's use of humour in one of these texts. Comment on how the narrative voice and the language are used to satirise the writer's chosen target.

Independent research

A number of the texts quoted in the activities above are taken from novels written after 1990. They have also been chosen to relate in theme to the four topic areas for Section B of this Unit – 'Relationships', 'Identifying Self', 'Journeys' and 'War'. Look back through them and choose two or three of these novels to read in full, in order to illuminate your study of literature in Section B.

Summary of your learning in Part 2

In this part you have developed your skills of analysing unprepared prose in the following areas:

• making your own interpretation of meaning rather than waiting to be told
• identifying the writer's focus in a text
• appreciating how writers make precise choices of language to create the meaning they want
• commenting on how and why writers create setting
• commenting on the techniques writers use to create and convey character
• commenting on the use writers make of narrative viewpoint and voice
• commenting on the use writers make of syntax
• commenting on how writers shape your attitude to a text.

Copy this list of skills. Use a tick system to show how confident you are at present of being able to apply each of them: 3 ticks = 'very confident', 2 ticks = 'gaining more confidence', 1 tick = 'lacking confidence'. This self-evaluation should lead, if necessary, to a programme of skill revision before you move on to further work on prose analysis in Part 3.

Writing in the exam

The highest marks in the exam are awarded for 'evaluative' responses: that is, for showing what meaning *you* find in the text, and how your understanding of it has been shaped. Do not be afraid to commit yourself to making your own interpretation and evaluation; the meaning of a text is not fixed before you read it, and its effectiveness is a matter for you to decide.

3 Unprepared poetry and prose: Independent approaches

This part encourages you to approach unprepared analysis of poems and prose passages in a creative and questioning way.

Unit 3 builds on your work at AS by putting the emphasis on the *interpretation* and *evaluation* of texts. The activities below will support you in taking an independent approach to Section A. They suggest ways of working that help you to be open-minded as you explore new texts.

Assessment objectives

The higher bands of AO2 (which accounts for 30 marks out of the 40 available) reward your personal response to a poem or a prose passage in Section A, and your ability to make your own meaning by the way you interpret it. The Band 5 requirements state that the student:

- provides an evaluative and analytical, critical understanding of a literary text which enables a sophisticated response
- evaluates features of structure, form and language effectively
- evaluates the text and demonstrates a developed understanding of the meanings which enables an independent response.

The key words here are 'evaluates' (as opposed to 'examines') and 'independent'. These indicate the difference between an excellent and a good answer.

Making your own interpretation:
What does it mean to *me*?

The poem in Activity 26 is best studied first with one or more partners. You will each need a copy of it.

Activity 26

1 Read the poem opposite aloud.

2 Work together to develop an interpretation of the poem. Annotate your copy of it in the way shown on page 42. The annotations were made by two A-level students in 20 minutes; you can decide whether or not to follow their ideas.

Under a Ramshackle Rainbow

A dead tree.
On a rotten branch sit two wingless birds. Among leaves
on the ground a man is searching for his hands.
It is fall.

A stagnant marsh.
On a mossy stone sits the man angling. The hook
is stuck in the waterlily.
The waterlily is stuck in the mud.

An overgrown ruin.
In the grass the man sleeps sitting up. A raindrop descends
in slow-motion through space.
Somewhere in the grass a pike flounders.

A dry well.
At the bottom lies a dead fly. In the wood nearby
a spider gropes through the fog.
The man is trapped in the spiderweb on the horizon.

An abandoned ant hill.
Above a little woodmarsh floats the man. The sun
is just going down. The man has already stopped growing.
The ants gather on the shore.

Ingemar Gustafson, translated from the Swedish by May Swenson

Under a Ramshackle Rainbow ●———— Combination of ruin and beauty – a paradox

1st line of each stanza is an image of death in Nature

● A dead tree.
On a rotten branch sit two wingless birds. Among leaves on the ground a man is searching for his hands. ●———— Birds and man are alike – both are mutilated

Two meanings of 'fall'? Autumn and fall of man, biblical?

● It is fall.

A stagnant marsh.
On a mossy stone sits the man angling. The hook is stuck in the waterlily.
The waterlily is stuck in the mud. ●

Everything is 'frozen', immobile, 'stagnant', 'stuck in the mud'

The images in this stanza like those in a haiku – man angling, waterlily, mossy stone

Same pattern as 1st line

● An overgrown ruin.
In the grass the man sleeps sitting up. A raindrop descends

A wider perspective

● in slow-motion through space.
Somewhere in the grass a pike flounders. ●———— Painfully clinging to life

Each stanza built up in the same way

● A dry well.
At the bottom lies a dead fly. In the wood nearby a spider gropes through the fog.
The man is trapped in the spiderweb on the horizon. ●

Like a horror film, or a nightmare

An abandoned ant hill.
Above a little woodmarsh floats the man. The sun ●———— The man's dead now

Just evening? – or the sun could be dying

● is just going down. The man has already stopped growing.
The ants gather on the shore. ●———— Ants on the march!

Ideas	Questions
• Describing the end of the world? • An allegory – could be a warning about man destroying the environment	• Is there meant to be a time-scale in the poem? • Is there meant to be any development in the poem, or is it just 5 snapshots of the same thing?

Writing in the exam

As long as your annotations are purposeful, 10 to 15 minutes working in this way on your poem or prose passage before you begin to write your answer will be time well spent.

3 Sum up the ideas about meaning you have arrived at. Then relate these to the structure, form and language of the poem. How effectively does the poet's style create and convey the themes you have identified?

4 Share your ideas in a class discussion. Justify your own interpretation by close reference to what you have found in the text and your opinions about the way it is written.

5 If you have found this poem interesting, write a detailed analysis of it. As you develop your own interpretation, explain how other readers could read the poem in different ways, and why.

Note:

Annotating a text with a partner or in a small group is a powerful way of reading. Use it as often as you can to ask questions about new texts. Remember that your annotations will always be *provisional*: they record your developing response and do not commit you to a firm view. Find the method that works best for you, and become familiar with it so that you can use a version of it in the exam.

Activity 27

1 Read the complete short story below.

The *Snow Child* by Angela Carter

Midwinter – invincible, immaculate. The Count and his wife go riding, he on a grey mare and she on a black one, she wrapped in glittering pelts of black foxes; and she wore high, black, shining boots with scarlet heels, and spurs. Fresh snow fell on snow already fallen; when it ceased, the whole world was white. 'I wish I had a girl as white as snow,' says the Count. They ride on. They come to a hole in the snow; this
5   hole is filled with blood. He says: 'I wish I had a girl as red as blood.' So they ride on again; here is a raven, perched on a bare bough. 'I wish I had a girl as black as that bird's feather.'

As soon as he completed her description, there she stood, beside the road, white skin, red mouth, black hair and stark naked; she was the child of his desire and the Countess hated her. The Count lifted her up and sat her in front of him on his saddle but the Countess had only one thought: how shall I get rid of her?

10   The Countess dropped her glove in the snow and told the girl to get down to look for it; she meant to gallop off and leave her there but the Count said: 'I'll buy you new gloves'. At that, the furs sprang off the Countess's shoulders and twined round the naked girl. Then the Countess threw her diamond brooch through the ice of a frozen pond. 'Dive in and fetch it for me,' she said; she thought the girl would drown. But the Count said: 'Is she a fish, to swim in such cold weather?' Then her boots leapt off the Countess's
15   feet and on to the girl's legs. Now the Countess was as bare as a bone and the girl furred and booted; the Count felt sorry for his wife. They came to a bush of roses, all in flower. 'Pick me one,' said the Countess to the girl. 'I can't deny you that,' said the Count.

So the girl picks a rose; pricks her finger on the thorn; bleeds; screams; falls.

20   Weeping, the Count got off his horse, unfastened his breeches and thrust his virile member into the dead girl. The Countess reined in her stamping mare and watched him narrowly; he was soon finished.

Then the girl began to melt. Soon there was nothing left of her but a feather a bird might have dropped; a bloodstain, like the trace of a fox's kill on the snow; and the rose she had pulled off the bush. Now the Countess had all her clothes on again. With her long hand, she stroked her furs. The Count picked up the
25   rose, bowed and handed it to his wife; when she touched it, she dropped it.

'It bites!' she said.

2 Annotate a copy of the text in a small group as you share your responses to this story. Use a method that works well for you all.

3 Write EITHER an individual OR a joint analysis of *The Snow Child*. Evaluate Angela Carter's use of structure, form and language to convey her themes as you understand them.

Questioning the text:
What meaning is there beneath the surface?

Unprepared texts may not be exactly what they seem on first reading. This is not because they contain 'hidden meanings' or a secret code that the reader has to unlock. It is more likely that the poet or writer is creating a narrator or a persona who addresses you in a way that reflects their particular view of things. This will not necessarily be the same as the writer's.

Activity 28

1 Read the text below. It is the opening of an American novel written in 1972 which became a best seller and attracted a cult following.

Key term

• unreliable narrator

From *The Dice Man* by Luke Rhinehart

I am a large man, with big butcher's hands, great oak thighs, rock-jawed head, and massive, thick-lens glasses. I'm six foot four and weigh close to two hundred and thirty pounds; I look like Clark Kent, except that when I take off my business suit I am barely faster than my wife, only slightly more powerful than men half my size, and leap buildings not at
5 all, no matter how many leaps I'm given.

As an athlete I am exceptionally mediocre in all major sports and in several minor ones. I play daring and disastrous poker and cautious and competent stock market. I married a pretty former cheerleader and rock-and-roll singer and have two lovely, non-neurotic and abnormal children. I am deeply religious, have written the lovely first-rate pornographic novel Naked Before the World, and am not now nor have I ever
10 been Jewish.

I realize that it's your job as a reader to try to create a credible consistent pattern out of all this, but I'm afraid I must add that I am normally atheistic, have given away at random thousands of dollars, have been a sporadic revolutionary against the governments of the United States, New York City, the Bronx and Scarsdale, and am still a card-carrying member of the Republican Party. I am the creator, as most of you
15 know, of those nefarious Dice Centers for experiments in human behaviour which have been described by the Journal of Abnormal Psychology as 'outrageous', 'unethical' and 'informative'; by the New York Times as 'incredibly misguided and corrupt'; by Time magazine as 'sewers', and by the Evergreen Review as 'brilliant and fun'. I have been a devoted husband, multiple adulterer and experimental homosexual; an able, highly praised analyst, and the only one ever dismissed from both the Psychiatrists Association of
20 New York (PANY) and from the American Medical Association (for 'ill-considered activities' and 'probable incompetence'). I am admired and praised by thousands of dicepeople throughout the nation but have twice been a patient in a mental institution, once been in jail, and am currently a fugitive, which I hope to remain, Die willing, at least until I have completed this 543-page autobiography.

Take it further

Make a class collection of poems and prose passages which address the reader in the voice of EITHER (a) a first-person narrator, OR (b) a persona or a third person which seems not to be the same as the writer's voice. Practise analysing them in order to explore why the writer wants to create this perspective. Sometimes the effect will be ironic: the writer will be shaping your view of the narrator/persona without using direct authorial comment.

2 Give a first response to *The Dice Man* extract in a small group. Everyone should jot down three impressions they get of the narrator here and one statement about the writer's possible purposes in presenting him like this.

3 Compare your responses. Do you find the narrator's voice amusing? likeable? irritating? self-contradictory? difficult to pin down? Is there evidence that this may be an *unreliable narrator*, whom you should not take entirely on trust?

4 Read the poem opposite in a small group. Read it aloud twice. The second time, take one stanza each.

5 Discuss what you think this poem is about. As you do so, take account of the voice in the poem. Is it personal? objective? judgemental? non-judgemental? a mixture of these? Do all readers have to adopt the same attitude to Sadie and Maud?

Sadie and Maud

Maud went to college.
Sadie stayed at home.
Sadie scraped life
With a fine-tooth comb.

5 She didn't leave a tangle in.
Her comb found every strand.
Sadie was one of the livingest chits
In all the land.

Sadie bore two babies
10 Under her maiden name.
Maud and Ma and Papa
Nearly died of shame.

When Sadie said her last so-long
Her girls struck out from home.
15 (Sadie had left as heritage
Her fine tooth-comb.)

Maud, who went to college,
Is a thin brown mouse.
She is living all alone
20 In this old house.

Gwendolyn Brooks

6 Compare the way in which Luke Rhinehart and Gwendolyn Brooks choose to present their texts to the reader. *The Dice Man* is written in the voice and from the viewpoint of a first-person narrator, and uses the genre of **autobiographical fiction**. 'Sadie and Maud' is written in the voice and from the viewpoint of a third-person narrator and uses the genre of a ballad. How do these literary techniques help you to *interrogate* the texts rather than read them unquestioningly?

Key term

• autobiographical fiction

Using prior reading:
What can I bring as a reader to this text?

Your prior reading of poems and prose fiction puts you in a strong position to analyse unprepared texts. Some A-level students find this hard to believe and are apprehensive about tackling unprepared texts. This is understandable. Remember, though, that you have considerable experience of different kinds of texts to draw on when faced with a new challenge. The key is to tap into this accumulated experience and use it relevantly as you plan and write your response. Activity 29 gives you practice in doing so.

Activity 29

1 Read the text opposite. It is from a novel written in 1996. The two characters are Larry Freeman, a Los Angeles policeman, and his friend, Jack Parlabane, a journalist nicknamed 'Scotland' who is on the trail of a crime story. He wants Larry's advice.

From *Quite Ugly One Morning* by Christopher Brookmyre

A strange scent in the nostrils, stronger all the time. The feeling of being on to something big but not knowing what it was. A lot of corpses and the broken traces of a connection; like discovering short stretches of an overgrown path through a dense forest, but not yet able to see where those stretches came from or were leading to.

5

Lieutenant Larry Freeman had been nervous. Larry was about seven feet tall with shoulders 'the size of a Kansas prairie', as his wife put it, a frightening sight in black shades and a black, bald head. And Larry was never nervous.

'Something in the air then, big man?'

'Uh-huh,' he had said slowly in that rumbling burr you could feel in your own diaphragm. 'Remember man, cops like the sound of openin' a fresh can of beer when the case is closed. The sound of openin' a fresh can of worms don't fill their heart with joy, know what I'm sayin'? Now I ain't sayin' there's dirty cops in my precinct, but cops gotta talk to snitches and there's gotta be some give and take. And no news travels faster than a secret.

10

15

'You gotta be careful what yo askin' and who yo askin', Scotland. Somebody starts playin' join-the-dots with a bunch of random stiffs and whole lotta people get trigger-happy. Maybe you ain't even connectin' anythin' to them or to stiffs they got anythin' to do with, but they don't know that and they ain't gonna stop to ask if they get you in their sights.'

20

'You're saying I should back off? Forget it all?'

'That's up to you, man. Maybe it's too late to back off. But you better be watchin' your back. I was you, I'd get me a gun.'

Parlabane shook his head.

'You know how I feel about guns. I couldn't carry one of those things around with me, forget about it.'

25

'Yeah, but I'd have one all the same. Keep it where I could get to it in a hurry. I got a spare one in the john. In a plastic bag taped under the cistern lid. Someone catches me off-guard at home, I got a chance if he lets me take a leak or I can just make it to the bathroom. Mitch Casey keeps one in his ice box.'

30

'What, so he's got a chance if the bad guy asks for a beer? You're all fucking crazy.'

'You ain't from L.A., Jack.'

Writing in the exam

When you are faced with an unprepared poem or prose passage, remember that you will have read other texts that use similar stylistic techniques. Capitalise on this. Making explicit or implicit links with your prior reading, or with your prescribed texts, will provide a thoughtful context for your response to the unprepared poem/ passage.

2 Discuss with a partner the genre of this text and the **genre conventions** Christopher Brookmyre is using here. Draw on your prior reading knowledge to comment on:
  • the way Brookmyre characterises Larry through (a) his description of his appearance, (b) his idiolect, and (c) his attitudes to the police and to crime
  • the extensive use of dialogue to move the narrative forward
  • the use of figurative language, syntax and tone in the first paragraph.

3 Work together to add 10–15 lines to the end of this passage. Invent your own content or develop the plot by introducing one of the 'trigger-happy' characters about whom Larry says, 'they ain't gonna stop to ask if you get in their sights'.

4 Exchange your writing with another pair's. Make an evaluation of their use of genre conventions to present plot and character.

5 Read the poem opposite.

6 Fill in a copy of the table below to help you respond to E.E. Cummings's use of the sonnet form here.

'i thank You God for most this amazing'

i thank You God for most this amazing
day:for the leaping greenly spirits of trees
and a blue true dream of sky and for everything
which is natural which is infinite which is yes

(i who have died am alive again today,
and this is the sun's birthday;this is the birth
day of life and of love and wings:and of the gay
great happening illimitably earth)

how should tasting touching hearing seeing
breathing any – lifted from the no
of all nothing – human merely being
doubt unimaginable You?

(now the ears of my ears awake and
now the eyes of my eyes are opened)

E.E. Cummings

Conventional sonnet	Cummings's version of the sonnet
Often on the theme of love	
Often addresses an unseen listener	
Often makes strong use of imagery	
Structured in 14 lines, often 3 quatrains and a couplet rhyming ababcdcdefefgg; rhythm normally based on iambic pentameter	
Usually orthodox spelling, punctuation, grammar and *graphology*	

7 Compare your completed table with a partner's. Then use your knowledge of conventionally written sonnets to discuss what Cummings is doing in this poem. You could look at, for example, Shakespeare's 'Shall I compare thee to a summer's day?' and Elizabeth Barrett Browning's 'How do I love thee? Let me count the ways'.

Do you think that, by modifying the normal sonnet form, Cummings is making new meanings that gain impact from the unorthodox way in which he writes? Or does his poem seem to you merely gimmicky?

8 If you have found the texts in this activity interesting, write a detailed analysis of one of them. Explain how the writer/poet makes use of a particular genre to shape your response.

Using comparison:
How does this text illuminate that one?

Your work for Section A does not require you to make comparisons between texts. However, exploring related poems or prose passages is an excellent way of deepening your response to an individual text. This is particularly true when analysing literature from the past. Activity 30 demonstrates a comparative method that you can apply to your own choices of poetry or prose.

Activity 30

1 Read the two poems below. 'An Elegy', published in 1640, is thought to have been occasioned by a serious illness.

Long Distance

Though my mother was already two years dead
Dad kept her slippers warming by the gas,
put hot water bottles her side of the bed
and still went to renew her transport pass.

5 You couldn't just drop in. You had to phone.
He'd put you off an hour to give him time
to clear away her things and look alone
as though his still raw love were such a crime.

He couldn't risk my blight of disbelief
10 though sure that very soon he'd hear her key
scrape in the rusted lock and end his grief.
He *knew* she'd just popped out to get the tea.

I believe life ends with death, and that is all.
You haven't both gone shopping; just the same,
15 in my new black leather phone book there's your name
and the disconnected number I still call.

Tony Harrison

An Elegy

Since you must go, and I must bid farewell,
    Hear, mistress, your departing servant tell
What it is like: and do not think they can
    Be idle words, though of a parting man;
5 It is as if night should shade noon-day,
    Or that the sun was here, but forced away;
And we were left under that dark hemisphere,
    Where we must feel it dark for half a year…
My health will leave me; and when you depart
10   How shall I do, sweet mistress, for my heart?
You would restore it? No, that's worth a fear,
    As if it were not worthy to be there:
Oh, keep it still; for it had rather be
    Your sacrifice, than here remain with me.
15 And so I spare it: come what can become
    Of me, I'll softly tread unto my tomb;
Or like a ghost walk silent among men,
    Till I may see both it and you again.

Ben Jonson

2 Annotate a copy of these poems to bring out (a) their similar themes, and (b) their different uses of structure, form and language to convey these themes. Use your own method of notation.

3 Draw on your annotations to complete a copy of the table on page 48. Some entries about 'Long Distance' have been made: you can build on the ideas or take your own approach. Your main task is to make entries about 'An Elegy'.

	Long Distance	*An Elegy*
Subject matter	1 Father can't come to terms with his wife's death 2 Poem's speaker takes a sceptical view of this – but finds he's behaving in the same way when his father dies	
Themes	1 Love outlasts death 2 Superstitious belief by the poem's speaker in an afterlife, despite his agnosticism	
Language	1 Voice of the poem's speaker has a frank, direct, colloquial register (sounds northern) – addressing the reader/reflecting aloud on own experience 2 Figurative language – two strong uses of metaphor in a poem mainly without imagery: 'still raw love', 'my blight of disbelief' – picks out the poem's central ideas	
Form and structure	1 Narrative form in stanzas 1–3; change of focus and rhyme scheme in stanza 4 to show how the poem's speaker is both unlike and like his father 2 Quatrains with a regular rhyme scheme in stanzas 1–3 and basic iambic pentameter – a formal structure, perhaps to celebrate the traditional 'love conquers death' theme, while at the same time questioning it	

Take it further

Throughout your A2 course, try to read a range of poems from recent anthologies. Among the best of these are *Staying Alive* and *Being Alive*, both edited by Neil Astley and published by Bloodaxe Books. The poems are arranged thematically and will give you plenty of material for comparison, as well as for choosing individual poems on which to practise writing analyses.

4 Read the two extracts below and on page 49. The first is from a novel written in 1984. The second is from a novel written in 1771. In each extract the narrator is passing an evening in a strange city.

From *Money* by Martin Amis

He dropped me off on Broadway. Eleven o'clock. What can a grown male do alone at night in Manhattan, except go in search of trouble or pornography?

Me, I spent an improving four hours on Forty-Second Street, dividing my time between a space-game arcade and the basement gogo bar next door. In the arcade
5 the proletarian ghosts of the New York night, these darkness-worshippers, their terrified faces reflected in the screens, stand hunched over their controls. They look like human forms of mutant moles and bats, hooked on the radar, rumble and wow of these stocky new robots who play with you if you give them money. They'll talk too, for a price. *Launch Mission, Circuit Completed, Firestorm, Flashpoint, Timewarp,*
10 *Crackup, Blackout!* The kids, tramps and loners in here, they are the mineshaft spirits of the new age. Their grandparents must have worked underground. I know mine did. In the gogo bar men and women are eternally ranged against each other, kept apart by a wall of drink, a moat of poison, along which mad matrons and bad bouncers stroll.

15 At eleven thirty or thereabouts the old barmaid said to me, 'See? She's talking to you, Cheryl's talking to you. You want to buy Cheryl a drink?'

I paid the ten and said nothing. The old barmaid in her brown condom, she might have been last night's sister. That's my life: repetition, repetition. True, the chicks on the ramp provided some variety. None of them wore any pants. At first I assumed
20 that they got paid a lot more for this. Looking at the state of the place, though, and at the state of the chicks, I ended up deciding they got paid a lot less.

From *Humphry Clinker* by Tobias Smollett

Without further preamble, I was persuaded to go to a ball… I sat a couple of
long hours, half stifled, in the midst of a noisome crowd; and could not help
wondering, that so many hundreds of those that rank as rational creatures, could find
entertainment in seeing a succession of insipid animals, describing the same dull
5   figure* for a whole evening, on an area, not much bigger than a tailor's shop-board…
The continual swimming of these phantoms before my eyes gave me a swimming
of the head; which was also affected by the fouled air, circulating through such a
number of rotten human bellows – … and I dropt senseless upon the floor…

I no sooner got home, than I sent for Dr Ch_____, who assured me, I needed not be
10 alarmed, for my swooning was entirely occasioned by an accidental impression of
fetid effluvia* upon nerves of uncommon sensibility. I know not how other people's
nerves are constructed; but one would imagine they must be made of very coarse
materials, to stand the shock of such a horrid assault. It was, indeed, *a compound of
villainous smells*, in which the most violent stinks, and the most powerful perfumes,
15 contended for the mastery. Imagine yourself a high exalted essence of mingled
odours, arising from putrid gums, imposthumated* lungs, sour flatulencies, rank arm-
pits, sweating feet, running sores and issues, plasters, ointments and embrocations,
hungary-water spirit of lavender, … and sal volatile; besides a thousand frowzy
steams, which I could not analyse. Such is the fragrant ether we breathe in the polite
20 assemblies of Bath – Such is the atmosphere I have exchanged for the pure, elastic,
animating air of the Welsh mountains – I wonder what the devil possessed me –

* describing the same dull
figure: doing a repetitive
dance
* fetid effluvia: stinking
sewage
* imposthumated: diseased

HACKNEY ASSEMBLY.

5 Follow the same procedure as in question 2 above. Decide which of the two
    extracts to prepare a detailed analysis of; use the other to bring out relevant points
    through comparison.

6 Write a detailed analysis of EITHER 'An Elegy' OR one of the prose extracts above.
    Show how the poet's/writer's use of structure, form and language creates and
    conveys the meaning you find in it.

Take it further

Use the poetry and
prose texts in Parts
1 and 2 above for
'analysis through
comparison'. Many
of them have been
chosen because they
are (a) related to each
other in subject matter
and theme, and (b)
linked to the topic
areas for Section B.
It is a good strategy
to work across both
Sections A and B;
the texts in each will
illuminate one another
in thought-provoking
ways.

Using writing to help you read

Your appreciation of poets' and prose writers' techniques will be deepened by becoming a creative writer yourself, especially if you work regularly with a writing partner. Activities 31 and 32 suggest some ways of getting started.

Activity 31

1 Read one of the poems on this page to a partner. Then listen to your partner read the other poem to you.

Man in Space

All you have to do is listen to the way a man
sometimes talks to his wife at a table of people
and notice how intent he is on making his point
even though her lower lip is beginning to quiver,

5 and you will know why women in science
fiction movies who inhabit a planet of their own
are not pictured making a salad or reading a magazine
when the men from earth arrive in their rocket,

10 why they are always standing in a semicircle
with their arms folded, their bare legs set apart,
their breasts protected by hard metal disks.

Billy Collins

To Virgil*

Lead me with your cold, sure hand,
make me press the correct buttons
on the automatic ticket machine,
make me not present my ticket upside down
5 to the slit mouth at the barriers,

then make the lift not jam
in the hot dark of the deepest lines.
May I hear the voice on the loudspeaker
and understand each syllable
10 of the doggerel of stations.

If it is rush-hour, let me be close to the doors,
I do not ask for space,
let no one crush me into a corner
or accidentally squeeze hard on my breasts
15 or hit me with bags or chew gum in my face.

If there are incidents, let them be over,
let there be no red-and-white tape
marking the place, make it not happen
when the tunnel has wrapped its arms around my train
20 and the lights have failed.

Float me up the narrow escalator
not looking backward, not losing my balance
or letting go of your cold, sure hand.
Let there not be a fire
25 in the gaps, hold me secure.
Let me come home to the air.

Helen Dunmore

2 Use anything you like about these poems to write a poem of your own. Set yourself a line limit. Draft and redraft it until you are satisfied it is good enough to be considered for publication.

3 Exchange poems with your partner. Ask questions, make comments, and suggest possible changes. Work together to plan a short analysis of one of them as if it were an unprepared poem in the Section A exam.

* Virgil: a classical poet and Dante's guide to the underworld in *The Divine Comedy*

Activity 32

1 Select a passage from one of your prescribed novels for Section B which interests you because of the way it is written. Using a similar style, write EITHER on a subject of your own choice OR a continuation of the passage as if you were the novelist.

2 Exchange your writing with a partner's. Compare your partner's work with the prescribed text and comment on its effectiveness.

3 Read the prose passage below. It is the opening of a novel written in 2005.

> **From *A Long Way Down* by Nick Hornby**
>
> *Martin*
>
> Can I explain why I wanted to jump off the top of a tower-block? Of course I can explain why I wanted to jump off the top of a tower-block. I'm not a bloody idiot. I can explain it because it wasn't inexplicable: it was a logical decision, the product
> 5 of proper thought. It wasn't even a very serious thought, either. I don't mean it was whimsical – I just mean that it wasn't terribly complicated, or agonized. Put it this way: say you were, I don't know, an assistant bank manager, in Guildford. And you'd been thinking of emigrating, and then you were offered the job of managing a bank in Sydney. Well, even though it's a pretty straightforward decision, you'd still have to
> 10 think for a bit, wouldn't you? You'd at least have to work out whether you could bear to move, whether you could leave your friends and colleagues behind, whether you could uproot your wife and kids. You might sit down with a bit of paper and draw up a list or pros and cons. You know:
>
> *CONS – aged parents, friends, golf club.*
>
> 15 *PROS – more money, better quality of life (house with pool, barbecue, etc.), sea, sunshine, no left-wing councils banning 'Baa-Baa-Black Sheep', no EEC directives banning British sausages, etc.*
>
> It's no contest is it? The golf club! Give me a break. Obviously your aged parents give you pause for thought, but that's all it is – a pause, a brief one, too. You'd be on
> 20 the phone to the travel agents within ten minutes.
>
> Well, that was me. There simply weren't enough regrets, and lots and lots of reasons to jump.

4 Martin is one of four strangers in Hornby's novel who meet on top of the same tower-block with the same intention. Each narrates their own story and their 'reasons to jump'. In the end, none of them actually does so.

Write EITHER the next few paragraphs of Martin's narrative OR the start of a new narrative by one of the other three. Invent the character and write in a style that reflects it.

5 Exchange your writing with a partner's. Ask questions, make comments, and suggest possible changes. You could go on to write a short analysis of EITHER your partner's writing OR your own.

Making your own choice of material: Self-help for unprepared analysis

Making your own choice of poems and prose passages to analyse will benefit your work at A2 in several ways. It helps you develop connections between your studies for Sections A and B of this unit. It allows you to draw on the poetry and prose you already know so that the material is not all entirely new. It puts you in the position of an examiner making suitable choices of unprepared texts and therefore increases your understanding of the nature of the task. Activity 33 shows how you can make practical use of these reading contexts.

Activity 33

1 Select a passage from one of your prescribed novels for Unit 3 Section B that you think you could write about in substantial detail. Plan a detailed analysis of it, without making any reference to the plot or characters in other parts of the novel.

Use the example below from *Captain Corelli's Mandolin* to guide you.

From *Captain Corelli's Mandolin* by Louis de Bernières

I, Carlo Piero Guercio, testify that in the Army I found my family. I have a father and mother, four sisters, and three brothers, but I have not had a family since puberty. I had to live among them secretly, like one who conceals leprosy. It was not their fault that I was made into a thespian. I had to dance with girls at festas, I had to flirt

5 with girls in the playground of the school and when taking the evening passeggiata in the piazza. I had to answer my grandmother when she asked me what kind of girl I would like to marry and whether I wanted sons or daughters. I had to listen with delight to my friends describing the intricacies of the female pudenda, I had to learn to relate fabulous histories of what I had done with girls. I learned to be more lonely

10 than it ought to be possible to feel.

In the Army there was the same gross talk, but it was a world without women. To a soldier a woman is an imaginary being. It is permissible to be sentimental about your mother, but that's all. Otherwise there are the inmates of the military brothels, the fictitious or unfaithful sweethearts at home, and the girls at whom one catcalls in the

15 streets. I am not a misogynist, but you should understand that to me the company of a woman is painful because it reminds me of what I am not, and of what I would have been if God had not meddled with my mother's womb.

I was very lucky at first. I was not sent to Abyssinia or North Africa, but to Albania. There was no fighting to speak of and we were blissfully oblivious to the notion that

20 the Duce might order us to invade Greece… With the Juliana Division I enjoyed every moment. No civilian can comprehend the joy of being a soldier. That is, quite simply, an irreducible fact. A further fact is that, regardless of the matter of sex, soldiers grow to love each other; and, regardless of the matter of sex, this is a love without parallel in civil life. You are all young and strong, overflowing with life, and

25 you are all in the shit together.

Notes for an analysis

Focus: First-person narrator's feelings about (a) his homosexuality = unhappiness when growing up (b) the Army = happiness as a young adult

Themes: (a) the loneliness/anguish of a 'thespian' in mixed society (b) Fate rather than society and others' attitudes is responsible: 'if God had not meddled with my mother's womb' (c) celebration of the close, collective life of the military

Uses of language:

(a) The force of the narrator's bitter feelings conveyed in para 1 by:

- figurative language: 'like one who conceals leprosy'
- his use of the euphemism 'thespian', suggesting he accepts society's judgement of him
- repetition of syntactical forms, which has a cumulative effect: 'I had to... I had to'
- increasingly sarcastic, embittered tone: 'intricacies of the female pudenda', 'had to learn to relate fabulous histories of what I had done with girls'
- the last sentence with its flat, dejected rhythm and alliteration of 'learned to be more lonely', which conveys a sense of finality.

(b) The narrator's frustration with his sexual orientation and his antipathy to women conveyed in para 2 by:

- emotive/derogatory language: 'inmates of the military brothels', 'girls at whom one catcalls in the streets'
- the imperative tone, anxious that the reader should empathise: 'you should understand'
- sense of anger in the choice of the pejorative verb 'meddled' to describe God

(c) Relief at finding a congenial life in the Army conveyed in para 3 by:

- the simple, unambiguous statement 'I enjoyed every moment'
- marked change of tone – 'an irreducible fact. A further fact is' – shows that he is now more sure of, and at ease with, himself
- use of superlatives: 'a love without parallel'
- use of the collective pronoun – 'you are all' – shows he has 'found my family'.

Form and structure:

(a) Narrator presents the passage in the form of a legal document: 'I, Carlo Piero Guercio, testify that' – shows the life-changing importance to him of finding his 'family' (fellow soldiers)

(b) Para 1 gives a cursory, reluctant summary of his childhood – coldly factual – family members referred to only by their titles, not names: 'four sisters, and three brothers' – reinforces the theme of alienation

(c) Para 2 marks a moving on – 'it was a world without women' – a growing sense of the narrator finding his real identity ('of what I would have been')

(d) Para 3 marks an arrival at a destination – 'blissfully oblivious', 'joy', 'overflowing with life': the diction has strong positive overtones now and the more varied, confident sentence structures reflect the discovery of happiness ('you are all in the shit together') – passage ends with the key word 'together' – feeling of alienation has been transformed into a sense of belonging.

2 Use the approach shown above to prepare analyses of extracts from your prescribed novels. This is a good way of exploring these in relation to your Section B topic area, as well as excellent practice for Section A.

3 Draw on your private reading, particularly of novels, to provide practice material for unprepared analysis. Build up a class collection of extracts that you think will challenge you and others in new ways. Make copies and keep them readily available. You could do the same with the completed analyses, in order to see how others are working and to learn from this.

Summary of your learning in Part 3

In this part you have developed your skills of analysing unprepared poetry and prose in the following areas:

- reading unprepared texts in an active, questioning way
- making your own individual interpretation of poems and prose passages
- annotating unprepared texts in a purposeful way before beginning to write
- making use of your prior reading to interpret and evaluate unprepared texts
- comparing and contrasting two texts in order to deepen your response to a single poem or prose passage.
- using creative writing to respond to a text from a practitioner's point of view
- choosing your own material to practise unprepared analysis
- linking your work in Section A with your study of prescribed texts in Section B
- making a personal judgement, or evaluation, of an unprepared text
- giving due weight to how other readers might interpret an unprepared text.

Copy this list of skills. Use a tick system to show how confident you are at present of being able to apply each of them: 3 ticks = 'very confident', 2 ticks = 'gaining more confidence', 1 tick = 'lacking confidence'. This self-evaluation should lead, if necessary, to a programme of skill revision before you sit the Section A exam.

4   Tackling Section A of the exam

> ## Assessment objectives
>
> To assess your essay on unprepared poetry or prose, the examiners use a mark scheme based on these two assessment objectives:
> - AO1 (10 marks) Articulate creative, informed and relevant responses to literary texts, using appropriate terminology and concepts, and coherent, accurate written expression.
> - AO2 (30 marks) Demonstrate detailed critical understanding in analysing the ways in which structure, form and language shape meanings in literary texts.
> See page 4 for what these assessment objectives mean in practice.

In Section A of the exam you will choose to answer an essay question on EITHER an unprepared poem OR an unprepared prose extract.

Section A is worth 40 marks (40% of the marks for Unit 3). You are recommended to spend around 1 hour 15 minutes of your total 2 hours 45 minutes on this task.

When you started to write about an unprepared poem or prose extract at AS, you had to answer straightforward questions requesting short, well-focused answers on aspects of poetic form, language and technique. At A2 you are asked to write an extended essay without the props offered at AS level.

When you are preparing for this section of the exam, it is important to look at a range of texts from different historical periods.

- The poem could come from a historical range as early as the mid-sixteenth century, provided it is quite short and approachable in terms of language and content.
- For the purposes of the exam, prose means prose fiction: a novel or short story. The novel as a form really only establishes itself as a genre by the eighteenth century, so it is unlikely that you will be presented with anything earlier than that.
- You may find that one of the texts was published after 1990.

The exam question

Your exam question will contain the instruction: 'Comment on and analyse how the writer's choices of structure, form and language shape meaning.' The focus is therefore very firmly on your ability to write effectively about literature and to be aware of *how* writers write.

The key words in the question are 'comment', 'analyse' and 'structure, form and language'.

Comment

Identifying and illustrating a particular feature of the text is not enough; go on to say what you feel about it as a reader.

- Your own personal response is as valuable as anyone else's provided it derives directly from the words on the page and is supported with suitable evidence.
- Aim to provide an honest but informed opinion that derives directly from the writing.

Analyse

This means:

- developing the comment by saying how effective the writing is in your opinion
- showing what effect the writer has achieved
- showing how he or she has done it
- showing how it contributes to the poem/extract as a whole
- showing what it contributes to the crafting of the text.

Structure, form and language

You will be familiar by now with the meaning of structure and form in both poetry and prose texts, but here are some brief reminders.

- The *form* of a poem refers to generic features such as being in the form of a sonnet, dramatic monologue, ballad, ode, free verse, etc. The forms of prose that are relevant for the exam are the novel and short story.
- *Structure* refers to the internal workings of the writing. So the form of a sonnet can be structured according to whether it is a Shakespearean or Petrarchan one, as well as many other variations. You might refer to matters such as verse structure, line length, rhythm and rhyme schemes. In prose you are likely to be dealing with the different conventions writers employ such as sentence and paragraph structure, and divisions between narrative, description and dialogue. The kind of narrator or point of view presented should also be regarded as a feature of structure to be explored.
- *Language* is the essential tool all writers employ. In both poetry and prose, the kind of imaginative use of language employed in imagery, metaphor and simile will be an essential focus of your analysis. The writer's use of diction, tone and voice, as well as the use of sound devices such as alliteration and assonance, will similarly feature in your discussion. Analysis of prose style may well focus on the features dealt with under 'structure', but deal with specific examples of how the words on the page work for the reader.

In order to achieve good marks in the unprepared question, therefore, you need to identify key features of structure, form and language, illustrate them clearly and comment on and analyse the effects they have on you as a well-informed reader.

Overall, the examiner is looking for a well-considered personal response to the poem or prose extract, and one in which you demonstrate your pleasure and enjoyment in reading literature.

Choosing poetry or prose

Your first task in the exam is to read the material and choose whether to tackle poetry or prose. You have a free choice. Spend a few minutes making your decision.

Consider each of the following issues:

- Am I more confident in writing about poetry or prose?
- Would I feel happier writing about a complete text (the poem) rather than an extract?

- Would I prefer to write about a twentieth- or twenty-first-century text rather than one written earlier?
- Does one of the texts look more immediately approachable than the other?
- Does one of the texts suggest a wider range of literary features to write about?

Remember that something that has immediate appeal may not yield so much material as a piece that takes more than one reading to reveal its potential.

Answering the question on poetry

Think about the structure and content of your answer before you begin to write.

Structure

You need to organise your ideas to guide the examiner through your thought processes.

- Begin with an introduction providing an overview of the poem's content and theme.
- Continue by discussing what the poem is about and showing how the poet has presented the content through use of language, form and structure.
- Remember the 'point, quotation, comment' sequence in demonstrating your knowledge of how to write about poetry.
- Work through the poem in sequence, stanza by stanza, section by section, or use whatever method is appropriate (but avoid merely telling the examiner what the poem is about).
- Make sure there is a section on *structure*, *form* and *language*. They do not have to be in that order, and you may well find some overlap between them.
- Make sure you end by including your own personal response. It can be effective to echo your opening remarks in your conclusion.

Content

You will apply your knowledge of the analysis of poetry, both unprepared and your set texts, in finding the appropriate things to write.

- Make sure you include reference to, illustration of, and critical and analytical comments on the key features of poetic technique that are relevant to the poem you are dealing with.
- Include your informed personal response, deriving from the ways in which you feel the poet has dealt with the subject matter and used features of structure, form and language to address it.

Activity 34

1 Read the sample exam question below. Then read the poem and work out your own response to it. Think about the ways in which the poet develops the feelings, ideas and situation. Remember that your answer should include some discussion of the form, language and structure of the poem.

Read 'Letter to Barbados' by Ted Walker, published in 1973.

Comment on and analyse how the writer's choices of structure, form and language shape meaning.
(40 marks)

2 Read the essay on page 58 and then the examiner's comments. Discuss as a class what you can learn from the analysis and the examiner's comments about how to:
- make your own interpretation of an unprepared poem
- compare the range of interpretations that emerge (are they all valid?)
- comment on the poet's use of diction, relating this to the theme of the poem
- comment on the poet's use of imagery, relating this to the theme of the poem
- integrate quotations into your comments
- use appropriate literary terms
- express yourself clearly.

The examiner used the following detailed mark scheme when assessing this essay. In your discussion, identify how the bands for each AO relate to the quality of the writing.

Band	Mark	AO1 – Articulate creative, informed and relevant responses to literary texts, using appropriate terminology and concepts, and coherent, accurate written expression
1	0–3	• Makes limited relevant comment • Makes limited use of critical literary terminology • Writes with minimal clarity but with technical lapses • Responds with limited originality and creativity.
2	4–7	• Makes relevant comment with some insight • Makes some appropriate use of critical terminology to make the response more specific • Uses accurate written expression with some technical lapses • Responds with some originality and creativity.
3	8–10	• Responds with a sustained argument in an informed and relevant manner • Makes confident and appropriate use of critical terminology to refine arguments and evaluate the text • Writes accurately with sustained fluency, coherence and confidence • Constructs an original and creative response in a well-developed argument.

Letter to Barbados

Dear far-off brother, Thank you for yours,
And for the gift you send of little shells.
Evening. It has been an April day
Like any you remember. I guess
How you miss the English spring, the way   5
A shower-cloud over a hillside spills

Between sunlight and sunlight, slowly.
Is it half a year since you've been gone?
While you gather up windfall nutmegs,
My white magnolia flowers fly   10
Withering from the twig like cotton rags
I must rake up tomorrow from the lawn.

I wonder what news you want to hear:
That everything remains as it was
Before you left? That we are well? That   15
Swallows, like molecules of summer,
Warm on the wall behind the dovecote?
All is satisfactory in this house.

I read over again what you tell me.
Outside your window you've had grapefruits   20
Ripening through winter; there's a calf
You love to let suck your fingers. I
Relish these images of your new life,
Though the dinning sun above you hurts

My eyes as I gaze. Easier for you,   25
Perhaps, to think back to the shadow
Of this temperate, darkening garden,
Where I sit and look for my last few
Doves to come home. They will soon swoop down,
Just as you recall they always do,   30

From the roof; each full throat soon will soothe
Nightfall once more. This morning I made
A first cut of the grass since autumn.
It smelt sweet in the sun, in the swathe
Where I left it to dry. I fetched my gun   35
And sought out a sickly dove and killed

It clean, and let it warm where it fell.
Whether it is white, loosened feathers
I glimpse in the half-dusk or blossoms
Lifting with the wind I cannot tell   40
But I am glad to have you share them.
There are words not used between brothers,

And you will understand if I send
No more than these, the shrivelling details
Of another lost and uneventful day.   45
The birds are folded now. I shall stand
A moment more in the dead grass we
Walked on. My hands close cold over shells.

Ted Walker

Band	Mark	AO2 – Demonstrate detailed critical understanding in analysing the ways in which structure, form and language shape meanings in literary texts
1	0–5	• Shows a limited understanding of the approaches to literary text • Identifies some features of structure, form and language • Shows a limited understanding of meanings.
2	6–11	• Shows limited critical understanding of literary text • Comments on some features of structure, form and language • Shows some understanding of the meanings.
3	12–17	• Demonstrates some critical understanding of literary text • Shows some awareness of features of structure, form and language • Provides evidence of a clear understanding of the meanings.
4	18–23	• Demonstrates a developed critical understanding of literary text • Examines features of structure, form and language effectively • Analyses the text and demonstrates a developed understanding of the meanings.
5	24–30	• Provides an evaluative and analytical, critical understanding of literary text which enables a sophisticated response • Evaluates features of structure, form and language effectively • Evaluates the text and demonstrates a developed understanding of the meanings which enables an independent response.

Good overview

Discourse marker suggests a higher-band student

Identifies more ambiguity: Who exactly has been displaced?

Discourse marker suggests a higher-band student

'Letter to Barbados' is exactly what the title says it is: a letter to another country that we assume the narrator comes from. In the poem the poet explores the complex relationship between family, homeland and displacement. In this essay I will consider the form, language and structure of the poem to get to a deeper understanding of the poem.

Firstly, it should be noted that the poem is in the first person. The narrator (possibly the poet Ted Walker) writes to his brother, who is in Barbados, while the narrator remains in England. It could be read that the narrator comes from Barbados, because this is referred to in the title of the poem, although it is not mentioned again. However it could be also the living place of the brother and not the poet's land. This at first appears to be a factual title, simple describing the form of the poem, but in fact gives deeper understanding of what the poem expresses. The letter 'to Barbados' not just the 'far-of brother'. This therefore includes the whole country in the poem; the latter being a discussion of his relationship to Barbados, and his current displacement from it (or his brother's displacement in it) combined with the narrator's first-person's voice makes it highly personal and emotive, engaging the reader even more in the narrator's plight.

The form of the poem is quite rigid. There are eight stanzas, each of which contains six lines. This rigid form highlights the narrator's feelings, possibly by their contrast with what he is saying. The strong emotions felt in the poem are expressed in a highly controlled and formalised pattern, which ironically prompts in the reader a questioning of what the narrator is saying — we can see in the final few stanzas a hint that all is not as idyllic as has first been suggested. The narrator is in strong control of his feelings by putting them in a rigid form, that will not allow the deep emotions to spill over into the poem directly; everything is hidden behind the 'shrivelling details'.

Similarly, the rhyme scheme also adds to the sense of unease and discomfort experienced behind the poem. There is a rough rhyme pattern of abcacb, although this is quite often disrupted. Also, these rhymes are only half-rhymes such as 'shells' and 'spills' or 'was' and 'house'. Only a couple of times are there direct rhymes such as 'day' and 'way'. This subverts the pleasure and expectation that we should feel when rhyme is used in a poem. The use of half-rhyme makes it ambiguous about what is about to follow and adds to the general atmosphere and tone of unease underneath the pleasurable appearance, perhaps highlighting the silence behind the poet's words, the unsaid.

AO2: Unsubtle way of signalling his intentions rather than just doing it through discussion and illustration

Clear development of issues initially raised in the introduction, acknowledging some ambiguities

Addresses form

Addresses poetic technique (language)

Addresses language

The language of the poem similarly creates an atmosphere and helps to directly express the feelings and emotions felt. The poet opens clearly as a letter 'Dear far-off brother'. The fact that he is writing to a brother immediately brings the issue of family into the poem. The close ties of blood make this more emotive and important; the narrator is looking back to the family, homeland and past that he has left for the 'English spring'. Similarly, the use of 'far-off' reinforces the idea that he cannot return and is displaced from his country Barbados. Is this poem an elegy for a past life that the narrator can no longer achieve in England?

Discourse marker suggests a higher-band student

Perhaps, but perhaps not. Does the poet in fact originally come from England, and it is the brother who is in Barbados, in a culture he does not recognise? Perhaps. The narrator is at home in England; he certainly feels comfortable in it, shown by the similes of 'like molecules of summer'. This positive, life-affirming sense of the poem juxtaposes with the uneasy sense of silence behind it. Likewise the ambiguity of the narrator's roots and the brother's home adds to the dark feelings expressed.

The language of this poem also has another contrast in it: between that of the everyday and the literary or more metaphorical. Often in this poem there are short, direct sentences that appear completely non-literary, for example 'All is satisfactory in this house'. This makes this statement ironically jump out to the readers for being a non-poetic line in quite an image-filled poem. The ordinary diction and short syntax makes us also question the statement's validity – is all well, or is there something wrong?

Addresses language

The everyday diction contrasts with the similes such as 'withering from the twig like cotton rags'. This simile, like many of the others in the poem, is drawn from the natural world – the narrator is very aware of the details of the landscape, both in England ('a shower-cloud') and in Barbados ('windfall nutmeg'). This concentration on the detail and beauty of the natural world ties the poem very closely to the landscape, emphasising the theme of the two distinct landscapes of the countries and the ambiguous dance between them. The sensory language such as 'it smelt sweet' shows the all-empowering sensory delight that the narrator experiences in the land, even as he remains dislocated from it.

Addresses structure

The structure of the poem moves like that of a letter, hence the title, including in the first line 'Thank you for yours' suggesting that the brother has sent a letter previously from Barbados with a gift of 'little shells'. The poem however does not then continue to read like a letter, but rather begins to sound more like an elegy. The third stanza starts with the rhetorical question 'I wonder what news you want to hear?' This direct question however does not feel totally addressed to the brother. Rather he is turning back to himself in a reflective moment. He then continues to list possible questions that the brother wants answering (and interestingly does not answer them) and discussing the brother's previous letter, with the details of 'grapefruits'. At this point in the poem, the narrator appears to be moving away from the brother to look at his own questions. The letter (and poem) is now a reflection of his relationship to his country and family, with the hint that it 'hurts'; the reflection is painful. There is an unmentioned break.

Only in the final few lines is there an oblique reference to this divide with 'there are words not used between brothers'. The poet has found in the sensual but 'shrivelling details' a way of avoiding directly addressing the divide between the two brothers. The poem has moved from hiding in the descriptions of the landscape to refer in an enigmatic way to his broken relationship with his brother.

Discourse marker suggests a higher-band student

Similarly, the structure of the poem undermines our expectation as to what will happen. The reference to the 'last few/Doves' perhaps provides some hope for the narrator, but this is immediately contradicted in the next stanza when the 'sickly dove' is killed. The image of peace and hope that is the dove has been ended.

Discourse marker suggests a higher-band student

Likewise, the symbolic gift of the shells changes in its relationship to the narrator. At first they appear as a 'gift'; a symbol of the family and love. However, in the final line the narrator's 'hands close cold over the shells'. The 'cold' feel emphasises the possible negative connotation, but it remains unclear whether the poet's hand is crushing the stones, destroying his link to the family, or if he finds in the coolness a refreshing reminder of family and country.

Discourse marker suggests a higher-band student

In conclusion, this poem explores with depth and ambiguity the narrator's relationships to the brother, Barbados and England. Its rich sensory description belies the uncertainty and break at its heart, making it an enigmatic and powerful poem, getting an emotional reaction from the reader.

Examiner's comments

This is an excellent essay that any student would be happy to produce under timed conditions, and which impresses the examiner for the insights shown into both the content of the poem and the ways in which it works.

AO1

This would clearly be placed in the top band (Band 3).

This is an informed and relevant response (it is not being assessed for creativity) and is accurately and coherently written.

The writing is well sustained, is always relevant and develops an interesting personal response to the poem.

There is effective use of critical terminology. What is impressive about this writer is his ability to use his analysis of structural features of the poem to develop his interpretation.

AO2

This would also be placed in the top band (Band 5).

Although the writer has signalled his intentions in a somewhat unsubtle way in his introduction by referring to form, language and structure, he nevertheless provides a subtle discussion, which is consistently analytical in showing how form, language and structure shape meaning. He is therefore demonstrating critical understanding throughout. He is also demonstrating an evaluative approach, which would lead to a high mark for this AO.

3 a Now read the beginning of another essay on the same poem, together with the examiner's comments.

'Letter to Barbados' depicts the distance between two close brothers. The first line of the poem is quite prosaic, 'Dear far off brother', yet due to the layout of the piece it is obvious it is a poem; there are 6 lines per stanza and an even number (8) of stanzas. This gives the poem regularity. However, the lack of rhyme and use of enjambement shows the poet battling with his emotions. When a poet uses enjambement and lacks a structured rhyme scheme, it suggests he is trying to let his thoughts and feelings dictate the form of the poem. In contrast to this the strict length of the stanzas and the pentameter (usually 9 syllables per line) show Walker is trying to keep a check on his senses and not let his feelings completely take over the poem.

Examiner's comments

This writer has used some appropriate literary language in her opening remarks by referring to the stanza form, the lack of rhyme, the use of enjambement and the pentameter. She has also linked these literary features to a personal interpretation of the poem by referring to and commenting on the emotions that are on display.

She has misread the term pentameter (a ten-syllable line) as she then (correctly) points out that the lines are mostly nine syllables in length.

She has also assumed that the emotions being expressed in the poem are those of the poet, as opposed to a narrator/persona. Compare the more open approach at this point in the first essay above.

b Continue the essay from this point. You should include detailed comments on the poet's:
- choices of diction
- use of imagery – metaphor, simile and personification
- use of voice
- use of structural elements – word order, line arrangement, stanza form
- use of sound to reinforce meaning.

Relate these aspects of style to the theme of the poem. End your analysis by evaluating how effectively the poet has conveyed his themes to you.

Answering the question on prose

Think about the structure and content of your answer before you begin to write.

Structure

You need to organise your ideas to guide the examiner through your thought processes.

- Begin with an introduction that provides an overview of the extract's content and theme.
- Continue by discussing what the extract is about, and showing how the writer has presented the content through use of language, form and structure.
- Remember the 'point, quotation, comment' sequence when demonstrating your knowledge of how to write about prose.
- Work through the passage in sequence, paragraph by paragraph, section by section, or whatever is appropriate (but avoid merely telling the examiner what the passage is about – do not tell the story).
- Make sure there is a section on structure, form and language. But they do not need to be in that order, and you may well find some overlap between them.
- Make sure you end by including your own personal response. It can be effective to echo your opening remarks in your conclusion.

Content

- Apply your knowledge of the analysis of prose, both unprepared and in the novels you have studied as set texts, in finding appropriate things to say.
- Make sure you include reference to, illustration of and critical and analytical comments on the key features of technique as they fit the extract you are dealing with.
- Include your informed personal response, deriving from the ways in which you feel the writer has dealt with the subject matter and used features of structure, form and language to address it.

Activity 35

1 Read the sample exam question below. Before you consider the student's work, read the prose extract and work out your own response to it. Think about the ways in which the writer develops the feelings, ideas and situation here. Remember that your answer should include some discussion of the form, language and structure of the extract.

> Read carefully the following extract. It is taken from the novel *A Change of Climate* by Hilary Mantel, published in 1994 and set in Norfolk in 1980. Ralph and Anna Eldred are concerned about their son, Julian, who has dropped out of university and has been spending much of his time with a girl called Sandra Glasse who lives with her mother in a remote cottage near the coast.
>
> Comment on and analyse how the writer's choice of structure, form and language shape meaning. (40 marks)

From *A Change of Climate* by Hilary Mantel

The week after Easter the winds were so violent that they seemed likely to tear up small trees by the roots. There was never a moment, day or night, when the world was quiet.

Mrs Glasse had no telephone, so Ralph couldn't contact her to arrange a time to meet.

'Should I drive over with you?' Anna said.

5 'No. It would look like a deputation. As if we'd come to complain about her.'

'You wonder what sort of woman she can be,' Anna said. 'Strange life they lead.'

His car joined the coast road at Wells. The sky was patchy, clouds moving fast, rushing above him as he skirted the dusky red walls of Holkham Hall: parting now and then to reveal a pacific blue. The sea was not visible at once; but as the road turned he saw on the broken line
10 of the horizon a strip of grey, indefinite, opaque.

It was ten o'clock when he rattled down the stony incline to the Glasses' house. The door opened before he had switched off the engine. Mrs Glasse stood waiting in the doorway.

His first thought: how young she is, she can't be more than thirty-five, thirty-six. She was pale, straight-backed, red-haired: the hair a deeper red than her daughter's, long and fine.

15 The wind ripped at his clothes as he stepped out of the car, billowing out his jacket like a cloak. 'This weather!' Mrs Glasse said. She smiled at him. 'Hello, Julian's dad.'

It was a low house, old; its bones protested, creaked under the onslaught of the weather. He heard its various sounds, as she stood hesitating inside the door; he thought, it is a house like a ship, everything in movement, a ship breasting a storm. 'On your left there,' Mrs Glasse said.
20 'Go in the parlour. There's a fire lit, and the kettle's on.'

'You might have been expecting me,' he said.

He sat by the fire, in a Windsor chair, waiting for her to bring them tea. The wind dropped; it was as if a noisy lout had left the room. In the sudden silence he heard the mantel clock ticking. She returned. Handed him a mug. 'I didn't put sugar in. Did you want it? No, I didn't
25 think you were the sugar sort.'

'Goodness,' he said. 'What does that mean?'

She pushed her hair back. 'Sugar's for comfort,' she said.

'You think I don't need comfort?'

Mrs Glasse didn't reply. She pulled up a stool to the fire. Ralph half-rose from his chair;
30 'Thanks, I'm comfortable here,' she said.

'That clock up there.' Ralph shook his head. 'We had one just like it at home when I was a boy. It was my father's. His pride and joy. He wouldn't let anyone else touch it.'

'You're not going to tell me,' said Mrs Glasse drily, 'that it stopped the day he died?'

'No, not exactly. My mother threw it out.'

35 'That was extreme.'

'For her, yes, it was. She couldn't stand the chime.'

'Did she ever mention it? In his lifetime, I mean?'

'I shouldn't think so. She was a self-effacing woman. At least, she effaced herself before him.'

She had fine hands, Mrs Glasse; the calloused hands of a woman used to outdoor work, but
40 still white, long-fingered. They were hands that rings might adorn, and that one did adorn: a plain red-gold wedding band, an old ring, one that might have been in a family for generations. Her skin had begun to line a little round the eyes: so many years of looking into the wind. All this he saw in the vibrant light that spilled into the room, morning light: sliding over cream walls, turning them the colour of butter.

2 Read the essay below and then the examiner's comments. Discuss as a class what you can learn from the analysis and the examiner's comments on how to:
- make your own interpretation of an unprepared prose passage
- compare the range of interpretations that emerge (are they all valid?)
- identify and comment on literary features in the writing by using appropriate literary terms
- be clear about specific features of the writer's style
- comment on aspects of features such as narrative, description, dialogue and characterisation
- integrate quotations into your comments
- express yourself clearly.

When assessing this essay, the examiner used the same detailed mark scheme as the one used for the unprepared poem (pages 57 and 58). In your discussion, identify how the bands for each AO relate to the quality of the writing.

Hilary Mantel explores the characters of Ralph and Mrs Glasse by careful working of dialogue, first-person perspective and significant and intricate detailing of setting in order to give the reader a complex picture of the situation depicted.

> He sets his agenda very clearly in his opening remarks

Perhaps the most prominent aspect of this prose is the significance of the environment as seen by Ralph. Although it is not a first-person account, Mantel focuses the writing on this character's perspective and so the descriptions of the wind are subjectively illustrated and reflect the mood of the character.

Mantel uses adjectives such as 'violent' to describe the wind but the writer's primary linguistic use is the employment of verbs which gather together to form an intense sense of movement and noise. Ralph's whole world seems to be loud and turbulent. The winds threaten to 'tear up' small trees, the tousling clouds in the sky are 'moving fast' and 'rushing'. The car Ralph drives noisily 'rattles' towards the Glasses' house and again the gate 'ripped' his clothes, 'billowing' his jacket. All these verbs create a landscape in which everything is in movement, not smooth motion, but jerky action.

> He goes on to explore some aspects of language – there follows some detailed exemplification of this aspect of the writing

The subjectivity of this piece means that the reader must accept the character of Ralph's account of the environment (even if it is not in first person, it follows his perspective). So Ralph's perception of the world around him inevitably reflects his own state of mind. Mantel does not give us a psychological insight into this character's emotions, but by showing us his perception the reader can make an accurate analysis of him as a person. Hence, when we learn that the wind 'seemed likely' to destroy the trees and there never seemed to be a moment 'when the world was quiet', Mantel successfully communicates that this character is troubled and the environment seems to add to his frustration. The writer describes its effects on him in terms of annoyance and irritation: 'the onslaught of the weather'.

> What is interesting about the response here is that it not only deals with language very precisely, but says something about the character Ralph, from whose viewpoint the passage is written

> Next he provides us with some insights into language and how it relates to form

The character's distress is tempered by a new intrigue in the character of Mrs Glasse. Consequently the writing becomes less hectic and jerky, the sentences lengthen and smooth out as Ralph instantly notices specific and personal details about the woman he meets. The description of Mrs Glasse also contrasts to that of the environment he has surveyed on his journey. We learn she is 'pale' in juxtaposition to the 'patchy' clouds and 'dusky' walls of Holkham Hall. Her hair is 'deep' red and 'fine', both rather admiring adjectives. Also, Ralph conceives of her house in metaphorical and mysterious terms, with the simile: 'he thought, it is a house like a ship'. This element of Ralph's perception introduces an imagination, triggered by the character of Mrs Glasse, so it seems clear she and her personal setting at home had an 'effect' on this protagonist.

This connection between the characters is strengthened and assured when they engage in apparently spontaneous but rather intimate conversation about Ralph's family and the significance of a clock that he spies in her house – which signals a joining of like minds.

> He demonstrates more insight into the way in which the extract develops and hence moves towards offering an overview

> The concluding remarks bring the reader satisfyingly back to the beginning of the passage and the discussion

Finally, the weather that has troubled Ralph from the beginning softens, brightens and mellows when he is in her home. The lexical choice is entirely positive and contrasting to the earlier frustrating violence: 'vibrant light... spilled into the room'. The walls are sensuously turned the colour of 'butter'.

Examiner's comments

AO1

This essay is articulate, accurately written, informed and relevant. It is a comparatively short essay (although there is a page of planning that has not been reproduced here), and its concision is one of its strengths.

The expression is very clear.

There is good use of terminology. Some sophisticated concepts are explained very well, with great clarity in precise (although not necessarily over-technical) language.

A mark in Band 3 would be awarded.

AO2

The essay shows great sensitivity to different ways in which the writer achieves her effects for the reader. It is analytical and evaluative.

There is a strong sensitivity to language and structural devices in the writing.

A mark in Band 5 would be awarded.

3 a Now read the start of another essay on the same extract, together with the examiner's comments.

It is quite apparent that the whole text is a way for Hilary Mantel to describe the relationship of Julian with his parents growing ever weaker.

From the outset, we realise that there is an ominous tone to the piece. The 'violent' winds suggest an unrest about the situation and is a foreshadowing device for the confrontation about to occur. The idea that the small trees are being 'torn up by the roots' creates a metaphor for the family tree of the Eldreds: their family connection is already 'small' and its foundations are being torn up by the wind (Mrs Glasse). This idea is exaggerated by the lack of telephone that Mrs Glasse has. When we consider that Julian spends all his time with there we realise that his parents are losing all connection with him.

Examiner's comments

This is an attempt at an overview that does not quite work because the writer seems to have addressed the contextualisation provided in the preamble to the question rather than anything specific in the passage itself.

But the writer redeems himself in the next section: 'From the outset, we realise that there is an ominous tone to the piece...'. He goes on to provide some examples to illustrate this.

b Continue the essay from this point. Include detailed comments on the writer's:
- choices of language
- use of imagery
- use of narrative
- use of description in setting the scene
- use of dialogue
- use of structural elements – sentence and paragraph structure.

End your analysis by evaluating how effectively the writer has developed the situation between the two characters and how she might have made you want to read on.

Activity 36

Consider all the students' essays and examiners' comments in this section.

1 What have you learned about the assessment process?

2 How has it helped you to plan your own writing?

3 Do you think you can write essays as effective as these?

4 If you think that their work is better than yours, what do you have to do to move up to the top two bands?

B Paired texts

This section introduces the prose fiction texts and poetry collections on which your work for Section B will be based. It gives you guidance on how to make connections and comparisons between texts, how to set them in the context of the time when (or about which) they were written, and how to consider them from the perspective of a modern reader.

Writing in the exam

You have to answer on *at least* two texts from your topic group. You will be asked to 'analyse the connections and comparisons between at least two texts you have studied'. It is expected that you will prepare three texts and then decide if you wish to refer in the exam to all of these or to two of them.

1   Introduction to Section B

Unit 3 allows a wide choice of texts for Section B. The essential requirements are as follows.

- Texts will be drawn from *one* topic group: 'Relationships' OR 'Identifying Self' OR 'Journeys' OR 'War'.
- Each topic group lists three prose and three poetry texts. A selection must be made from these. It must include prose *and* poetry.
- The specification states: '*Three* texts are selected within the group from a choice of six... It is not necessary to study the three texts in the same level of detail.'
- At least **one** of the texts for study must have been published *after* 1990. This can be prose or poetry.

Possible combinations of texts

Your texts could be made up of:

- two prose texts and one poetry text OR
- two poetry texts and one prose text.

Remember that post-1990 literature must be included.

Each topic group is arranged to make possible a study of both modern literature and literature from the past. Three of the topic groups are arranged to make possible a study of texts exclusively from after 1990.

Assessment objectives

Examiners use four assessment objectives for Section B. They are:

AO1: (10 marks) Articulate creative, informed and relevant responses to literary texts, using appropriate terminology and concepts, and coherent, accurate written expression

AO2: (10 marks) Demonstrate detailed critical understanding in analysing the ways in which structure, form and language shape meanings in literary texts out

AO3: (20 marks) Explore connections and comparisons between different literary texts, informed by interpretations of other readers

AO4: (20 marks) Demonstrate understanding of the significance and influence of the contexts in which literary texts are written and received

Combining texts: examples from one of the topic groups

The six texts listed for the topic group 'Identifying Self' are:

Prose	Poetry
Behind the Scenes at the Museum*: Atkinson *Great Expectations*: Dickens *Life of Pi**: Martel	*Taking Off Emily Dickinson's Clothes**: Collins *The Wife of Bath's Prologue and Tale*: Chaucer *The Fat Black Woman's Poems*: Nichols
* Texts marked with an asterisk are post-1990	

Possible combinations include:

Combination A	**Combination B**	**Combination C**
Behind the Scenes at the Museum* *Great Expectations* *The Fat Black Woman's Poems*	*Behind the Scenes at the Museum** *Life of Pi** *Taking Off Emily Dickinson's Clothes**	*Great Expectations* *Taking Off Emily Dickinson's Clothes** *The Wife of Bath's Prologue and Tale*

Combination A would allow you to compare (a) prose with prose (b) prose with poetry (c) one post-1990 text with two pre-1990 texts.

Combination B would allow you to compare (a) prose with prose (b) prose with poetry (c) three post-1990 texts.

Combination C would allow you to compare (a) poetry with poetry (b) poetry with prose (c) one post-1990 text with two pre-1990 texts.

Other combinations could be created. Work some of them out yourself.

Influences on your choice

You will choose your three texts in consultation with your teacher. Your choice could be guided by the following considerations.

- **The topic groups**. It may be that the subject matter of texts in a given topic group is particularly appealing or likely to introduce you to new areas of interest.
- **The focus of comparison**. It may be that you and your teacher choose to explore texts that are related principally by *theme*, or by *genre*, or by *period*, or by *context*. The chosen focus of comparison will point you to suitable texts.
- **The balance of prose and poetry in Unit 3**. It may be that, if you have chosen to concentrate on one genre for Section A, you and your teacher want to foreground the other for Section B.

Connections, comparisons, contexts

Section B emphasises the links you can find between texts and the way you choose to explore these links. The key terms in the specification are 'connections', 'comparisons' and 'contexts'. You will be rewarded for being able to:

- explore *connections* between texts across different periods or within the same period
- make *comparisons* between texts, taking account of other readers' interpretations
- show the importance of the *contexts* in which texts are written and read.

2   Comparing texts by theme, genre and period

This part shows you how to make connections and comparisons between texts in terms of their themes and their genres. In addition, it gives you guidance on how to compare texts across time.

How to use the activities in Part 2

The activities in this part are a combination of text-specific and generic. The text-specific activities use pairs of texts to illustrate various ways of making comparisons. The generic activities ask you to apply the same skills to other texts you may be studying.

You will benefit from working on a range of activities, not just those that apply to your own texts. The skills of comparing themes, genres and periods can be transferred. The text-specific activities use passages and poems that are printed in full, so they can also be used as unprepared texts – consolidating your work for Section A as well as helping you prepare for Section B.

Most activities focus on single extracts and poems, before drawing in the prescribed texts as a whole and other texts in a topic group. This is to help clarify the process of comparison. It is not the only way of making connections between texts; the specification encourages you to develop your own approaches and to range widely across your chosen texts in your exam response.

Comparing prose with prose: *Captain Corelli's Mandolin* and *Tess of the d'Urbervilles* (post-1990 and pre-1990)

Activities 37 and 38 focus on key passages from these novels which are connected by theme. They also illustrate some stylistic differences between prose fiction written before and after 1990. They will be useful to you in studying any prose texts and should be undertaken together.

Activity 37

1 Read the extract below from near the end of *Captain Corelli's Mandolin*. Pelagia, the central female character, is confronting the loss of her hopes of happiness with Captain Corelli.

From *Captain Corelli's Mandolin* by Louis de Bernières

All my home is nothing but sadness and silence and ruin and memory. I have been reduced, I am my own ghost, all my beauty and youth have shrivelled away, there are no illusions of happiness to impel me. Life is a prison of poverty and aborted dreams, it is nothing but a slow progress to my place beneath the soil, it is a plot by God to disenchant us with the flesh, it is nothing but a brief flame in a bowl of oil between one darkness and another that
5   ends it.

I sit here and remember former times. I remember music in the night, and I know that all my joys have been pulled out of my mouth like teeth. I shall be hungry and thirsty and longing forever. If only I had a child, a child to suckle at the breast, if I had Antonio. I have been eaten up like bread. I lie down in thorns and my well is filled with stones. All my happiness was smoke.

Across AS and A2

For Activities 37 and 38, you may wish to refer back to your work on narrative technique earlier in the course. Material on the use of narrative point of view and narrative voice can be found in the AS Student Book on pages 55–60 and on pages 33–36 of this book.

2 Discuss with a partner de Bernières' narrative technique here. Focus on:
- the use of a first-person point of view and voice
- the tone and mood of the passage
- the extensive use of imagery, particularly metaphor
- the syntax and overall structure of the passage.

3 Share your responses in class discussion. Then evaluate the effectiveness of this passage in portraying a woman broken by unhappiness.

4 If *Captain Corelli's Mandolin* is one of your chosen texts:

a Create a 'fortunes graph' for Pelagia. It should show how she is 'reduced... [to] my own ghost' in the course of the narrative. Plot four or five points on the graph which you think mark decisive shifts in her fortunes, and provide a key to explain them.

b Work outwards from the extract above to consider the different kinds of love presented in *Captain Corelli's Mandolin*: heterosexual love, homosexual love, love between members of a family, love of country, and so on. Does love lead to fulfilment or to tragedy? How successful is de Bernières in presenting love in the context of war?

Activity 38

1 Read the extract below from near the end of *Tess of the d'Urbervilles*. Tess, the central female character, is confronting the loss of her hopes of happiness with Angel Clare. They have reached Stonehenge in their flight from the police, who are pursuing Tess to arrest her for murder.

From *Tess of the d'Urbervilles* by Thomas Hardy

When they saw where she lay, which they had not done till then, they showed no objection, and stood watching her, as still as the pillars around. He went to the stone and bent over her, holding one poor little hand; her breathing now was quick and small, like that of a lesser creature than a woman. All waited in the growing light, their faces and hands as if they were silvered, the remainder of their figures dark, the stones glistening green-gray, the Plain still a

5 mass of shade. Soon the light was strong, and a ray shone upon her unconscious form, peering under her eyelids and waking her.

'What is it, Angel? she said, starting up. 'Have they come for me?'

'Yes, dearest,' he said. 'They have come.'

'It is as it should be,' she murmured. 'Angel, I am almost glad – yes, glad! This happiness could not have lasted. It

10 was too much. I have had enough; and now I shall not live for you to despise me!'

She stood up, shook herself, and went forward, neither of the men having moved.

'I am ready,' she said quietly.

2 Discuss in a small group Hardy's narrative technique here. Compare and contrast it with de Bernières'. Focus on:
- the use of a third-person point of view and voice
- the mixture of description and dialogue
- the tone and mood of the passage
- the use of simile and metaphor
- the syntax and overall structure of the passage.

3 Share your responses in class discussion. Then compare the effectiveness of Hardy's portrayal of a woman broken by happiness with de Bernières'.

Can you relate the stylistic differences between these passages to the different periods in which they were written? Are there aspects of de Bernières' text which show that it is from a modern novel, written more than a century after Hardy's?

4 If *Tess of the d'Urbervilles* is one of your chosen texts:

a Create a 'fortunes graph' for Tess. It should show how her fortunes rise and fall in the course of the narrative. Plot four or five points on the graph that you think mark decisive shifts in her fortunes, and provide a key to explain them.

b Work outwards from the extract above to consider how Hardy presents individuals in relation to the social and moral conventions of nineteenth-century England. To what extent, and in what ways, are Tess and Angel seen as victims of these conventions? How successful is Hardy in his attempt to present Tess as 'a pure woman'?

Activity 39

This activity applies to prose texts in any topic group.

Choose an extract from near the end of your prose text(s) that shows the central character to have changed in the course of the narrative. Discuss as a class the writer's narrative technique, and compare it with at least one earlier point in the text.

Then draw a graph to show and explain why the central character changes. To what extent are these changes caused by (a) purely outside influences, (b) the way in which the character reacts to them?

Activity 40

This activity applies to texts in the topic group 'Relationships'.

'Literature about love is invariably sad. It shows that the price we pay for love in youth is an age spent grieving at its loss.'

Compare and contrast at least two texts from the topic group 'Relationships' in the light of this comment. Focus your comparison on the themes of the text and the way these are developed by the writer. You might consider:

- the definition of 'love' given in each text
- the way 'grieving' is presented in each text
- how each writer guides the reader's response.

Writing in the exam

You will be given a comment, or 'proposition', as a starting point for your answer. Bear in mind that:
- the comment is intended to focus your ideas about your chosen texts, not to prompt a discursive essay on the topic rather than the texts
- you are free to challenge or disagree with the assumptions in the comment.
You have had experience of this kind of question in Section B of the Unit 1 exam. The same strategies apply.

Independent research

During the A2 course you should try to read at least one other novel by the prose writer(s) you are studying. Your teacher will be able to suggest suitable choices.

Take it further

Bring in a further text from the topic group 'Relationships' to compare with the texts used for Activities 37 and 38. You could compare the way Daisy is presented in *The Great Gatsby* with the sympathetic portrayals of Pelagia and Tess by de Bernières and Hardy. You could compare Carol Ann Duffy's exploration of the pleasures and pains of love in *Rapture* with the varied experiences of lovers in any of the three prescribed novels.

Writing in the exam

In developing comparisons between two or more texts, you will be taking a broader view than in Section A, where close focus on a single text is required. Make sure, however, that you do not rely on general statements alone and leave the text behind. It is necessary to analyse structure, form and language in specific detail. The best answers to a Section B question will combine an overview with close attention to the way the texts are written.

Comparing poetry with poetry: *Metaphysical Poetry* and *Rapture* (pre-1990 and post-1990)

Activities 41 and 42 focus on key poems from these texts and which are connected by theme. They also illustrate some stylistic differences between a seventeenth-century poem and a post-1990 one. They will be useful to you in studying any poetry texts and should be undertaken together.

Across AS and A2

For Activities 41 and 42 you may wish to refer back to your work on the use of imagery and structure in poetry earlier in the course. Relevant material can be found in the AS Student Book on pages 12–24 and 34–7, and on pages 12–17 of this book.

Key terms

- **second-person voice**
- **realism**
- **conceit**
- **paradox**

Activity 41

1 Read the seventeenth-century poem opposite.

2 'Love, all alike, no season knows nor clime,/ Nor hours, days, months, which are the rags of time'. Discuss as a class what you think Donne is saying about love and time (a) in this couplet, and (b) in the poem as a whole.

Then explore the poetic techniques he uses to convey this theme. Focus on:
- the way the poem's speaker addresses the sun directly, using the **second-person voice**
- the use of a specific setting to create **realism**
- the conversational register of the poem and its varied syntax
- the use of imagery, particularly in stanza 3.

3 Discuss as a class the aspects of structure, form and language in 'The Sun Rising' that mark it out as a poem from the past. Focus on:
- the references to the seventeenth-century context – look at (a) social/cultural references such as 'court huntsmen' (line 7) and 'alchemy' (line 24), (b) historical references such as 'both th'Indias of spice and mine' (line 17), and (c) linguistic usages such as 'Call country ants to harvest offices' (line 8)
- the grammar and syntax, some of which is highly compressed
- the use of **conceits** – that is, images that combine together ideas which would normally be considered incongruous
- the use of a structure based on argument as well as emotion, which often leads to **paradox** – for example, 'Shine here to us, and thou art everywhere' (line 29).

These stylistic features are typical of metaphysical poetry. Donne's poetry is also typified by wit, exuberance and explicitness about love and sex. Do you think Donne's style (a) enhances the way he conveys his theme that love can transcend time, or (b) works against it?

The Sun Rising

Busy old fool, unruly sun,
    Why dost thou thus,
Through windows and through curtains call on us?
Must to thy motions lovers' seasons run?
    Saucy pedantic wretch, go chide
    Late schoolboys and sour prentices,
  Go tell court huntsmen that the King will ride,
  Call country ants to harvest offices;
Love, all alike, no season knows nor clime,
Nor hours, days, months, which are the rags of time.

    Thy beams so reverend and strong
    Why shouldst thou think?
I could eclipse and cloud them with a wink,
But that I would not lose her sight so long:
    If her eyes have not blinded thine,
    Look, and tomorrow late tell me
  Whether both th'Indias of spice and mine
  Be where thou left'st them, or lie here with me.
Ask for those kings whom thou saw'st yesterday,
And thou shalt hear, all here in one bed lay.

    She'is all states, and all princes I,
    Nothing else is.
Princes do but play us, compared to this
All honour's mimic, all wealth alchemy;
    Thou sun art half as happy' as we,
    In that the world's contracted thus.
  Thine age asks ease, and since thy duties be
  To warm the world, that's done in warming us:
Shine here to us, and thou art everywhere;
This bed thy centre is, these walls thy sphere.

John Donne

4 If *Metaphysical Poetry* is one of your chosen texts:

a Compare and contrast 'The Sun Rising' with the following poems in the collection: 'To His Coy Mistress' by Andrew Marvell, 'A Song' by Thomas Carew and 'Song: To Lucasta, Going Beyond the Seas' by Richard Lovelace. What similarities and differences are there in the way these poets deal with a common theme?

b Work outwards from the poem on p70 to consider how Donne and other metaphysical poets such as George Herbert present divine as well as secular love. How do they vary their style when addressing God as opposed to a lover? Do you find one of these kinds of poetry more successful than the other, or are they equally effective?

Key term

• poetic sequence

Activity 42

1 Read the post-1990 poem opposite.

2 'Time hates love, wants love poor,/ but love spins gold, gold, gold from straw.'

Discuss as a class what you think Carol Ann Duffy is saying about love and time (a) in this couplet, and (b) in the poem as a whole.

Then explore the poetic techniques she uses to convey this theme. Focus on:
• the way the poem's speaker uses the first-person-plural voice
• the use of a specific setting to create realism
• the use of imagery, particularly for purposes of contrast
• the use of the sonnet form.

Hour

Love's time's beggar, but even a single hour,
bright as a dropped coin, makes love rich.
We find an hour together, spend it not on flowers
or wine, but the whole of the summer sky and a grass ditch.

For thousands of seconds we kiss; your hair
like treasure on the ground; the Midas light
turning your limbs to gold. Time slows, for here
we are millionaires, backhanding the night

so nothing dark will end our shining hour,
no jewel hold a candle to the cuckoo spit
hung from the blade of grass at your ear,
no chandelier or spotlight see you better lit

than here. Now. Time hates love, wants love poor,
but love spins gold, gold, gold from straw.

Carol Ann Duffy

3 Discuss as a class the use of structure, form and language in 'Hour'. Focus on:
• the references to the twenty-first-century context – look at (a) the setting for the poem, (b) social/cultural references such as 'no chandelier or spotlight' (line 12), and (c) linguistic usages such as 'hold a candle' (line 10)
• the grammar and syntax, some of which is highly compressed
• the use of conceits
• the use of a structure based on argument as well as emotion, which often leads to paradox – for example, 'love spins gold, gold, gold from straw'.

What evidence is there that Duffy is using some of the stylistic features typical of metaphysical poetry in a modern way? Do you think her style (a) enhances the way she conveys her theme that love can transcend time, or (b) works against it?

4 If *Rapture* is one of your chosen texts:

a Compare and contrast 'Hour' with the following poems in the collection: 'Fall', 'Wintering', 'Unloving'. What similarities and differences can you find in Duffy's treatment of love in these poems? Consider structure, form and language as well as subject matter and themes.

b Work outwards from the poem above to consider how Duffy makes use of the **poetic sequence** in *Rapture*. How effective is her technique of using a wide range of poetic forms in the collection? How well do you think the collection works as the narrative of a love affair?

Take it further

Bring in a further text from the topic group 'Relationships' to compare with the texts used for Activities 41 and 42. You could compare the way modern poets in *Emergency Kit* explore erotic love with the way the same theme is treated by seventeenth-century poets such as Donne, Carew and Rochester in *Metaphysical Poetry*. You could compare the free verse forms chosen by some poets in *Emergency Kit* with the more traditional forms and structures typically used by seventeenth-century poets.

Writing in the exam

Try to include in your answer more than one approach to the topic set. You can, for example, base part of your comparison on subject matter and themes, part of it on style, part of it on the writers' contexts, part of it on different readers' interpretations, and so on.

Independent research

During the A2 course you should try to read other collections by the poets you are studying. Your teacher will be able to make suitable suggestions.

Across AS and A2

For Activity 45 you may wish to refer back to your work on comparing prose with poetry earlier in the course. Relevant material can be found on pages 41–54 of this book.

Activity 43

This activity applies to poetry texts in any topic group.

1 Choose at least two poems from your poetry text(s) that deal with a similar theme in different ways. Discuss as a class the poets' techniques and evaluate their effectiveness.

2 Write a comparative analysis of two or more poems that take different approaches to a common theme. Explain which poem you find the most effective.

Activity 44

This activity applies to texts in the topic group 'Relationships'.

'In dealing with "rapture" in relationships, writers put the emphasis in different places. Some show how it is short-lived rather than long-lasting; some show the reverse. Some writers show both.'

Compare and contrast at least two texts from the topic group 'Relationships' in the light of this comment. Focus your comparison on the themes of the texts and the way these are developed by the writer. You might consider:

- how far this comment seems true of your chosen poet(s), and in what ways
- how far this comment seems true of your chosen novelist(s), and in what ways
- how each writer guides the reader's response.

Comparing prose with poetry:
The Great Gatsby and *Emergency Kit* (pre-1990)

Activity 45 shows you how to illuminate themes in a prose text by connecting it with poetry. It also highlights some basic stylistic differences between poems and prose. It will be useful to you in studying any poetry and prose texts. (Remember that in the exam you will have to write about at least one post-1990 text).

Activity 45

1 Read the extract on page 73 from near the end of *The Great Gatsby*. It marks the point at which Jay Gatsby is facing the failure of his attempt to persuade Daisy, the love of his life, to leave her husband. The narrator is Gatsby's friend and neighbour, Nick.

From *The Great Gatsby* by F. Scott Fitzgerald

I couldn't sleep all night; a fog-horn was groaning incessantly on the Sound, and I tossed half-sick between grotesque reality and savage, frightening dreams. Toward dawn I heard a taxi go up Gatsby's drive, and immediately I jumped out of bed and began to dress – I felt that I had something to tell him, something to warn him about, and morning would be too late.

5 Crossing his lawn, I saw that his front door was still open and he was leaning against a table in the hall, heavy with dejection or sleep.

'Nothing happened,' he said wanly. 'I waited, and about four o'clock she came to the window and stood there for a minute and then turned out the light.'

His house had never seemed so enormous to me as it did that night when we hunted through the great rooms for
10 cigarettes. We pushed aside curtains that were like pavilions, and felt over innumerable feet of dark wall for electric light switches – once I tumbled with a sort of splash upon the keys of a ghostly piano. There was an inexplicable amount of dust everywhere, and the rooms were musty, as though they hadn't been aired for many days. I found a humidor on an unfamiliar table, with two stale, dry cigarettes inside. Throwing open the french windows of the drawing-room, we sat smoking out into the darkness.

15 'You ought to go away,' I said. 'It's pretty certain they'll trace your car.'

'Go away now, old sport?'

'Go to Atlantic City for a week, or up to Montreal.'

He wouldn't consider it. He couldn't possibly leave Daisy until he knew what she was going to do. He was clutching at some last hope and I couldn't bear to shake him free.

2 Discuss with a partner the way Scott Fitzgerald presents the death of Gatsby's relationship with Daisy here. Focus on:
- the use of Nick's narrative viewpoint and voice
- the strained dialogue between Nick and Gatsby
- the mood of the extract
- the descriptions of Gatsby's house.

3 Share your responses in class discussion. Then read the extract opposite from the poem 'This Dead Relationship' from *Emergency Kit*.

4 Discuss as a class the way the speaker in the poem uses (a) voice, (b) imagery and (c) form and structure to convey the theme that 'I am this thing's twin./ One of us is dead'.

This Dead Relationship

I carry a dead relationship around everywhere with me.
It's my hobby.
How lucky to have a job that's also my hobby,
To do it all the time.

5 A few people notice, and ask if they can help carry this thing.
But, like an alcoholic scared they will hear the clink of glass in the bag,
I refuse – scared they'll smell rottenness,
Scared of something under their touch
That will cave in, a skin over brown foam on a bad apple.
10 I cram this thing over the threshold
Into the cold and speechless house,
Lean against the front door for a moment to breathe in the dark,
Then start the slow haul to the kitchen.
Steel knives catch the moonlight on white tiles […].

15 This dead relationship. This dead and sinking ship.
Bulbs lie, unplanted, on a plate of dust.
Dry and puckered pouches, only slightly mouldy;
Embalmed little stomachs but with hairy, twisted fingers,
Waiting for something to happen without needing to know what it is.
20 When it happens everything else in the universe can start.

This dead relationship.

I am this thing's twin.
One of us is dead
And we don't know which, we are so close.

Katherine Pierpoint

Take it further

Bring in a further text from the topic group 'Relationships' to compare with the texts used for Activity 45. You could compare the way the prescribed poets and novelists present relationships from different points of view. This includes the way relations between the sexes are explored from a male perspective in *The Great Gatsby* and *Metaphysical Poetry*, from a female perspective in *Rapture*, and from both perspectives in *Captain Corelli's Mandolin*.

Writing in the exam

Remember that the literary terms used to comment on prose and poetry are not exclusive to either genre. What is sometimes referred to as 'the language of poetry analysis' – metaphor, simile, tone, mood, and so on – applies equally to prose. What is sometimes referred to as 'the language of prose analysis' – viewpoint, voice, syntax, structure, and so on – applies equally to poetry.

5 Compare the poem's theme and style with the extract from *The Great Gatsby* on p73. You might consider:
  - the tone and mood of each text
  - the use and effect of imagery in each text
  - the different viewpoint in each text
  - the different structural features of the prose passage and the poem.

6 If *The Great Gatsby* is one of your chosen texts, explore how you can interpret Jay Gatsby's experience of love by reference to Katherine Pierpoint's poem. Use as a starting point these quotations:
  - 'It's my hobby… [I] do it all the time'
  - 'A few people notice, and ask if they can help … But… I refuse – scared'
  - 'Waiting for something to happen… When it happens everything else in the universe can start'.

Activity 46

This activity applies to texts in any topic group.

1 Choose a poem and an extract from a prose text you are studying which illuminate each other in interesting ways. Discuss as a class how these texts can be related in theme and style, following the same procedure as in Activity 45.

2 Create a note-diagram that summarises the similarities and differences. You could make a spider diagram for themes and a style grid to go with it, or use your own version of a mind map. Use this as a plan for writing a comparative analysis of your chosen texts, highlighting whatever aspects you think are important. Make sure you include specific comment on the differences between prose and poetry.

Activity 47

This activity applies to texts in the topic group 'Relationships'.

'I carry a dead relationship around everywhere with me'. (Katherine Pierpoint, 'This Dead Relationship', see page 73.)

Compare and contrast at least two texts from the topic group 'Relationships' in the light of this quotation. Focus your comparison on the themes of each text and the way these are developed by the writer. You might consider:

- the reasons why a relationship 'dies' in the texts you choose
- the emotional consequences of the 'dead relationship' presented by each writer
- the language used by each writer to convey this theme
- how each writer guides the reader's response.

Writing in the exam

You will not be penalised in the exam for writing about two texts. When commenting on a poetry collection, however, it is a bad strategy to limit yourself to one or two poems in it. Be prepared to refer to the collection as a whole, at the same time as you illustrate your points by specific analysis of the text.

Comparing prose with prose: *Behind the Scenes at the Museum, Life of Pi* (post-1990) and *Great Expectations* (pre-1990)

Activities 48 and 49 focus on extracts from these texts that illustrate the genre of autobiographical fiction and the use of first-person narration. They will be useful to a study of any prose texts and should be undertaken together.

Activity 48

1 Read the two extracts below.

The first is from *Behind the Scenes at the Museum*. At this point in the story Ruby, the first-person narrator, has just been conceived.

> ### From *Behind the Scenes at the Museum* by Kate Atkinson
>
> I'm wide awake too, turning somersaults and floating in the ocean of Bunty. I tap my naked heels together three times and think, there's no place like home.
>
> Next morning George is in an uncharacteristically good mood (his night on the tiles – with Walter – was satisfying) and he prods my sleeping mother awake.
>
> 5 'How'd you like breakfast in bed, Bunt?' Bunty grunts.
>
> 'How about a bit of sausage? Black pudding?' Bunty moans, which George takes to mean 'yes' and he saunters off down to the kitchen while Bunty has to run to the bathroom. For a second she thinks she sees Scarlett smiling in the bathroom mirror in full Technicolor, but the image disappears as she vomits. Leaning her hot, prickling forehead against the cold tiles, a terrible idea forms in Bunty's head – she's pregnant!
> 10 (Poor Bunty – throwing up every morning at every pregnancy. No wonder she was always telling us that she was sick of us.) She sits abruptly down on the toilet and mouths a silent Munch-like scream – it can't be (yes, yes, yes, Bunty's going to have a baby! Me!). She throws the nearest thing (a red shoe) at the mirror and it breaks into a million splintery pieces.
>
> I'm hanging like a pink-glass button by a thread. Help. Where are my sisters? (Asleep.) My father?
> 15 (Cooking breakfast). Where's my mother?

The second extract is from *Life of Pi*. At this point in the story Pi, the first-person narrator, has just found out that his family, who own a zoo in India, have decided to emigrate to Canada.

> ### From *Life of Pi* by Yann Martel
>
> Why do people move? What makes them uproot and leave everything they've known for a great unknown beyond the horizon? Why climb this Mount Everest of formalities that makes you feel like a beggar? Why enter this jungle of foreignness where everything is new, strange and difficult?
>
> The answer is the same the world over: people move in the hope of a better life.
>
> 5 The mid-1970s were troubled times in India. I gathered that from the deep furrows that appeared on Father's forehead when he read the papers. Or from snippets of conversation that I caught between him and Mother and Mamaji and others. It's not that I didn't understand the drift of what they said – it's that I wasn't interested. The orang-utans were as eager for chapattis as ever; the monkeys never asked after the news from Delhi; the rhinos and goats continued to live in peace; the birds twittered; the clouds carried rain; the
> 10 sun was hot; the earth breathed; God was – there was no Emergency in my world.

Across AS and A2

For Activities 48 and 49, you may wish to refer back to your work on the use of first-person point of view and voice earlier in the course. Relevant material can be found in the AS Student Book on pages 55–60, and on pages 33–36 of this book.

2 Discuss as a class the narrative techniques used by the two writers here. Fill in a copy of the table below to show what you decide.

NARRATIVE TECHNIQUES		
	Behind the Scenes at the Museum	*Life of Pi*
Narrative viewpoint		
Narrative voice		
Use of tenses		
Choices of language		
Syntax and overall structure of extract		
Relationship created between narrator and reader		

3 Both these extracts are from autobiographical fiction. Use your completed tables to compare and contrast the two writers' use of this genre. Are their purposes the same? How well do you think they succeed in achieving their purposes, as you understand them?

4 If *Behind the Scenes at the Museum* or *Life of Pi* are among your chosen texts, compare their principal themes with those of another novel from the topic group 'Identifying Self'. You might consider:
- how the past shadows and shapes the present
- how childhood experience is presented
- how the theme of guilt and innocence is handled
- how the central character finds an identity in the course of the novel.

Activity 49

1 Read the extract below from *Great Expectations*. Pip, the narrator, is an orphan. He is describing a Christmas dinner at which his grown-up sister, her husband Joe, Uncle Pumblechook and others are present. Pip has recently stolen food from Mrs Joe's pantry.

From *Great Expectations* by Charles Dickens

Among this good company I should have felt myself, even if I hadn't robbed the pantry, in a false position. Not because I was squeezed in at an acute angle of the table-cloth, with the table in my chest, and the Pumblechookian elbow in my eye, nor because I was not allowed to speak (I didn't want to speak), nor because I was regaled with the scaly tips of the drumsticks of the fowls, and of those obscure corners of pork of which the pig, when living, had
5 had the least reason to be vain. No; I should not have minded that if they would only have left me alone. But they wouldn't leave me alone. They seemed to think the opportunity lost, if they failed to point the conversation at me, every now and then, and stick the point into me. I might have been an unfortunate little bull in a Spanish arena, I got so smartingly touched up by these moral goads.

It began the moment we sat down to dinner. Mr Wopsle said grace with theatrical declamation – as it now appears
10 to me, something like a religious cross of the Ghost in Hamlet with Richard the Third – and ended with the very proper aspiration that we might be truly grateful. Upon which my sister fixed me with her eye, and said, in a low reproachful voice: 'Do you hear that? Be grateful.'

'Especially,' said Mr Pumblechook, 'be grateful, boy, to them which brought you up by hand.'

Mrs Hubble shook her head, and contemplating me with a mournful presentiment that I should come to no good,
15 asked: 'Why is it that the young are never grateful?' This moral mystery seemed too much for the company until Mr Hubble tersely solved it by saying: 'Naturally vicious.' Everybody then murmured, 'True!' and looked at me in a particularly unpleasant and personal manner.

2 Discuss as a class the use Dickens makes here of first-person narrative. Focus on:
- the way Pip, as an adult looking back on this episode, recreates the discomfort he felt as a child
- the way the adult Pip presents this episode humorously
- the way the adult Pip's voice guides your response to the other characters
- the way Dickens shapes your response to Pip both as an adult and a child.

3 Look back over the three extracts above from *Behind the Scenes at the Museum*, *Life of Pi* and *Great Expectations*. Compare and contrast the writers' use of first-person narrative to achieve their purposes as you understand them.

4 Summarise the range of narrative techniques you have identified in your work on Activities 48 and 49. Do you think some of these are more characteristic of modern novels than of novels written in the past? If so, try to be clear about what they are and the way in which they work. Refer to your wide reading as well as your prescribed texts.

5 If *Great Expectations* is one of your prescribed texts, compare Dickens' use of the first-person voice with the way in which the first-person voice is used by at least one other prose writer or poet in the topic group 'Identifying Self'. You might consider:
- the writer's purposes
- what is distinctive about the first-person voice
- how the first-person voice is created
- how the first-person voice positions the reader in relation to the text.

Base your comparison on extracts from the texts you choose and which you think are typical of their style.

Activity 50

This activity applies to texts in any topic group.

'Whether it's prose or poetry, literature written post-1990 is rarely as satisfying as literature from the past. It has less depth, and the novelists and poets seem to want to play clever tricks with the reader rather than just saying clearly what they mean.'

Compare and contrast a post-1990 text with an earlier text in the light of this comment. Focus your comparison on:

- the subject matter and themes of the texts
- the ways in which subject matter and themes are presented to the reader
- your response to the claim that post-1990 literature lacks 'depth'
- your response to the claim that post-1990 writers 'play clever tricks'.

Include in your writing a personal evaluation of the post-1990 text(s) you are studying.

Take it further

Bring in a poetry text from the topic group 'Identifying Self' to compare with the novels used for Activities 48 and 49. You could compare the use of a female persona in *The Wife of Bath's Tale* or *The Fat Black Woman's Poems* with the use of a female narrator in *Behind the Scenes at the Museum*. You could compare the way Grace Nichols presents the experience of displacement with the way Yann Martel presents this in *Life of Pi*.

Writing in the exam

When comparing texts written before and after 1990, guard against making sweeping statements about 'modern' and 'older' literature, especially judgemental ones. Activity 50 below deliberately uses such a statement as a springboard for writing. A weak answer would be written in the same general terms. A good answer would comment on and evaluate each text in terms of its writer's purposes and the extent to which these are achieved, irrespective of dates.

Comparing prose with poetry: *Small Island* and *The General Prologue to the Canterbury Tales* (post-1990 and pre-1990)

Activities 51 and 52 illustrate writers' presentation of character in different genres. They also show some stylistic differences between prose and poetry from different times. They will be useful to the study of any prose and poetry texts and should be undertaken together.

Activity 51

1 Read the extract below from *Small Island*. Queenie Bligh, the narrator at this point in the novel, has a West Indian lodger, Gilbert. His wife has just arrived from Jamaica to join him. Mr Todd, Queenie's white neighbour, disapproves. The setting is London in 1948.

From *Small Island* by Andrea Levy

I knew he'd be round, as soon as that woman, Gilbert's wife, left her trunk in the road for all to see. A woman. You don't see many coloured women. I'd seen old ones with backsides as big as buses but never a young one with a trim waist. His head popped out of his door then darted back in again. Probably went to get his shoes.

5 I was right. Not five minutes after Gilbert had taken the trunk inside he was on the doorstep. 'Mr Todd,' I said, 'what can I do for you?'

Another darkie, that's what the look on his face said. The motley mixture of outrage, shock, fear, even – nostrils flaring, mouth trying to smile but only managing a sneer. 'Yes. I just wanted a quick word with you, Mrs Bligh, about your paying guests.'

10 I bet he did. He'd have told that horrible sister of his that more coloureds had just turned up. How many is it now? they'd have said to each other. Fifty? Sixty? 'You'll have to speak to her, Cyril,' she'd have told him, before bemoaning how respectable this street was before they came. They'd have got all those words out – decent, proper – polished them up and made them shine, before blaming Mrs Queenie Bligh
15 for singlehandedly ruining the country. They were the same during the war, although even they couldn't blame me for that. Too many Poles. Overrun by Czechs. Couldn't move for Belgians. And as for the Jews. They moaned about Jews even after we knew what the poor beggars had been through. They were all right in their own country, Mr Todd reasoned, but he wanted none of them down our street. He'd never
20 forgiven me for taking in Jean. Bombed out. Her family dead. Sweetheart blown to no-one-there in North Africa. Why not? She was company even when she started going out all night and coming in with the milk. He asked, bold as anything, what she did for a living. I told him she was a nurse – you know, on night duty. Choked on his cup of tea before enquiring if I was very sure of that.

2 Discuss as a class how the narrator, Queenie, characterises Mr Todd in this extract. Focus on:
   • her descriptions of his appearance
   • her representation of his way of speaking
   • the tone of her narrative
   • how her narrative conveys her opinion of Mr Todd to the reader.

3 Explore how the writer, Andrea Levy, characterises Queenie in this extract. What impressions do you get of her personality from (a) her idiolect, (b) her colloquial register, and (c) her attitude towards people of different nationalities? How does Levy present her as a likeable character whose attitudes the reader is encouraged to share?

4 In this extract, Levy is dealing with the theme of racial prejudice in post-war England. One of her purposes is to satirise – that is, to criticise through humour and ridicule – people like Mr Todd. How do her techniques of characterisation help her to achieve this? How effective do you find these techniques?

5 If *Small Island* is one of your chosen texts:

a Compare Queenie as a narrator with Hortense and/or Gilbert and/or Bernard. What differences are there in the perspectives they provide for the reader and in their narrative styles? Why do you think Levy chooses to tell the story by using four narrators whose accounts are interleaved in the course of the novel?

b Work outwards from the extract above to consider how *Small Island* explores the conflicts between two cultures in post-war England. How does Andrea Levy use humour and satire to convey cultural difference and conflict? Do you find some sections of the novel more effective than others in presenting this theme?

Take it further

Remind yourself of the difference between analysing characterisation and 'character study' by looking back to pages 30–2 of this book. Then choose two leading characters in the prose text(s) you are studying. Write a comparative analysis of the way they are presented to the reader. You might comment on their similarities to and differences from Andrea Levy's method of characterising Mr Todd in the extract in Activity 51.

Activity 52

1 Read the extract below from *The General Prologue to the Canterbury Tales*. The narrator, Chaucer himself in the persona of a pilgrim on his way to Canterbury Cathedral, is describing one of his travelling companions, the Miller.

From *The General Prologue* to the Canterbury Tales (545–566)

The MILLERE was a stout carl for the nones;	*stout carl*: muscular bloke; *for the nones*: indeed
Ful byg he was of brawn, and eke of bones.	*eke*: also
That proved wel, for over al ther he cam,	*over al ther he cam*: wherever he went
At wrastlynge he wolde have alwey the ram.	*the ram*: the first prize in a wrestling match
5 He was short-sholdred, brood, a thikke knarre;	*thikke knarre*: strongly built hard man
Ther was no dore that he nolde heve of harre,	*nolde heve of harre*: couldn't lift off its hinges
Or breke it at a rennyng with his heed.	*at a rennyng*: running at full tilt; *heed*: head
His berd as any sowe or fox was reed,	*sowe*: female pig; *reed*: red
And therto brood, as though it were a spade.	
10 Upon the cop right of his nose he hade	*cop right*: very tip
A werte, and theron stood a toft of herys,	*werte*: wart; *herys*: hairs
Reed as the brustles of a sowes erys;	*erys*: ears
His nosethirles blake were and wyde.	*nosethirles*: nostrils; *blake*: black
A swerd and a bokeler bar he by his syde.	*swerd and a bokeler*: sword and small shield
15 His mouth as greet was as a greet forneys.	*forneys*: oven
He was a janglere and a goliardeys,	*janglere*: noisy gossip; *goliardeys*: buffoon
And that was moost of synne and harlotries.	*of synne and harlotries*: scandalous, obscene
Wel koude he stelen corn and tollen thries;	*stelen*: steal; *tollen thries*: take three times his due
And yet he hadde a thombe of gold, pardee.	*thombe of gold*: talent for making money
20 A whit cote and a blew hood wered he.	
A baggepipe wel koude he blowe and sowne,	*sowne*: play on
And therwithal he broghte us out of towne.	*broghte us*: i.e. at the head of the procession

Geoffrey Chaucer

Take it further

If your chosen texts include one of the prescribed works by Chaucer, it is important to listen to readings of them in the original Middle English. Sources include: http://www. bl.uk/learning/langlit/ changlang/activities/ lang/chaucer/ chaucerpage1.html and the audio book of *The Wife of Bath's Prologue and Tale* read by Elizabeth Salter (Cambridge University Press).

Take it further

Bring in a further text from the topic group 'Journeys' to compare with those used in Activities 51 and 52. You could compare the way Andrea Levy presents the experience of migration and exile with the way this theme is presented in *Reef* or *The Final Passage*. You could compare the use made of point of view and voice in *The Terrorist at my Table* with the narrative techniques in *The General Prologue to the Canterbury Tales* or any of the prescribed novels.

2 Once you have absorbed the meaning, listen to this extract being read aloud in **Middle English** dialect. Then try reading it aloud yourself with a partner. Take it in turns to read the 11 sentences.

3 Discuss as a class how the poem's narrator characterises the Miller in this extract. Focus on:
  • the detailed descriptions of his appearance
  • the colloquial language and the use of the vernacular
  • the way in which the sound of words echoes their meaning
  • how the narrator's opinion of the Miller is conveyed.

4 In this extract, Chaucer the pilgrim is the narrator. Chaucer the poet is the writer. How effective do you think the writer's technique is?

5 Compare Chaucer's characterisation of the Miller with Levy's characterisation of Mr Todd and Queenie. Which makes the stronger impact on you? You might consider:
  • the way in which the reader is positioned in relation to each text
  • the way in which each writer guides the reader's response
  • some specific differences between prose and poetry
  • some specific differences between a post-1990 text and a text from the past.

6 If *The General Prologue to the Canterbury Tales* is one of your chosen texts:

  a Compare the characterisation of the Miller with the characterisation of the following: the Knight, the Prioress, the Pardoner. Are Chaucer's techniques the same in each case? How does he use irony and the rhyming couplet form to present his imagined characters to the reader?

  b Work outwards from the extract on page 79 to consider Chaucer's use of a journey of pilgrimage in *The General Prologue to the Canterbury Tales*. How is this device intended to give variety and coherence to the text? Do you find it effective, or is it just a weak strategy for assembling a diverse group of characters who would not otherwise meet?

Activity 53

This activity applies to texts in the topic group 'Journeys'.

'Journeys can be both outward and inward; in the best literature, a journey between places is also a journey into the self.'

Compare and contrast at least two texts in the light of this comment. Focus your comparison on:
• the nature of the 'journey' described in each text
• your understanding of each writer's purposes
• whether the definition of 'journeys' above applies to each text equally well
• how you respond to the evaluative comment 'in the best literature…', above.

Remember that, in tasks that ask you to compare texts 'in the light of this comment', you are free to challenge or disagree with the assumptions made in the comment.

Writing in the exam

Look at the range of Section B questions in the Sample Assessment Materials for this Unit (pages 115–129). With the help of your teacher, devise two or three similar questions for your topic group. Pay particular attention to the comment or 'proposition' you invent. Keep in mind your particular texts, so that the comment is (a) clearly relevant to them and (b) neither too vague nor too contentious. Work as a class to plan *different kinds* of answers to them.

Comparing poetry with poetry: *101 Poems Against War* and *Legion* (pre-1990 and post-1990)

Activities 54 and 55 focus on key poems from these texts that treat a common theme in different ways. They also illustrate some stylistic differences between two kinds of poetry. They will be useful to the study of any poetry texts and should be undertaken together.

Activity 54

1 Read the poem opposite. It was published in 1964.

2 Discuss as a class how this poem presents a comment on war. Focus on:
- the situation described in lines 1–23 – who might the poem's speaker be? Whereabouts might he be? What seems to have happened in the world at large?
- how 'the strange horses' make a difference to the community – what way of life does the community now embrace? Why have they turned their backs on technology? In what ways do you think 'Our life is changed' (line 53)?
- why this poem has been included in a collection entitled *101 Poems Against War*
- what kind of poem this is and how it might be read – as a narrative poem? As a dramatic monologue? As a fable?

The Horses

Barely a twelvemonth after
The seven days war that put the world to sleep,
Late in the evening the strange horses came.
By then we had made our covenant with silence,
But in the first few days it was so still   5
We listened to our breathing and were afraid.
On the second day
The radios failed; we turned the knobs; no answer.
On the third day a warship passed us, heading north,
Dead bodies piled on the deck. On the sixth day   10
A plane plunged over us into the sea. Thereafter
Nothing. The radios dumb;
And still they stand in corners of our kitchens,
And stand, perhaps, turned on, in a million rooms
All over the world. But now if they should speak,   15
If on a sudden they should speak again,
If on the stroke of noon a voice should speak,
We would not listen, we would not let it bring
That old bad world that swallowed its children quick
At one great gulp. We would not have it again.   20
Sometimes we think of the nations lying asleep,
Curled blindly in impenetrable sorrow,
And then the thought confounds us with its strangeness.

The tractors lie about our fields; at evening
They look like dank sea-monsters couched and waiting.   25
We leave them where they are and let them rust:
'They'll moulder away and be like other loam'.
We make our oxen drag our rusty ploughs,
Long laid aside. We have gone back
Far past our fathers' land.   30
          And then, that evening
Late in the summer the strange horses came.
We heard a distant tapping on the road,
A deepening drumming; it stopped, went on again
And at the corner changed to hollow thunder.   35
We saw the heads
Like a wild wave charging and were afraid.
We had sold our tractors in our fathers' time
To buy new tractors. Now they were strange to us
As fabulous steeds set on an ancient shield   40
Or illustrations in a book of knights.
We did not dare go near them. Yet they waited,
Stubborn and shy, as if they had been sent
By an old command to find our whereabouts
And that long-lost archaic companionship.   45
In the first moment we had never a thought
That they were creatures to be owned and used.
Among them were some half-a-dozen colts
Dropped in some wilderness of the broken world,
Yet new as if they had come from their own Eden.   50
Since then they have pulled our ploughs and borne our loads,
But that free servitude still can pierce our hearts.
Our life is changed; their coming our beginning.

Edwin Muir

Key term

- narrative perspective

3 'The Horses' describes 'That old bad world that swallowed its children quick/ At one great gulp' (lines 19–20) and its aftermath. Explore the way Edwin Muir develops this theme. You might consider:

- his use of (a) a persona to narrate the poem, (b) a rural setting for the poem
- how he shifts the **narrative perspective** to describe in sequence (a) the recent past, (b) the present, (c) the remote past, (d) the present
- his use of imagery that makes reference to the Bible and Christianity – for example, 'as if they had come from their own Eden' (line 49), 'The seven days war that put the world to sleep' (line 2), 'that free servitude' (line 52), 'as if they had been sent/ By an old command' (lines 43–44)
- the speaker's choices of language and tone of voice.

4 If *101 Poems Against War* is one of your chosen texts:

a Compare 'The Horses' with the following poems in the collection: 'A Refusal to Mourn the Death, by Fire, of a Child in London' by Dylan Thomas, 'Fears in Solitude' by S.T. Coleridge, and 'On Being Asked for a War Poem' by W.B. Yeats. In what ways can they be read as 'Poems Against War'? How do they take different and unusual approaches to this subject?

b Work outwards from the poem on page 81 to consider how the poets in *101 Poems Against War* use a variety of poetic forms. Choose three poems that contrast markedly in form and structure. How effective do you find each in making a protest against war?

Activity 55

1 Read the poem below from *Legion* by David Harsent. This collection was published in 2005. In a sequence of linked poems, Harsent 'offers reports from an unnamed war zone', according to the publisher's note.

Harp Strings

(i)

Then we had iron rain, nine days without break or let, the rain
that is nothing more nor less than rain of the season
spilling into our songs as 'fist of nails' or 'harp strings'
5 or 'love of solitude'. Should we have guessed they would gain
ground under that cover? Well, look, the reason
we turned to our bottling and sewing, to pot-luck and make-good,
is simple enough to tell: the rain only ever brings
music in mist or sweet bafflement or rain-dreams. There's a birch-wood
10 on the outskirts, silver poles no thicker than a man, where the rain swings
and shudders, wind-blown walking rain, and their top-to-toe
silver-grey, and the steel of their sidearms, and bone-
ash mixed with clay slapped to their cheeks and necks is how
they came among us, backed by the wind, the stain
15 of their last battle carried like a blazon on the brow.

(ii)

The rain washed everything, took everything downhill, a log-jam,
a slurry, that side-slipped to the river. White water rang
on broken boulders and roared in the mid-stream slam,
20 then it all went clear. We've owned to it since; we were wrong
to see nothing dark in the rain. All this has gone into song.

David Harsent

2 Discuss as a class how this poem presents a comment on war. Focus on:
- the situation described in lines 1–14 – who might the poem's speaker be? Who might 'we' and 'they' be? What has happened in the war zone?
- how the rain has influenced the outcome of the conflict
- what kind of poem this is and how it might be read – as a narrative poem? As a dramatic monologue? As a nature poem?

3 'Harp Strings' describes a battle in which the elements and the season play a major part. Explore the way David Harsent develops this theme. You might consider:
- his use of (a) a persona to narrate the poem, and (b) a rural setting for the poem
- how the poem's perspective changes in part (ii)
- his use of imagery that makes reference to the songs of the speaker's community. See, for example, the poem's title, lines 3–4 and line 19
- the speaker's choices of language and tone of voice.

4 Compare the ways in which 'Harp Strings' and 'The Horses' can be read as protests against war. Harsent and Muir deal with a common theme in quite different ways. Summarise these. Then make an evaluation of the poems. How effective is each in achieving its purposes, as you understand them? Which of them conveys its anti-war theme more memorably for you?

5 If *Legion* is one of your chosen texts:

a Compare 'Harp Strings' with the following poems in the collection: 'Chinese Whispers', the five poems entitled 'Despatches', 'Snapshots (1)', 'Snapshots (2)', and 'Mascot'. How does Harsent use different poetic forms and structures to explore his principal theme? Do you find some of these more effective than others?

b Work outwards from the poem on page 82 to consider Harsent's use of the poetic sequence as an organising principle in *Legion*. How does the title of the collection connect the individual poems together? How well does the range of poetic forms in the collection combine to present a realistic narrative of modern warfare?

Take it further

Bring in a novel from the topic group 'War' to compare with the poetry texts in Activities 54 and 55. You could compare the view of war presented in *The Ghost Road* or *The Kite Runner* with the one presented by David Harsent in *Legion*. You could compare the way in which Pat Barker or Khaled Hosseini draw on historical events to shape their narratives with the use of historical context by poets in *Here to Eternity* or *101 Poems Against War*.

Activity 56

This activity applies to texts in the topic group 'War'.

'War is a timeless subject. The best poems and novels about war reflect this; the less accomplished provide us with only a limited picture.'

Compare and contrast at least two of your chosen texts in the light of this comment. Focus your comparison on:
- each writer's purposes, as you understand them
- the ways in which subject matter and theme are presented to the reader
- your response to the claim that war is 'a timeless subject'
- your response to the evaluative terms 'best', 'less accomplished' and 'limited picture'.

Writing in the exam

If you are comparing poetry with poetry, remember that poets can use structure, form and language in very different ways. Avoid making general assumptions or statements about poetry as a genre. Always relate your comments on the style of a poem to its particular theme and context.

Writing a comparative analysis of prescribed texts

This sub-section gives you guidance on how to construct an essay based on two prescribed texts. There is no single 'right way' of doing this: you will decide for yourself on the best approach to take in the light of the exam question you are given. However, some general principles need to be followed in order to meet the four assessment objectives for Section B. Activity 57 helps you understand what they are and suggests how to build a response that takes account of them.

Activity 57

1   Read the question below, which applies to the topic group 'Identifying Self'.

> 'Texts only work well if the reader can identify herself or himself with the situations, the people, the crises and the personal dilemmas that are presented in them. To want to read more, the reader has to feel personally involved.'
>
> Comment on and analyse the connections and comparisons between at least two texts you have studied in the light of this assertion.
>
> In your response, ensure that at least one text is a post-1990 text.
>
> You should demonstrate what it means to be considering texts as a modern reader in a modern context, and that other readers at other times may well have had other responses.

The guidance that follows uses *Great Expectations* ('GE') and *Taking off Emily Dickinson's Clothes* ('TOEDC') as exemplar texts.

2   Read the detailed paragraph plan below for a sample response to this question.

> *Introductory paragraph:* Contrast the genres of GE and TOEDC – autobiographical fiction and poetry in the form of free verse. Relate these genres to the time in which the texts were written – mid-nineteenth century, early twenty-first century. State that they explore 'personal dilemmas', etc in very different ways and address different kinds of reader – they need to be compared in the light of this.
>
> *First main paragraph:* Show how GE presents 'situations, people, crises, dilemmas' through a fictional narrative that appeals to readers' common experience of childhood and growing up – the reader feels 'personally involved' because the experiences described are universal (fear of the unknown, search for an identity, being rejected in love, etc).
>
> *Second main paragraph:* Show how TOEDC presents 'situations, people, crises, dilemmas' through autobiographical poems that strike a chord with the reader's everyday experience – the reader feels 'personally involved' because the experiences described are commonplace (eating a meal, taking a walk, driving in the car, etc).
>
> *Third main paragraph:* Show how GE provides a wide variety of experience and characters/stories within one narrative – mainly describes Pip's inner life but also incorporates love stories, a mystery story, tragic deaths etc – a great deal for the reader to 'identify' with.
>
> *Fourth main paragraph:* Show how TOEDC is less varied in the range of experience it presents – mainly describes Collins' thoughts and feelings in response to ordinary events and situations – quote Collins saying he writes about things 'you don't hear much about in poetry': this is what the reader is asked to 'identify' with.

Fifth main paragraph: Show how GE is varied in its style and language – **pathos**, **broad comedy**, melodrama, tragedy, satire – helps to make the reader feel 'personally involved' on a number of levels.

Sixth main paragraph: Show how TOEDC is less varied in its style and language – quote Collins saying he deliberately confines himself to 'a blue jeans kinda style' – the reader will feel 'personally involved' if he/she responds to this colloquial register and tone but it risks becoming repetitive.

Concluding paragraph: Quote other readers' responses to Dickens: largely favourable in all age-groups; the novel was highly popular in Victorian times and still is. Quote other readers' responses to Collins; admired on the 'college circuit' and among younger readers, limited range of subject matter and technique. Personal view: engaged in a personal and imaginative way far more strongly by Dickens – Collins seems merely whimsical, amusingly ironic but detached.

3 Discuss as a class how well this plan is likely to lead to an essay in which the writer:
- compares and contrasts the texts throughout
- addresses the subject matter and principal themes of the texts
- refers to the texts in specific detail
- analyses and compares the structure, form and language of the texts
- sets the texts into their contexts
- refers to other readers' interpretations and responses
- makes a personal evaluation of the texts
- answers the question set.

4 Make your own detailed paragraph plan for an essay on two or three of your texts, using the plan above as a model. Remember that one of these must be post-1990. Use the bullet points in question 3 above as a checklist to ensure that you are meeting the requirements of the four assessment objectives for Section B.

5 Read the passage below. It is taken from the completed essay based on the plan quoted above.

Great Expectations and _Taking off Emily Dickinson's Clothes_ involve the reader with personal experience in different ways. Dickens' novel takes the form of autobiographical fiction in which the central character, Pip, tells his own story from an adult point of view:

> My sister, Mrs Joe, with black hair and eyes, had such a prevailing redness of skin that I sometimes used to wonder whether it was possible she washed herself with a nutmeg instead of soap.

The narrative is retrospective, though Pip recreates his experiences, particularly of childhood, in an imaginative, dramatic style which engages the reader strongly with the events he describes. A good example is the first episode in the book where Pip is suddenly attacked by the convict:

> 'Oh, don't cut my throat, sir,' I pleaded in terror. 'Pray don't do it, sir.'
>
> 'Tell us your name,' said the man. 'Quick!'
>
> 'Pip, sir.'
>
> 'Once more,' said the man, staring at me. 'Give it mouth!'

Here the narrative captures the shock and terror of a young boy confronted by every child's nightmare – having their name demanded for no clear reason by an adult stranger who threatens to harm them. Pip's feeling of being controlled by unknown, or half-understood, forces continues throughout the book and is one reason why the reader identifies with him so strongly. Not knowing exactly who we are and searching for an identity ('Tell us your name') is a universal human experience.

Billy Collins' poems seem autobiographical, but they present personal experience in a manner that is detached and philosophical rather than intense or dramatic:

> I am wondering what became of all those tall abstractions
> that used to pose, robed and statuesque, in paintings
> ('The Death of Allegory')

He reflects on his experiences by inviting the reader to see commonplace events in a new light, as in the poem 'Insomnia', which begins with the speaker counting sheep and ends with:

> I picture all the fish in creation
> leaping a fence in a field of water,
> one colorful species after another.

It is typical of Collins to introduce a surreal note into poems that are basically about everyday, even mundane, subjects. He has said, 'In a poem, I want the reader to know they've been taken on an imaginative journey.' This is a good description of the pattern of his poems: the reader is asked to share his way of seeing things and either smile with recognition ('You know: the driving rain, the boots by the door,/ small birds searching for berries in winter') or be surprised by a disturbing insight ('Just another Wednesday/ you whisper,/ then holding your breath,/ place this cup on yesterday's saucer/ without the slightest chink').

6 Discuss as a class how well this extract develops the content of the first and second main paragraphs in the plan above. Evaluate the way in which the writer:
  - compares and contrasts the two texts
  - combines general statements with specific textual illustration
  - employs reference and quotation
  - uses appropriate literary concepts and terms
  - expresses herself clearly and fluently
  - constructs suitable paragraphs.

7 Turn the paragraph plan you made in question 4 on p85 into a complete essay. Use the bullet points in question 6 above as a checklist to ensure you are meeting the four assessment objectives for Section B.

8 Look back over your work in this sub-section. Draw up a list of the principles and practices you need to follow when writing a comparative analysis of prescribed texts. Use this to help you plan and write essays in the future.

3 Comparing texts in their contexts

This part shows you how to make connections and comparisons between texts related by context. It gives you guidance on how to set prescribed texts into context.

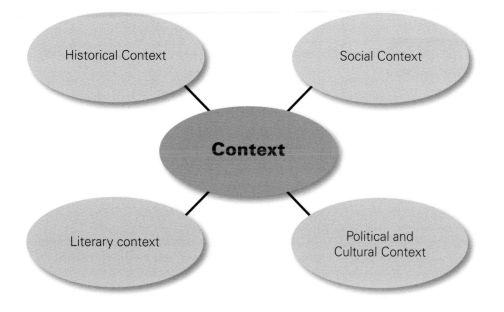

What is meant by 'context'?

There are two main kinds of context in which you need to set your texts when making a comparative study: **the context of production** and **the context of reception**.

The context of *production* relates to the circumstances in, or about which, a text is written. For example, some writers explore the *historical context* of the First World War or the Second World War; some writers explore the *social context* of racial or gender attitudes at particular times; some writers explore the *cultural context* of politics or religion; some writers work within a *literary context* by using genres such as tragedy or the poetic sequence. All the activities in this part of the book help you explore the context of production.

The context of *reception* relates to the way in which a text is interpreted by different readers over time. Various factors influence this, principally the assumptions about life and literature held by readers at different periods. This applies, for example, to nineteenth-century readers of Charles Dickens or Thomas Hardy. It applies equally to modern readers of Geoffrey Chaucer or Carol Ann Duffy, including yourself. Activities that help you explore the context of reception are to be found in Part 4 on pages 101–112 below.

How to use the activities in Part 3

The activities in this part, as in the previous part, are a combination of text-specific and generic. You can use them in the same way. You will benefit from working on a range of activities, not just those that apply to your own texts.

Exploring the historical context of texts: *The Ghost Road* and *Here to Eternity*

Activities 58 and 59 show you how to set two prescribed texts from the topic group 'War' into their historical context. They should be undertaken together. You can apply a similar method to your own texts.

Activity 58

1 Read the extract below from near the end of *The Ghost Road*. The setting is France in 1918. Billy Prior is waiting to lead his men in an offensive against a German-held canal. Wilfred Owen is a fellow officer in the same action.

From *The Ghost Road* by Pat Barker

There is to be no retirement under any circumstances. That was the order. They have tied us to the stake, we cannot fly, but bear-like we must fight the course. The men were silent, staring straight ahead into the mist. Talk, even in whispers, was forbidden. Prior looked at his watch, licked dry lips, watched the second hand crawl
5 round to the quarter hour. All around him was a tension of held breath. 5.43. Two more minutes. He crouched further down, whistle clenched between his teeth.

Prompt as ever, hell erupted. Shells whined over, flashes of light, plumes of water from the drainage ditches, tons of mud and earth flung into the air. A shell fell short. The ground shook beneath them and a shower of pebbles and clods of earth peppered
10 their steel helmets. Five minutes of this, five minutes of the air bursting in waves against your face, men with dazed faces braced against it, as they picked up the light bridges meant for fording the flooded drainage ditches, and carried them out to the front. A gasp for air, then noise again, but further back, as the barrage lifted and drummed down on to the empty fields…

15 Prior was about to start across the water with ammunition when he was himself hit, though it didn't feel like a bullet, more like a blow from something big and hard, a truncheon or a cricket bat, only it knocked him off his feet and he fell, one arm trailing over the edge of the canal.

He tried to turn to crawl back beyond the drainage ditches, knowing it was only a
20 matter of time before he was hit again, but the gas was thick here and he couldn't reach his mask. Banal, simple, repetitive thoughts ran round and round his mind. *Balls up. Bloody mad. Oh Christ.* There was no pain, more a spreading numbness that left his brain clear. He saw Kirk die. He saw Owen die, his body lifted off the ground by bullets, describing a slow arc in the air as it fell. It seemed to take for ever
25 to fall, and Prior's consciousness fluttered down with it. He gazed at his reflection in the water, which broke and reformed and broke again as bullets hit the surface and then, gradually, as the numbness spread, he ceased to see it.

2 Discuss in a small group the way Pat Barker shapes the reader's response to the First World War in this extract. Focus on:
  - the use of narrative point of view in paragraphs 1 and 2
  - the way the narrative voice moves between the conventional third person and free indirect style throughout the extract
  - the use of imagery
  - the use of syntax.

3 Share your responses in class discussion. How effective do you find Barker's use of style and language to be in giving you a perspective on war?

4 Read the extract on page 89 from one of Wilfred Owen's letters to his mother from the battlefield in France.

Pat Barker cites Owen's letters as a primary source in her research for *The Ghost Road*. Owen was an officer in the 2nd Manchester Regiment, which was wiped out in the attack on the Sambre–Oise canal described above. He was killed in this action on 4 November 1918, one week before the Armistice that ended the war.

Tues: 16 January 1917   *[2ⁿᵈ Manchester Regt., B.E.F.]*

My own sweet Mother,

I am sorry you have had about 5 days letterless. I hope you had my two letters 'posted' since you wrote your last, which I received tonight. I am bitterly disappointed that I never got one of yours.

I can see no point in deceiving you about these last 4 days. I have suffered seventh hell.

I have not been at the front.

I have been in front of it.

I held an advanced post, that is, a 'dug-out' in the middle of No Man's Land.

We had a march of 3 miles over shelled road then nearly 3 along a flooded trench… High explosives were dropping all around us, and machine guns spluttered every few minutes. But it was so dark that even the German flares did not reveal us.

Three quarters dead, I mean each of us three-quarters dead, we reached the dug-out, and relieved the wretches therein. I then had to go forth and find another dug-out for a still more advanced post where I left 18 bombers. I was responsible for other posts but there was a junior officer in charge.

My dug-out held 25 men tight packed. Water filled in to a depth of 1 or 2 feet, leaving say 4 feet of air.

One entrance had been blown in and blocked.

So far, the other remained.

The Germans knew we were staying there and decided we shouldn't.

Those fifty hours were the agony of my happy life.

Every ten minutes on Sunday afternoon seemed an hour.

I nearly broke down and let myself drown in the water that was now slowly rising over my knees.

Towards six o'clock, when, I suppose, you would be going to church, the shelling grew less intense and less accurate: so that I was mercifully helped to do my duty and crawl, wade, climb and flounder over No Man's Land to visit my other post. It took me half an hour to move about 150 yards…

I allow myself to tell you all these things because <u>I am never going back to this awful post</u>. It is the worst the Manchesters have ever held; and we are going back for a rest.

I hear that the officer who relieved me left his 3 Lewis Guns behind when he came out. (He had only 24 hours in.) He will be court-martialled…

Don't pass round these sheets but have portions typed for Leslie, etc. My previous letter to you has just been returned. It will be too heavy to include in this.

Your very own Wilfred X

5 Discuss as a class Wilfred Owen's feelings and views about (a) the conditions in which fighting is taking place, (b) his responsibilities as an officer, and (c) his mother.

Then compare Owen's letter with Pat Barker's prose fiction text. What light does the letter shed on the novel? What light does the novel shed on the letter? Include in your comparison some comment about the style in which each text is written. Relate this to the two writers' different audiences.

Independent research

Try the following sources:

www.iwm.org.uk

www.historylearning
site.co.uk

www.bbc.co.uk/history

www.ww1battlefields.
co.uk

www.sassoonery.
demon.co.uk

6 If *The Ghost Road* is one of your chosen texts:

a Carry out research into:
- the history of the 2nd Manchester Regiment in the First World War
- the ill-fated attack on the Sambre–Oise canal in November 1918
- the friendship between Wilfred Owen and Siegfried Sassoon, fictionalised in Barker's earlier novel *Regeneration*.

Some research sources are suggested in the 'Independent research' box to the left.

b Once your research is complete, explore some of the differences between Barker's fiction and the facts on which it is based. You might consider:
- the way the narrative of *The Ghost Road* is built up and developed
- the use of the parallel stories of Billy Prior's First World War experiences and Dr Rivers' experiences (a) at Craiglockhart, (b) in Melanesia
- the use of a first-person narrative – i.e. parts of Billy's diary – combined with third-person omniscient point of view and voice
- the novel's focus on psychological states.

Activity 59

1 Read the poem opposite by Siegfried Sassoon, included in *Here to Eternity*.

Sassoon was a British infantry officer in the First World War. Like Wilfred Owen, he was hospitalised with shell-shock for a time and later returned to the front line. Like Owen, he was decorated for bravery. Unlike Owen, he survived the war.

2 Discuss in a small group the way Sassoon shapes the reader's response to the First World War in this poem. Focus on:
- the setting – how are the details of the tunnel evoked?
- the use of the rear-guard's viewpoint – how does this create realism?
- the narrative form of the poem – how does this convey a mixture of horror and pathos?
- the use of imagery – what effects are created by (a) 'his prying torch with patching glare' (line 2), (b) 'The rosy gloom of battle overhead' (line 7), (c) 'Dawn's ghost' (line 20), and (d) 'Unloading hell behind him' (line 25).

Then consider Sassoon's attitude to the rear-guard in this poem. How effectively do you think his attitude is conveyed?

Key term
- **parallel stories**

The Rear-Guard
(Hindenberg Line, April 1917)

Groping along the tunnel, step by step,
He winked his prying torch with patching glare
From side to side, and sniffed the unwholesome air.

Tins, boxes, bottles, shapes too vague to know;
A mirror smashed, the mattress from a bed;
And he, exploring fifty feet below,
The rosy gloom of battle overhead.

Tripping, he grabbed the wall; saw someone lie
Humped at his feet, half-hidden by a rug,
And stooped to give the sleeper's arm a tug.
'I'm looking for headquarters.' No reply.
'God blast your neck!' (For days he'd had no sleep,)
'Get up and guide me through this stinking place.'

Savage, he kicked a soft, unanswering heap,
And flashed his beam across the livid face
Terribly glaring up, whose eyes yet wore
Agony dying hard ten days before;
And fists of fingers clutched a blackening wound.

Alone he staggered on until he found
Dawn's ghost that filtered down a shafted stair
To the dazed, muttering creatures underground
Who hear the boom of shells in muffled sound.
At last, with sweat of horror in his hair,
He climbed through darkness to the twilight air,
Unloading hell behind him step by step.

Siegfried Sassoon

3 Read the extract below from *Sherston's Progress*, written by Sassoon in 1936.

From *Sherston's Progress* by Siegfried Sassoon

Shell-shock. How many a brief bombardment had its long-delayed after-effect in the minds of these survivors, many of whom had looked at their companions and laughed while inferno did its best to destroy them. Not then was their evil hour, but
5 now; now, in the sweating suffocation of nightmare, in paralysis of limbs, in the stammering of dislocated speech. Worst of all, in the disintegration of those qualities through which they had been so gallant and selfless and uncomplaining – this, in the finer types of men, was the unspeakable tragedy of shell-shock; it was in this that their humanity had been outraged by those explosives that were sanctioned
10 and glorified by the Churches; it was thus that their self-sacrifice was mocked and maltreated – they, who in the name of righteousness had been sent out to maim and slaughter their fellow-men. In the name of civilization these soldiers had been martyred, and it remained for civilization to prove that their martyrdom wasn't a dirty swindle.

4 Discuss as a class the feelings and views expressed here about (a) 'the unspeakable tragedy of shell-shock', (b) the role of the Church in the First World War I, and (c) civilisation.

Then compare the theme of this extract with the theme of 'The Rear-Guard'. What light does it shed on the poem, particularly on the last stanza? Include in your comparison some comment about the style in which each text is written, and relate this to Sassoon's purposes as you understand them.

5 If *Here to Eternity* is one of your chosen texts:
a Carry out research into:
  • the controversy Sassoon caused in the press and in parliament during 1917 by disowning his Military Cross and refusing to fight again
  • the background to Wilfred Owen's poem 'Dulce Et Decorum Est' (see *Here to Eternity* page 281) and why Jessie Pope was one of the readers it addressed
  • the death of Rudyard Kipling's son John in the First World War, which prompted his poem 'Epitaphs of War 1914–1918' (see *Here to Eternity* page 282).

Some research sources are suggested in the 'Independent research' box opposite.

b Once your research is complete, use it to illuminate the poems in *Here to Eternity* by Owen, Kipling, Sassoon and Isaac Rosenberg. You might consider:
  • their various attitudes towards patriotism and the war
  • the way their poems address both public and private concerns
  • the way their poems convey the psychological as well as the physical effects of war
  • the relationship between life and literature.

Take it further

Bring in a further text from the topic group 'War' to compare writers' use of historical context. You could compare the effect of war on friendships in *Spies* and *The Kite Runner*. You could compare poems about war in ancient times with poems about modern warfare in the prescribed poetry collections. Do attitudes to war change over time, and do poets in different eras treat the subject in different ways?

Writing in the exam

Discussing texts in their context will be part of the *comparison* you develop between them in your answer. Remember that the basic instruction you are given is 'comment on and analyse the connections and comparisons'. You need to comment on context in the light of this and not get sidetracked into a non-comparative account of historical, social, cultural or literary background.

Independent research

Try the following sources:
Siegfried Sassoon, *Memoirs of an Infantry Officer*;
Mad Jack, a 1970 BBC play about Sassoon in the First World War (see www. screenonline.org.uk/tv/ id/1242883/index.html);

Rudyard Kipling's autobiography *Something of Myself*, ed. Thomas Pinney;

www.1914-18.co.uk/ owen/dulce.htm

www.oup.com:80/ oxforddnb/info/ freeodnb/magazine/ october.

Activity 60

This activity applies to texts in any topic group.

Decide on a historical context that links your chosen texts in some way. It need not be a context from the distant past. It could relate to recent events such as war or political conflict, or to the social setting of the texts, or to their publishing history, or to the personal history of your writers.

Research the context you select, using the internet and/or bibliographical sources. Then develop a comparative study of how your texts can be related to each other within this context. Use Activities 58 and 59 to guide you. Bear in mind that historical context will be more important to some texts than to others.

Exploring the social context of texts:
The Wife of Bath's Prologue and Tale and
The Fat Black Woman's Poems

Activities 61 and 62 show you how to set two of the prescribed texts from the topic group 'Identifying Self' into their social context. They should be undertaken together. You can apply a similar method to your own texts.

Activity 61

1 Read the extract below and the poem opposite.

From *The Wife of Bath's Prologue* (593–608)

To chirche was myn housebonde born a-morwe   *born a-morwe*: carried the next day
With neighebores, that for hym maden sorwe;   *maden sorwe*: were in mourning
And Jankyn, oure clerk, was oon of tho.
5 As help me God, whan that I saugh hym go
After the beere, me thoughte he hadde a paire   *after the beere*: behind the coffin-board
Of legges and of feet so clene and faire
That al myn herte I yaf unto his hoold.   *yaf unto his hoold*: gave to him completely
He was, I trowe, twenty wynter oold,
10 And I was fourty, if I shal seye sooth;   *seye sooth*: tell the truth
But yet I hadde alwey a coltes tooth.   *coltes tooth*: the lustfulness of a young horse
Gat-tothed I was, and that bicam me weel;   *Gat-tothed*: gap-toothed (believed a sign of lechery)
I hadde the prente of seinte Venus seel.   *prente of seinte Venus*: mark of the goddess of love
As help me God, I was a lusty oon,
15 And faire, and riche, and yong, and wel bigon,   *wel bigon*: well provided for, affluent
And trewely, as myne housebondes tolde me,
I hadde the beste quoniam myghte be.   *quoniam*: 'you know what' (i.e. female genitalia)

Geoffrey Chaucer

Invitation

1
If my fat
was too much for me
I would have told you
5 I would have lost a stone
or two

I would have gone jogging
even when it was fogging
I would have weighed in
10 sitting on the bathroom scale
with my tail tucked in

I would have dieted
more care than a diabetic

But as it is
15 I'm feeling fine
feel no need
to change my lines
when I move I'm target light
Come up and see me sometime

20 **2**
Come up and see me sometime
Come up and see me sometime

My breasts are huge and exciting
amnions of watermelon
25   your hands can't cup
my thighs are twin seals
     fat as slick pups
there's a purple cherry
below the blues
30   of my black seabelly
there's a mole that gets a ride
each time I shift the heritage
of my behind

Come up and see me sometime

Grace Nichols

2 Compare in a small group the impressions given of the Wife of Bath and the Fat Black Woman. Focus on:
- their attitudes towards their femininity
- their attitudes towards their sexuality
- the distinctive voice each of them uses
- the way they can be seen to be alike.

3 Share your responses in class discussion. Then consider the social context of these poems. Chaucer was writing in the early 1390s. Grace Nichols published *The Fat Black Woman's Poems* in 1984. What does each poem's speaker imply about the society in which she lives and its view of (a) gender, (b) women's age and appearance, and (c) sex? How does each speaker project herself as a non-conformist and a rebel?

4 Compare as a class the use of structure, form and language in these poems. Focus on:
- the effect of informal and colloquial language in *The Wife of Bath's Prologue*
- the effect of the varied syntax and energetic rhythms in *The Wife of Bath's Prologue*
- the effect of informal and colloquial language in 'Invitation'
- the effect of a loose yet controlled structure in 'Invitation'.

If *The Wife of Bath's Prologue and Tale* is one of your chosen texts, carry out research into the prevailing attitudes in Chaucer's time to:
- the place of women in medieval society
- the role of a wife in marriage
- sex outside marriage.

Some research sources are suggested in the 'Independent research' box above.

Independent research

Try the following sources:
www.middle-ages. org/uk

www.channel4.com/ history/microsites/H/ history/guide12

Women in Medieval English Society by Mavis E. Mate, CUP, 1999.

Activity 62

1 Read the poem opposite and the extract from *The Wife of Bath's Tale* on page 94.

In the fairy tale on which *The Wife of Bath's Tale* (see page 94) is based, the Loathly Lady, having saved a young Arthurian knight's life, insists he should marry her to show his gratitude. When he protests that she is old and ugly, she asks him to think of the advantages of this.

Loveact

She enter into his Great House
her see-far looking eyes
unassuming

5 He fix her with his glassy stare
and feel the thin fire in his blood
awakening

Soon she is the fuel
that keep them all going

10 He/his mistresswife/and his
children who take to her breasts
like leeches

He want to tower above her
want her to raise her ebony
15 haunches and when she does
he think she can be trusted
and drinks her in

and his mistresswife
spending her days in rings
of vacant smiling
20 is glad to be rid of the
loveact

But time pass/es

Her sorcery cut them
like a whip

20 She hide her triumph
and slowly stir the hate
of poison in

Grace Nichols

From *The Wife of Bath's Tale* (1219–1239)

'Chese now,' quod she, 'oon of thise thynges tweye:	*Chese*: choose; *quod*: said
To han me foul and old til that I deye,	*han*: have; *foul*: ugly
And be to yow a trewe, humble wyf,	*trewe*: constant
And nevere yow displese in al my lyf;	*yow displese*: stray from you
5 Or elles ye wol han me yong and fair,	*fair*: beautiful
And take youre aventure of the repair	*take youre aventure… of me*: run the risk of
That shal be to youre hous by cause of me,	lovers queuing up at your house for me
Or in som oother place, may wel be.	
Now chese yourselven, wheither that yow liketh.'	*wheither*: whichever
10 This knyght avyseth hym and sore siketh,	*avyseth hym*: considers deeply; *siketh*: sighs
But atte laste he seyde in this manere:	
'My lady and my love, and wyf so deere,	
I put me in youre wise governance;	*governance*: control
Cheseth yourself which may be moost plesance,	*moost plesance*: most pleasurable
15 And moost honour to yow and me also.	*moost honour*: most honourable
I do no fors the wheither of the two;	*I do no fors*: I have no preference
For as yow liketh, it suffiseth me.'	*as yow liketh*: whatever you wish
'Thanne have I gete of yow maistrie,' quod she,	*of yow maistrie*: the upper hand over you
'Syn I may chese and governe as me lest?'	*Syn*: since; *governe as me lest*: do as I wish
20 'Ye, certes, wyf,' quod he, 'I holde it best.'	*holde*: believe
'Kys me,' quod she, 'we be no lenger wrothe…	*wrothe*: angry, at loggerheads

Geoffrey Chaucer

Writing in the exam

Note that the activities on context throughout this part encourage you to focus on the way texts are written. Writing about the context of production involves analysing structure, form and language as well as identifying themes.

At this point, the Loathly Lady turns into a desirable young woman and vows to be true to the knight. They make love joyfully and thereafter 'she obeyed hym in every thyng'. The Wife of Bath adds her wish that 'Jhesu Crist us sende/ Housbondes meeke, yonge, and fressh abedde'.

2 Compare as a class the way the theme of relations between a husband and wife is explored in these poems. Focus on:
   • the attitude of the slave-owner to his 'mistresswife' in 'Loveact'
   • her 'triumph' (line 24) – what do you think allows her to triumph?
   • the attitude of the young knight to the Loathly Lady in *The Wife of Bath's Tale*
   • the way she achieves 'maistrie' – what do you think allows her to 'gete… maistrie'?

3 Consider the social context of these poems. 'Loveact' is set in the Caribbean with its long history of white colonial rule. *The Wife of Bath's Tale*, though set in the time of King Arthur, is narrated by a middle-class medieval woman. What does each poem suggest about the society of the time and its view of (a) gender relations, (b) the balance of power in marriage, and (c) love in marriage?

Independent research

Try the following sources:
http://news.bbc.co.uk/ hi/english/static/ in_depth/uk/2002/race/ short_history_of_ immigration.stm#1972;

www.historyandpolicy. org/papers/policy- paper-45.html

4 Compare as a class the use of structure, form and language in 'Loveact' and 'Invitation'. Focus on:
   • the effect of Caribbean English dialect in 'Loveact'
   • the choice of a third-person voice in 'Loveact' by contrast with a first-person voice in 'Invitation'
   • the effect of imagery in 'Loveact' ('the thin fire in his blood', 'she is the fuel', 'Her sorcery cut them/ like a whip') compared with the imagery in 'Invitation' ('I'm target light', 'amnions of watermelon', 'purple cherry', 'black seabelly')
   • the tense, serious tone of 'Loveact' compared with light, expansive tone of 'Invitation'.

5 If *The Fat Black Woman's Poems* is one of your chosen texts, carry out research into race relations in England and the West Indies during the 1970s and 1980s. Some research sources are suggested in the 'Independent research' box to the left.

Activity 63

This activity applies to texts in any topic group.

Decide on a social context that links your chosen texts in some way. It could relate to their social setting, or to the communities described in the texts, or to the social attitudes your writers explore, or to the relationship between individuals and their backgrounds.

Research the context you select, using the internet and/or bibliographical sources. Then develop a comparative study of how your texts can be related to each other within this context. Use Activities 61 and 62 to guide you. Bear in mind that social context will be more important to some texts than to others.

Take it further

Bring in a prose text from the topic group 'Identifying Self' to compare writers' use of social context. You could compare the feminism of the Wife of Bath or the Fat Black Woman with the attitudes of the female narrator of *Behind the Scenes at the Museum*. You could compare the social background of nineteenth-century London presented in *Great Expectations* with the social background of twenty-first-century America presented in *Taking Off Emily Dickinson's Clothes*.

Exploring the political and cultural context of texts: *Reef* and *The Terrorist at my Table*

Activities 64 and 65 show you how to set two of the prescribed texts into their political and cultural context. They should be undertaken together. You can apply a similar method to your own texts.

Activity 64

1 Read the extract below from near the end of *Reef*. Triton, the narrator, has emigrated from his native Sri Lanka to England with his employer, Mister Salgado. Triton hopes to open a restaurant in London. Mister Salgado is concerned about the political upheavals in Sri Lanka and the safety of his estranged wife Nili, who is still living there.

From *Reef* by Romesh Gunesekera

One cold, wet afternoon we came back to discover a small snack-bar at the end of our road up for sale. Mister Salgado said, 'Here's your chance. Make it come true.' He invested the last of his savings in it. I painted it the colours of our tropical sea. Bought some wicker chairs and a blackboard for the menu. I put coloured lights outside and bucket lanterns inside. It was ready to grow. Mister Salgado beamed.

5   Then, in the summer of 1983, mobs went on the rampage in Colombo. We saw pictures of young men, who looked no different from me, going beserk on what could have been our main road. The rampant violence made the television news night after night for weeks. There had been nothing like it when trouble had broken out before, when books had been burned and the first skirmishes had started. Even during the insurgency of '71, the news had come only in drifts, distanced. But this time images of cruelty, the birth of a war, flickered on the screens across the
10   world as it happened. I remembered my fervent schoolmaster: his wobbly, black bicycle with its rust-eaten chain-guard, the schoolbook he always carried with him and the black umbrella that would bloom in the warm rain. I had found him in a ditch on the edge of our rice-field, that unsettled month which ended with me coming to Mister Salgado's house. His legs had been broken by a bunch of older boys who used to huddle in a hut in the schoolyard and chant the slogans of a shrinking world.

15   At the end of the summer, out of the blue one day, Tippy telephoned Mister Salgado. He was changing planes at Heathrow, heading for New York to do some deal. He said he got our number from Directory Enquiries; Tippy knew how things worked all over the world. He said it was wartime now, back home. 'Buggers are playing hell.' He talked about the political shenanigans, the posturing and the big money that was there to be made as always out of big trouble. 'Big bucks, boy,' he said. 'Bloody big bucks.' Right at the end he mentioned Nili. He said she was in a sanatorium off the Galle Road.
20   She was on her own… 'In a mess, men. Hopeless. You know how it is, machang… killing herself now. She has no one, really'.

Mister Salgado put the phone down and pressed his fingers to his temples. He repeated what Tippy had said to him. He told me he had to go and see her. 'I must go back.'

Independent research

Try the following sources:

http://www.archaeolink.com/sri_lanka_history.htm

http://news.bbc.co.uk/1/hi/world/south_asia/country_profiles/1168427.stm

http://thereport.amnesty.org/eng/regions/asia-pacific/sri-lanka

http://tracearchive.ntu.ac.uk/writers/gunesekera/

2 Discuss in a small group how this extract shows that the three characters, although displaced from their own country, still feel strong links with it. Focus on:
- the way Triton chooses to refurbish the snack-bar
- Triton's point of view and voice as he gives details of the political turmoil in Colombo, Sri Lanka's capital city
- the way Tippy, a Sri Lankan, conveys the news of events in his country
- Mister Salgado's decision to 'go back'.

3 If *Reef* is one of your chosen texts:

a Carry out research into the political and cultural context in which Romesh Gunesekera sets the story. Find out about the following:
- the end of British rule in 'Ceylon' and the granting of independence in 1948
- the causes of the Sri Lankan civil war
- the 'Tamil Tigers' and their role in the civil war
- the personal history of Romesh Gunesekera between 1970 and 1985.
- Some research sources are suggested in the 'Independent research' box to the left.

b Once your research is complete, consider the ways in which *Reef* explores the changes that took place in Sri Lanka during the period in which it is set. How does Gunesekera use (a) the relationship between Mister Salgado and Nili, (b) Triton's cooking, and (c) the coral reef that Mister Salgado is studying to reflect political and cultural shifts in Sri Lankan life during the 1970s and 1980s? What can you deduce about Gunesekera's own attitude towards these?

4 If your topic area is 'Journeys', compare the way at least two texts explore the theme of cultural difference. You might consider how your writers present:
- social differences between individuals and/or cultural differences between nations
- conflict between different ways of life
- the concept of community.

Activity 65

1 Read the poem opposite from the poetic sequence 'Lascar Johnny' in *The Terrorist at my Table*. Imtiaz Dharker's own background note to the sequence ends:

'*In the 1930s, twenty percent of Britain's maritime labour force was made up of Indian seamen, called Lascars. Many stayed on at ports like Glasgow, some as itinerant salesmen, peddling their wares in remote parts of Scotland.*'

Close

I'll tell you, I was like you once, not
knowing where to go or what
to do. In a place where no one
speaks your tongue, you are a child again.

See, go up from the dock,
turn left, then right, too many streets
to tell, you might
find a countryman to ask.

It might be hard to see, this time
of night, but when you reach the close
go up the stairs to the seamen's mission,
top floor, I think, three flights.

Then it is our own country.
People from our village
giving proper food and rice,
sometimes, God willing, a bed.

If you are fortunate enough to sleep,
the bed becomes a charpoy
that takes you home
to just outside your door.

And in the dawn, when you wake,
balanced between light and shade,
there is dew on your body
and woodsmoke begins to fold the stars away.

Imtiaz Dharker

2 Discuss in a small group how this poem shows that the speaker, Lascar Johnny, has been displaced from his own country. Focus on:
- the voice in which he speaks to his fellow countryman
- his references to searching and partial sight
- his references to food, sleeping and dreams
- the images in lines 21–24.

3 Compare the way Imtiaz Dharker presents the theme of exile and displacement in this poem with Romesh Gunesekera's treatment of the same theme in the extract from *Reef* above. Comment on how the reader is positioned in relation to each text and the effect of this.

4 If *The Terrorist at my Table* is one of your chosen texts:

a Carry out research into the cultural context Dharker uses for her collection. Find out about the following:
- the origin of the term 'Lascar'
- the Lascars in London and Glasgow during the 1930s
- Dharker's personal history of living in Pakistan, Britain and India
- Salman Rushdie's essay 'The Imaginary Homeland'.
- Some research sources are suggested in the 'Independent research' box opposite.

b Once your research is complete, consider how the poems in *The Terrorist at my Table* deal with the idea of 'home' as an attitude of mind rather than as a place defined by birth, nationhood or geography. Use as a starting point 'home moved house/ to bring me here' ('Call', from the poetic sequence 'The Habit of Departure').

Activity 66

This activity applies to texts in any topic group.

Decide on a political or cultural context that links your texts in some way. It could relate to the ways of life described in the texts, or to their political background, or to the cultural identity of your writers, or to their views about politics and religion.

Research the context you select, using the internet and/or bibliographical sources. Then develop a comparative study of how your texts can be related within this context. Use Activities 64 and 65 to guide you. Bear in mind that cultural context will be more important to some texts than to others.

Writing in the exam

It can be useful to support a comparative analysis by referring to research you have done into the background to texts. Make sure, though, that you do not make your answer unbalanced by protracting this and moving too far away from the principal task of exploring structure, form and language.

Independent research

Try the following sources:
www.lascars.co.uk

www.imtiazdharker.com

www.museumindocklands.org.uk

Take it further

Bring in further texts from the topic group 'Journeys' to compare writers' use of political and cultural context. You could compare the way racism and sexism are presented in *Small Island* with the way they are presented in *The Final Passage*. You could compare the way in which Geoffrey Chaucer and Imtiaz Dharker explore the individual's place in a mixed society in their poems.

Take it further

Bring in a further text from the topic group 'Relationships' to compare writers' use of literary context. You could compare the way in which de Bernières, Hardy and Scott Fitzgerald define 'tragedy' and present their central characters in a tragic light. You could compare Carol Ann Duffy's use of first-person point of view and voice in *Rapture* with John Donne's or Andrew Marvell's use of first-person point of view and voice in *Metaphysical Poetry*.

6 If your chosen texts include *Captain Corelli's Mandolin* and/or *Tess of the d'Urbervilles*, explore the way they set their narratives in the context of literary tradition. You might consider:

- how de Bernières uses Homer's *The Odyssey* as a background to events
- how de Bernières uses characters from Greek myth to provide parallels with his own characters
- how Hardy uses ideas from Greek tragedy as a background to events – take as a reference point 'Justice was done, and the President of the Immortals, in Aeschylean phrase, had ended his sport with Tess' (Chapter LIX)
- how Hardy challenges themes common in Christian literature in the nineteenth century – take as reference point the novel's sub-title 'A Pure Woman'.

Some research sources are suggested in the 'Independent research' box below.

Independent research

Try the following sources:

On *Captain Corelli's Mandolin*:

Louis de Bernières: The Essential Guide, Reynolds and Noakes, Vintage, 2002; *Classical and Modern Literature: A Quarterly*, Winter 2001, E.A. McDermott; *Captain Corelli Film Script*, S. Slovo, Vintage, 2002.

On *Tess of the d'Urbervilles*:

Tess of the d'Urbervilles: A Sourcebook, ed. S. McEathron, Routledge, 2005; *Thomas Hardy: His Career as a Novelist*, M. Millgate, The Bodley Head, 1971; *The English Novel: Form and Function*, D. Van Ghent, International Thomson, 1953.

Activity 68

This activity applies to texts in any topic group.

'When poets and novelists draw consciously on literary tradition, it can give an added dimension to their writing. On the other hand, it can act as a barrier to readers, who may feel they have too much work to do before making their own response.'

Compare and contrast at least two texts in the light of this comment. Concentrate on showing how your chosen writers *use* literary traditions rather than on explaining what these traditions are.

Writing in the exam

When you refer to contextual factors, try to integrate your material into your comparative analysis rather than put it in a separate section of your answer. This will show you are able to draw freely on different viewpoints about your texts. It will also prevent your answer from becoming too formulaic.

4 Comparing interpretations of texts

Section B requires you to show an awareness that your texts can be read and understood in more than one way. This part helps you explore how different responses can be made to:

- their themes
- their genres
- their contexts
- their effectiveness.

The purpose of your work is to develop your *own* interpretation of your chosen texts. To do this in an informed way, you need to consider first how other readers, past and present, find meaning in the texts. 'Meaning' is not a single entity or something that is fixed for all time. Meanings are multiple. They depend upon readers' responses. Readers' responses depend, in turn, on the assumptions about life and literature they bring to a text.

How to use the activities in Part 4

The activities are a combination of text-specific and generic. In each text-specific activity below, question 3 calls for detailed knowledge of a particular novel or poetry collection.

Interpretations of theme:
The Great Gatsby and *Metaphysical Poetry*

Activities 69 to 72 show how different responses can be made to writers' themes. They will be useful to you to illustrate how readers find different kinds of meaning in a text, and why.

Activity 69

1 Read the extract below from the end of *The Great Gatsby*. Gatsby has been shot dead by George Wilson, who mistakes him for his wife's lover. The narrator, Nick, who finds the body, reflects on what Gatsby's wealth and his pursuit of Daisy has been worth.

From *The Great Gatsby* by F. Scott Fitzgerald

Most of the big shore places were closed now and there were hardly any lights except the shadowy, moving glow of a ferryboat across the Sound. And as the moon rose higher the inessential houses began to melt away until gradually I became aware of the old island here that flowered once for Dutch sailors' eyes – a fresh, green breast of the new world. Its vanished trees, the trees that had made way for Gatsby's house, had once pandered in whispers to the last
5 and greatest of all human dreams; for a transitory enchanted moment man must have held his breath in the presence of this continent, compelled into an aesthetic contemplation he neither understood nor desired, face to face for the last time in history with something commensurate to his capacity for wonder.

And as I sat there brooding on the old, unknown world, I thought of Gatsby's wonder when he first picked out the green light at the end of Daisy's dock. He had come a long way to this blue lawn, and his dream must have seemed
10 so close that he could hardly fail to grasp it. He did not know that it was already behind him, somewhere back in that vast obscurity beyond the city, where the dark fields of the republic rolled on under the night.

Gatsby believed in the green light, the orgastic future that year by year recedes before us. It eluded us then, but that's no matter – to-morrow we will run faster, stretch out our arms farther… And one fine morning –

So we beat on, boats against the current, borne back ceaselessly into the past.

Writing in the exam

The exam question includes the instruction: 'In your response you should demonstrate what it means to be considering texts as a modern reader in a modern context and that other readers at other times may well have had other responses.'

Assessment objectives

AO3 requires you to make connections and comparisons between your texts in a way that is informed by the interpretations of other readers. It counts for 20 marks out of 60.

2 Discuss as a class the narrator's use of structure, form and language. Focus on:
- the narrative point of view and how it constructs a broad perspective of time
- the relationship created between past and present (look at the use of tenses)
- the images of colour, light and shade
- the use of paradox.

3 If *The Great Gatsby* is one of your chosen texts, consider how the above passage touches on themes you have found in the novel as a whole. These might include:
- romantic love
- the American Dream – the idea of a land of opportunity for all
- money
- appearance and reality.

Then discuss which themes you consider to be most prominent in the novel, and why. As you do so, take into account the following interpretation of *The Great Gatsby*. It suggests that Scott Fitzgerald is centrally concerned with issues of sexuality and gender.

From *Fitzgerald's The Great Gatsby*: by Nicolas Tredell

'*Gatsby*' vividly dramatizes the shifting definitions of masculinity and femininity and the uncertain roles of men and women in a society in transition. Tom Buchanan embodies – and here the verb 'embodies' seems especially apt – a powerful patriarchy threatened by social change; Daisy seems to find little satisfaction in the traditional roles of wife and mother but has no real alternative to them; Jordan Baker is a financially independent woman and sporting celebrity living a peripatetic life but she is harshly criticized and eventually rejected by Nick; Myrtle is a lower-middle class woman of great but stifled vitality; Wilson lacks key signs of conventional masculinity; Gatsby feels 'married' to Daisy but tries to break up Tom's marriage; and Nick is a sexually ambiguous figure.

Does this interpretation match your own? How persuasive do you find it?

Key terms

- **psychoanalytic criticism**
- **feminist criticism**
- **Marxist criticism**
- **new historical criticism**

Activity 70

This activity applies to texts in any topic group.

1 Find out about the way literary critics interpret texts from one or more of the following theoretical standpoints:
- *psychoanalytic criticism*
- *feminist criticism*
- *Marxist criticism*
- *new historical criticism.*

The 'Independent research' box below suggests suitable sources.

2 Make a theme-based comparison of two of your texts from *one* of these standpoints. How far does it conform to your own interpretation?

Independent research

Read *Critical Theory Today: A User-Friendly Guide* by Lois Tyson, 2006, or a similar introduction to critical theory such as *Literary Theory: An Introduction*, Terry Eagleton, 1983.

Activity 71

1 Read the extract opposite from Andrew Marvell's poem 'To His Coy Mistress'. The speaker is persuading his mistress to let him make love to her while they still have time.

2 Discuss as a class how Marvell develops the theme 'Now let us sport us while we may'. Focus on:

- the voice of the poem's speaker and the various tones he uses
- the way the speaker presents an argument based on logic
- the speaker's unusually varied imagery
- the effect of the rhyming couplets and the rhythms of the verse.

3 If *Metaphysical Poetry* is one of your chosen texts, consider how 'To His Coy Mistress' touches on themes you have found in other poems in the collection. These might include:

- erotic love as a defence against time
- the mistress as goddess
- the transience of human life
- love and death.

Then discuss which of these themes *you* consider to be most prominent in 'To His Coy Mistress', and why. As you do so, take into account the following interpretation of the poem by a feminist critic.

To His Coy Mistress

But at my back I always hear
Time's wingèd chariot hurrying near:
And yonder all before us lie
Deserts of vast eternity.
Thy beauty shall no more be found,   5
Nor, in thy marble vault, shall sound
My echoing song: then worms shall try
That long preserved virginity,
And your quaint honour turn to dust;
And into ashes all my lust.   10
The grave's a fine and private place,
But none, I think, do there embrace.
    Now, therefore, while the youthful glue
Sits on thy skin like morning dew,
And while thy willing soul transpires   15
At every pore with instant fires,
Now let us sport us while we may;
And now, like am'rous birds of prey,
Rather at once our time devour,
Than languish in his slow-chapped* power.   20
Let us roll all our strength, and all
Our sweetness, up into one ball:
And tear our pleasures with rough strife,
Thorough* the iron grates* of life,
Thus, though we cannot make our sun   25
Stand still, yet we will make him run.

Andrew Marvell

* slow-chapped: with slowly grinding jaws
* Thorough: through
* grates: bars of a cage

In the course of his invitation to his mistress, the speaker portrays her as alternately desirous and repulsive, but ultimately he identifies the female body as a loathsome symbol of human decay. Beginning with 'But at my back I always hear…', the speaker reveals his mistress to
5 be unworthy of complimentary description and revises her instead as a harbinger of death. This drastic shift from the language of praise to that of threat, from lust to disgust, heightens the poem's devaluation of its female subject… With witty, erotic conceits, the speaker mocks contemporary notions of virginity and expresses disgust at the female
10 body as a symbolic place of death. Rather than uphold the value of her virginity, he emphasises its 'quaint honour', an oxymoron in which 'honour' is negated by his use of 'quaint', a reference to female genitalia in medieval literature with which Marvell's audience would have been familiar. Though he notes how her 'willing soul transpires', the reference
15 is ironic: in the poem, there are no intimations of her honour, only bawdy physical descriptions.

Source: www.poets.org

Does this interpretation match your own? How persuasive do you find it?

Independent research

Try the following sources: www.poetrymagic. co.uk/literary-theory/ theory.html

Literary Theory: The Basics by H. Bertens, Routledge, 2001

Modern Criticism and Theory: A Reader by D. Lodge and N. Wood, Longman, 2008

Literary Theory and Criticism: An Oxford Guide, ed. P. Waugh, OUP, 2006.

Writing in the exam

Show the examiner you are aware that your texts can be interpreted in various ways. You could use phrases such as 'Some readers take the view that…', 'This feminist interpretation is based on…', 'Other critics put the emphasis on…', and 'Seen from a Marxist perspective, the text can be interpreted as…'.

Activity 72

This activity applies to texts in any topic group.

Go online to find critical approaches to literature that you may not have considered before. The 'Independent Research' box to the left suggests some suitable sites. Bring material from them into class and decide which are worth applying to your three texts in more detail. Then arrange for different people to adopt the viewpoints about textual themes to which your research has led you. Hold a class debate to put them to the test.

Interpretations of genre: *Life of Pi* and *The Wife of Bath's Prologue and Tale*

Activities 73 to 75 show how different responses can be made to writers' use of genre. They illustrate how the relationship between theme and genre can be interpreted in different ways.

Activity 73

1 Read the extract below from *Life of Pi*. Near the end of the novel, Pi is questioned by two shipwreck investigators about the sinking of the *Tsimtsum*. He has shared with the reader the story of how he survived in a lifeboat for more than six months, accompanied by a Bengal tiger named Richard Pearson. The investigators do not believe this story.

From *Life of Pi* by Yann Martel

'We want a story without animals that will explain the sinking of the Tsimtsum.'
'Give me a minute, please.'…
[Long silence]
'Here's another story.'
5 'Good.'

'The ship sank. It made a sound like a monstrous metallic burp. Things bubbled at the surface and then vanished. I found myself kicking water in the Pacific Ocean. I swam for the lifeboat. It was the hardest swim of my life. I didn't seem to be moving. I kept swallowing water. I was very cold. I was rapidly losing strength. I wouldn't have made it if
10 the cook hadn't thrown me a lifebuoy and pulled me in. I climbed aboard and collapsed.

'Four of us survived. Mother held on to some bananas and made it to the lifeboat. The cook was already aboard, as was the sailor… The sailor was young… His right leg was badly broken at the thigh. The bone stuck out of the flesh. He screamed with pain. We set his leg as best we could and we made sure he was eating and drinking. But his leg became
15 infected. Though we drained it of pus every day, it got worse. His foot became black and bloated.

'It was the cook's idea. He was a brute. He dominated us. He whispered that the blackness would spread and that he would survive only if his leg were amputated. Since the bone was broken at the thigh, it would involve no more than cutting through flesh and setting
20 a tourniquet. I can still hear his evil whisper. He would do the job to save the sailor's life, he said, but we would have to hold him. Surprise would be the only anaesthetic. We fell upon him. Mother and I held his arms while the cook sat on his good leg. The sailor writhed and screamed. His chest rose and fell. The cook worked the knife quickly. The leg fell off. Immediately Mother and I let go and moved away. We thought that if the restraint
25 was ended, so would his struggling. We thought he would lie calmly. He didn't. He sat up instantly. His screams were all the worse for being unintelligible. He screamed and we stared, transfixed. There was blood everywhere.

2 Discuss as a class the genre characteristics of this passage. Focus on aspects of its style that suggest a typical shipwreck narrative told by a survivor to a group of wide-eyed listeners – an 'ancient mariner' story, in other words. You might consider:

- the first-person voice and point of view
- the highly compressed narrative style and structure
- the foregrounding of dramatic and violent events
- the **stereotyping** of characters – 'He was a brute', 'I can still hear his evil whisper'
- the **clichéd language** – 'The sailor writhed and screamed', 'There was blood everywhere'.

3 If *Life of Pi* is one of your chosen texts, compare the above extract (and the rest of the story Pi tells to Mr Chibo and Mr Okamoto) with the castaway narrative that occupies the middle part of the book. Consider how this castaway narrative displays some genre characteristics of:

- an adventure story
- **magic realism**
- a **moral fable**
- a **religious allegory**.

Then discuss which of these genres *you* think Yann Martel makes the most effective use of, and why. As you do so, take into account the following analysis of theme and genre in the novel.

> [Martel] reawakens the central power of the story as yarn and legend, as the entertaining narrative told round the camp fire and handed between generations, designed to pass the night hours with captivating drama rather than to deliver political analyses on contemporary society… [In the novel as a whole] Martel takes different modes of discourse and genre, mutates their characteristics and mixes them together between a single set of covers… The castaway narrative balances elementary yet dramatic things happening (days passing, fish caught, rescue ships encountered) with moral self-discovery. Yet Martel's sense of humour, the constant revelations that things are not what they appear… means that we are entertained unconscious of what of human psychology is being exposed in the process. If entertainment is the primary ambition of the story and the primary desire of its reader, in the binary challenge with which Martel closes – to have an entertaining story or a factual story, to have a god whose presence can't be measured or to have a world ordered by rational science – there is only one positive conclusion.
>
> *Source*: www.thepequod.org.uk/essays/reviews/lop_ym.htm

Does this interpretation match your own? How persuasive do you find it?

Key terms

- **stereotype**
- **clichéd language**
- **magic realism**
- **moral fable**
- **religious allegory**

Activity 74

1 Read the extract below from the start of *The Wife of Bath's Tale*. The Wife is embarking on a narrative set in the time of King Arthur when 'Al was this land fulfild of fayerye' ('There were fairies in every corner of the land').

From *The Wife of Bath's Tale* (857–863, 882–898)

In th'olde dayes of the Kyng Arthour,
Of which that Britons speken greet honour,
Al was this land fulfild of fayerye.
The elf-queene, with hir joly compaignye,
5 Daunced ful ofte in many a grene mede.
This was the olde opinion, as I rede;
I speke of manye hundred yeres ago…

And so bifel it that this kyng Arthour
Hadde in his hous a lusty bacheler,
10 That on a day cam ridynge fro ryver;
And happed that, allone as he was born,
He saugh a mayde walkynge hym biforn,

Of which mayde anon, maugree hir heed,
By verray force, he rafte hire maydenhed;
15 For which oppressioun was swich clamour
And swiche pursute unto the kyng Arthour
That dampned was this knyght for to be deed,
By cours of lawe, and sholde han lost his heed –
Paraventure swich was the statut tho –
20 But that the queene and other ladyes mo
So longe preyeden the kyng of grace
Til he his lyf hym graunted in the place,
And yaf hym to the queene, al at hir wille,
To chese wheither she wolde hym save or spille.

Geoffrey Chaucer

2 Discuss as a class the genre characteristics of this extract. Focus on aspects of its style that suggest a fairy-tale romance. You might consider:
- the third-person voice and point of view
- the choice of King Arthur's court, Camelot, as a setting
- the fast-moving plot
- the morally loaded language.

3 If *The Wife of Bath's Prologue and Tale* is one of your chosen texts, compare the genre characteristics of the *Prologue* with the genre characteristics of the *Tale*. Comment on:
- the use in the *Prologue* of autobiographical fiction and the use in the *Tale* of imaginative fiction
- the use in the *Prologue* of a loose, anecdotal structure and the use in the *Tale* of an economical, plot-driven structure
- the use in the *Prologue* of earthy, colloquial language and the use in the *Tale* of courtly, philosophical language.

Then discuss how effective *you* find Chaucer's use of different narrative genres in this text as a whole. As you do so, take into account the following analysis of theme and genre in the poem.

> The romance of the Loathly Lady... suits the Wife better in respect of its concern with sovereignty in marriage, but in other respects seems alien to the character which her Prologue reveals in such detail... The more restrained idiom of the tale proper... suggests that a courtly narrator has replaced the Wife... Chaucer is failing to maintain the creative synthesis achieved – and, as it seems, dramatically represented – in *The Wife's Prologue*.
>
> This failure is most apparent in the discussion which occupies a quarter of the Wife's Tale. It might be conceded that the Wife could tell a fairy-tale, but not that she should become involved in a serious philosophical debate on the nature of 'gentillesse'. The woman who becomes enraged when another wife precedes her during the offertory, who cheats and deludes her husbands, seizing their wealth by force of 'maistrie' and even exacting payment for the use of her body, shows not the remotest interest in the ideal of gentle behaviour which forms the hub of her Tale... Chaucer has been unable to reconcile his philosophical interests with the individuality of the story-teller, and has chosen to accept inconsistency of character in order to develop his scholarly theme.
>
> *James Winny*
>
> Source: *The Wife of Bath's Prologue and Tale*, Cambridge, 1965

Does this interpretation match your own? How persuasive do you find it?

Activity 75

This activity applies to prescribed texts in any topic group.

Research and compare comments by literary critics about your writers' use of genre. Try to find a range of views about, for example, how well their choice of form suits the subject matter, how original their use of genre is, how effectively they adapt traditional genres to a modern context, and so on.

Then hold a class discussion based on your findings in which you express your *own* view about your writers' choice and use of genre. Does the chosen genre seem to be used in an imaginative or derivative, purposeful or formulaic way? Does it add to your interest in the text or inhibit your enjoyment of it?

Writing in the exam

The purpose of referring to critics' interpretations of your texts is to provide a context for stating your own. Avoid giving a list of views and leaving it at that. You should work references to other interpretations into your comparative analysis in a way that shows how they helped you arrive at your *own* view.

Interpretations of context:
Spies and *The Kite Runner*

Activities 76 to 78 show how different responses can be made to writers' use of context. They illustrate how the relationship between theme and setting can be interpreted in different ways.

Activity 76

1 Read the extract below from *Spies*. The adult narrator is recalling how, as a boy during the Second World War, he discovered a British pilot in hiding near his home. The pilot lost his nerve and hid underground in order to keep his secret from the community, who believed him to be a hero.

From *Spies* by Michael Frayn

'I heard the dogs barking at you,' he says. 'Aren't you scared of them?'

Another shrug.

'So if I said, "Here, take this bucket and go past the dogs, and fetch me some water from the well behind the Cottages…"?'

5 I nod. He makes no move to hand me a bucket, though.

He laughs. 'Yes, you'd go all right. You'd go like a shot. To get away from me. You'd go, but you wouldn't come back.'

I say nothing. He's said it for me.

'Poor kid,' he says in a different voice. 'But that's what happens. You start playing
10 some game, and you're the brave one, you're the great hero. But the game goes on and on, and it gets more and more frightening, and you get tired, because you can't go on being brave for ever. And then one night it happens. You're up there in the darkness five hundred miles from home and suddenly the darkness is inside you as well. In your head, in your stomach. You've cut out, like a dicky engine. You can't
15 think, you can't move. You can't see, you can't hear. Everything's drowned by this great scream of terror in the darkness, and the scream goes on and on, and it's coming out of *you*.'

He's started to weep. Between one word and the next, out of nowhere. I long to be anywhere else on earth. But of course I have to wait.

20 'So then the others have to get you home,' he whispers. 'They're as sick at heart as you are, and somehow they have to keep their nerve and get you home. They trusted you and you failed them. And afterwards you could never look at them again, you could never be with them. From that day on you're an outcast. There's no place for you anywhere any more.'

---

2 Discuss as a class how this passage shows the effect of war on an individual. Focus on:
   - the way the pilot conveys his feeling of being an 'outcast'
   - the pilot's use of the second-person voice to tell his own story
   - the images the pilot uses to describe his fear of fighting
   - the effect on the reader of Stephen's narrative interventions
   - the extent to which the pilot's story arouses your sympathy.

3 If *Spies* is one of your chosen texts:

   a Consider (a) Michael Frayn's reasons for introducing Uncle Peter as a character at this late stage in the novel, and (b) how Uncle Peter's story presents the reader with an additional context in which to place the events of the novel.

b Discuss how Frayn makes use of following contexts in *Spies*:
- the social context of England in the 1940s
- the historical context of the Second World War
- the political context of Jewish persecution during the 1930s and 1940s
- the literary context of boys' adventure stories published between the two world wars.

Which of these contexts do *you* find important to a balanced interpretation of the novel? How far do you agree with the Marxist critical view of *Spies* described below? (Marxist critics see literature as a product of its social context: hence a novel can be interpreted in sociological, or socio-psychological, terms.)

> The whole plot depends upon the social and emotional repression of Stephen as underdog – an oppression with which he colludes and which he even helps to sustain himself … Stephen's deeply ingrained feelings of social inferiority and his deference to adults and people he considers to be of higher social status than himself exert such a strong influence over his behaviour that they could be said to dictate the course of the action. For example, if Stephen were to reject Keith's assumed superiority instead of meekly subjugating himself, he would never have been drawn into the 'game' which goes so horribly wrong. If he had not felt himself superior to the man under the metal sheeting, the crisis would not have been precipitated by the boys tormenting the man. And if had not been cowed by the schoolboy solidarity that frowned upon tale-telling, both Keith's bullying of him and Mr Hayward's abuse of his family could have come to light and been dealt with.
>
> *Anne Rooney*
>
> Source: *York Notes on 'Spies'*, Pearson 2007

Does this interpretation match your own? How persuasive do you find it?

Activity 77

1 Read the extract below from *The Kite Runner*. The adult narrator, Amir, has just found out that his father Baba had a child by a 'Hazara' woman from the socially inferior Shi'a people within Afghanistan. Amir grew up thinking that the child, Hassan, was his servant when in fact he was his half-brother. As a boy, Amir betrayed Hassan's devotion to him and has never got over his guilt.

From *The Kite Runner* by Khaled Hosseini

How could [Baba] have lied to me all those years? To Hassan? He had sat me on his lap when I was little, looked me straight in the eyes, and said, *There is only one sin. And that is theft… When you tell a lie, you steal someone's right to the truth.* Hadn't he said those words to me? And now, fifteen years after I'd buried him, I was learning that Baba had been a thief. And a
5 thief of the worst kind, because the things he'd stolen had been sacred: from me the right to know I had a brother, from Hassan his identity, and from Ali [Hassan's assumed father, Baba's housekeeper] his honor. His *nang*. His *namoos*.

The questions kept coming at me: How had Baba brought himself to look Ali in the eye? How had Ali lived in that house, day in and day out, knowing he had been dishonoured by his master
10 in the single worst way an Afghan man can be dishonoured? And how was I going to reconcile this new image of Baba with the one that had been imprinted on my mind for so long, that of him in his old brown suit, hobbling up the Taheris' driveway to ask for Soraya's hand?

Here is another cliché my creative writing teacher would have scoffed at; like father, like son. But it was true, wasn't it? As it turned out, Baba and I were more alike than I'd ever known. We
15 had both betrayed the people who would have given their lives for us.

2 Discuss as a class how Khaled Hosseini sets Amir's attempt to come to terms with his father's deception in the context of:
- the social structures of Afghan life
- the cultural conventions of Afghan life
- the spiritual values of Afghan life.

How does the style and structure of this passage reflect Amir's sense that his personal world has come adrift from these contexts?

3 If *The Kite Runner* is one of your chosen texts:

a Consider Hosseini's reasons for (a) revealing Amir's blood-tie with Hassan at the mid-point in the novel, and (b) setting parts of the story in Afghanistan and parts of it in California.

b Discuss how far the novel's *political* context shapes the way you interpret it. As you do so, take account of the following extract from a review written in 2003 when *The Kite Runner* was first published.

> Whatever the truth of the claim [that *The Kite Runner* is] the first English-language Afghan novel, Hosseini is certainly the first Afghan novelist to fictionalise his culture for a Western readership, melding the personal struggle of ordinary people into the terrible historical sweep of a devastated country...
>
> Over the last three decades, Afghanistan has been ceaselessly battered by Communist rule, Soviet occupation, the Mujahideen and a democracy that became a rule of terror [under the Taliban]. It is a history that can intimidate and exhaust an outsider's attempts to understand, but Hosseini extrudes it simply and quietly into an intimate account of love, honour, guilt, fear and redemption that needs no dry history book or atlas to grip and absorb...
>
> The book [is] a sharp, unforgettable taste of the trauma and tumult experienced by Afghanis as their country buckled. [It] is about the price of peace, both personal and political, and what we knowingly destroy in our hope of achieving that, be it friends, democracy or ourselves.
>
> Amelia Hill, *The Observer*

Does this interpretation match your own? How persuasive do you find it?

Activity 78

This activity applies to prescribed texts in any topic group.

Research and compare comments by the writers of your texts about their choice and use of context. Try to find out, for example, why they chose to write about particular subjects, how their personal experience helped shape their texts, and what kind of readership they may have had in mind.

Then hold a class discussion based on your findings, in which you express your *own* view about how your writers use context. Does the chosen context appeal to a wide range of readers? Does it ask too much of readers? Does it provide new insights into the subject or recycle subject matter found in texts by other writers? Does it add to your interest in the text or inhibit your enjoyment of it?

Evaluations of texts: *The Final Passage* and *The General Prologue to the Canterbury Tales*

Activities 79 to 81 help you to comment on the effectiveness of texts as part of your interpretation of them. They will be useful to illustrate how readers make different value judgements.

Activity 79

1 Read the extract below from near the end of *The Final Passage*. Leila has come from her native Caribbean to make a new life in London. However, her husband has left her with a young child, Calvin, and she is facing Christmas alone in a strange country.

From *The Final Passage* by Caryl Phillips

People in the streets were busy, hurrying everywhere. They all rushed, for it was Christmas. The cars slushed past throwing up a spray of melted ice and water, leaving their tracks seemingly indelibly etched into the road. Then another car would come along and scratch the same message, then another, till they became like the people, one huge pattern of individual marks, each indistinguishable from the next, each reduced with the short passing of
5   time… to being a distant untraceable blur.

Leila stopped at a window and listened to her son speaking, though he could not as yet speak. She watched his image reflected in the glass as he spoke with unsurity.

'Mommy, is that Santa Claus there, that man with the white beard and moustache, that man with a red suit and a red face?'

10   She held Calvin so he would be able to see better. His short arm freed itself from being trapped between his own small body and his mother's breasts. It pointed out the man he was talking about.

'Him, mommy, that man there with the funny horse.'

Leila looked at her son, his eyes bright, his face eager for knowledge.

'Yes, Calvin, that's Santa Claus,' said Leila.

15   Calvin looked at her as she confirmed the man's identity, then he looked back at the man.

'Why is Santa Claus white?'

Leila could not answer her own question.

'He should be coloured. Why isn't Santa Claus coloured?'

Leila began to repeat herself like a record player stuck into a groove. She tore other parents' and other children's
20   attention away from the man. They just looked at her and moved away, saying nothing.

'Why isn't Santa Claus coloured?' she whispered.

---

2 Discuss in a small group the impact this extract makes on you. Comment on how effectively you think the writer:
  • evokes Leila's loneliness
  • evokes the urban surroundings
  • evokes Leila's feelings about being black.

3 Share your ideas in class discussion. Then hold a debate about the quality of Caryl Phillips' writing here. Decide which of these two views to adopt: (a) the writing is sensitive and moving, or (b) the writing is sentimental and contrived. Argue your case by making close reference to the text.

4 If *The Final Passage* is one of your chosen texts, consider how successful the novel is in using the idea of a journey to convey its themes. You might consider:
  • the use of Leila as a **focaliser** – that is, the character through whose eyes the events are seen
  • the way the Caribbean is compared and contrasted with England
  • the use of time in the novel
  • the concept of geographical (or 'outward') and personal (or 'inward') journeys.

Key term

• focaliser

Then read the extract below from a book review of *The Final Passage* when it first appeared in 1985.

Phillips uses the idea of a voyage to explore imperial constructs such as 'mother country', 'home', colonialism and post-colonialism. His theme is rootlessness and displacement, focalised through the central character Leila – black, searching for 'a better life', and ultimately defeated. The problem with the novel is Phillips' analysis of what, precisely, Leila is defeated by. A Caribbean culture that has sold out to capitalism and lost its soul in the process? False promises of prosperity in England (the novel is set in the 1950s when a cheap West Indian labour force was encouraged to migrate 'home')? A feckless husband whose idea of marriage is to impregnate his wife and then live with another woman he impregnated earlier? An over-possessive mother?

All these strands, and more, are examined in a novel that is relentlessly bleak and written in one, unvaried register. Phillips piles on the agony but fails to give a coherent account of the black experience of displacement and dislocation. By the end of the narrative, the reader is as worn out as Leila by misery and pain – and, like her, finally unenlightened.

Alan Sinclair

Source: *The Guardian*, 1985

Does this evaluation match your own? How persuasive do you find it?

Activity 80

1 Read the extract opposite from near the end of *The General Prologue to the Canterbury Tales*. A group of pilgrims has assembled at the Tabard Inn before setting off on their journey to Saint Thomas Becket's shrine in Canterbury. The narrator describes the Host of the Tabard and how he welcomes the pilgrims 5

2 Discuss in a small group the impact this extract makes on you. Comment on how effectively you think the writer:
  • creates a mood of sociability and good cheer
  • conveys the character of the Host 10
  • entertains the reader.

3 Share your ideas in class discussion. Then hold a debate about the quality of Chaucer's writing here. Decide which of these two views 15 to adopt: (a) the writing is lively and vividly descriptive, or (b) the writing is flat and lacking in linguistic variety. Argue your case by making close reference to the text.
20

From *The General Prologue to the Canterbury Tales* (747–768)

Greet chiere made oure Hoost us everichon,
And to the soper sette he us anon.
He served us with vitaille at the beste;
Strong was the wyn, and wel to drynke us leste.
A semely man OURE HOOSTE was withalle
For to been a marchal in an halle.
A large man he was with eyen stepe –
A fairer burgeys was ther noon in Chepe –
Boold of his speche, and wys, and wel ytaught,
And of manhod hym lakkede right naught.
Eek therto he was right a myrie man;
And after soper pleyen he bigan,
And spak of myrthe amonges othere thynges,
Whan that we hadde maad oure rekenynges,
And seyde thus: 'Now, lordynges, trewely,
Ye been to me right welcome, hertely;
For by my trouthe, if that I shal nat lye,
I saugh nat this yeer so myrie a compaignye
Atones in this herberwe as is now.
Fayn wolde I doon yow myrthe, wiste I how.
And of a myrthe I am right now bythoght,
To doon yow ese, and it shal coste noght.'

Geoffrey Chaucer

4 If *The General Prologue to the Canterbury Tales* is one of your chosen texts:

    a Consider how successful the poem is in creating and conveying character. You might consider:
  - the variety of characters portrayed
  - the way the portraits are sequenced and ***juxtaposed***
  - the way Chaucer, as pilgrim and poet, guides the reader's response
  - the use of irony, satire and compliment.

    b Read the extract below from a critical essay on *The General Prologue*.

> Chaucer's view of the world and of the human person was more uniform and stratified than ours. Furthermore, in a way that post-Renaissance sophistication made much less possible, the furnishings of a man's life were then closely articulated ***metonymies*** for the man himself. His being in nature, and description in literature, were still supported by those ***modalities***, and we thread our way to him through them.
>
> Chaucer's innovation in personal description was the inorganic, disordered, and inconsequent piling-up of details. That he could do this while depending upon what was still a rigidly systematic social and sacramental order is a large part of his charm, and the source of his illusion. The rubric of classical biography is used to introduce each figure. The formulary… persisted even to Chaucer's day: 'A KNYGHT *there was…*';… '*There was* also a NONNE, a PRIORESS…'; 'A FRANKLYN *was* in his compaignye…' and so on through the whole group, with slight verbal deviation. Only one paragraph is allotted each person described, which makes for an impressive straitening of presentation. And, for the most part, each description is intact, self-enclosed, 'framed' with very careful formality… Each person is a disarray of traits which, if we may use the word, 'repersonify', by virtue of several bold strokes.
>
> *Ralph Baldwin*
>
> Source: *Chaucer Criticism: Vol 1*, Notre Dame, 1960

Does this evaluation match your own? How persuasive do you find it?

Writing in the exam

A good exam answer will analyse and comment on two or more texts by:
- comparing the texts throughout
- including some material about their contexts of production and reception
- making some reference to other readers' and critics' views about them
- developing a coherent argument at sufficient length
- making a personal interpretation supported by textual reference and quotation.

Use these five points as a checklist when you write practice answers.

Activity 81

This activity applies to texts in any topic group.

Research and compare comments by literary critics about the effectiveness of your texts. Try to find a range of views about, for example, their treatment of the subject matter, the way structure, form and language are used, the kind of impact made on the reader, and so on.

Then hold a class discussion based on your findings in which you express your *own* view about how effective your texts are. Do they engage you strongly, or fail to appeal to your imagination? Do they use language in an original way, or language that is too obscure or too conventional? Do you judge your texts to be highly successful, undistinguished, or somewhere between the two?

5   Tackling Section B of the exam

In Section B of this unit you have studied three texts from one of the groupings: 'Relationships', 'Identifying Self', 'Journeys', or 'War'. It is important that you have studied one text from each of the genres of prose and poetry, and also that at least one of your texts should have been published after 1990.

In Section B of the exam you will write a sustained essay on at least two of the texts you have studied. Section B is worth 60 marks (60% of the marks for Unit 3).

The essay question

The question will start with a comment - a quotation offering a point of view with which you may or may not agree. This is called the *proposition*. Its purpose is to give you a starting point from which to construct your argument. There is likely to be an implied reference to the theme under which your choice of texts is grouped ('Relationships', 'Identifying Self', 'Journeys' or 'War'). There may be a reference to the genres (novels and poetry) that you have studied, and there may be reference to the writer or reader. You will see from the examples in the following pages how this works in practice.

Underneath the proposition will be an instruction that you should comment and analyse, followed by clear reminders to:

- make connections and comparisons between your texts (you are required to answer on at least two of them)
- consider contexts – what other people say about the texts you have studied, the contexts within which the texts were written and how they are regarded now
- write about at least one post-1990 text.

Assessment objectives

To assess your essay, the examiners use a mark scheme based on all four assessment objectives. See the beginning of this unit, page 4, for what these assessment objectives mean in practice.

The full marking scheme reproduced below indicates how the examiner applies the assessment objectives in detail. The grid is identical for each of the text groupings in Section B of the exam.

Writing in the exam

You should take clean copies of all three of your texts into the examination room with you. In an exam that is 2 hours 45 minutes long, you will probably have about 1 hour 30 minutes for this task. You should spend some of this time thinking about which essay you wish to tackle (from the choice of two) before putting pen to paper.

Band	Mark	AO1 – Articulate creative, informed and relevant responses to literary texts, using appropriate terminology and concepts, and coherent, accurate written expression
1	0–3	• Makes limited relevant comment • Makes limited use of critical literary terminology • Writes with minimal clarity but with technical lapses • Responds with limited originality and creativity.
2	4–7	• Makes relevant comment with some insight • Makes some appropriate use of critical terminology to make the response more specific • Uses accurate written expression with some technical lapses • Responds with some originality and creativity.
3	8–10	• Responds with a sustained argument in an informed and relevant manner • Makes confident and appropriate use of critical terminology to refine arguments and evaluate the text • Writes accurately with sustained fluency, coherence and confidence • Constructs an original and creative response in a well-developed argument.

Band	Mark	AO2 – Demonstrate detailed critical understanding in analysing the ways in which structure, form and language shape meanings in literary texts
1	0–3	• Shows a limited critical understanding of literary texts • Explores some features of structure, form and language • Shows a limited understanding of meanings.
2	4–7	• Shows some critical understanding of literary texts • Analyses features of structure, form and language • Shows some understanding of the meanings.
3	8–10	• Demonstrates a developed critical understanding of literary texts • Evaluates features of structure, form and language effectively to make relevant points • Evaluates the text and demonstrates a developed understanding of the meanings which enables an independent response.

Band	Mark	AO3 – Explore connections and comparisons between different literary texts, informed by interpretations of other readers
1	0–3	• Refers to one or more texts and identifies basic literary connections • Provides a basic presentation of ideas • Shows limited ability to interpret the texts.
2	4–7	• Makes well-selected connections between texts • Presents some ideas which do not reach full development • Shows a limited ability to consider that more than one interpretation of the texts is possible.
3	8–11	• Makes literary connections between the texts to inform the line of argument • Some evidence of an independent approach in the presentation of ideas • Shows an awareness of a variety of interpretations; with some exploration.
4	12–15	• Makes insightful and relevant literary connections between texts, supporting the line of argument • Demonstrates an independent approach in the presentation of well-developed ideas • Demonstrates an awareness of a variety of interpretations; with some analysis and evaluation.
5	16–20	• Demonstrates a cogent synthesis of literary connections between texts to develop a line of argument • Demonstrates an independent and original approach in the presentation of coherently developed argument • Demonstrates a developed awareness of a variety of interpretations; applies an open-minded approach when exploring and evaluating the texts.

Band	Mark	AO4 – Demonstrate understanding of the significance and influence of the contexts in which literary texts are written and received
1	0–3	• Shows a very limited awareness of the concept of a reader • Makes limited reference to the contextual influences that have affected how the texts have been received over time • Makes limited reference to the cultural and contextual factors that influenced texts when they were produced, without applying these facts very usefully in a literary way • Makes basic reference to the contextual framework within which they as readers can respond but this is not developed in a way that reflects on the understanding of texts under consideration.
2	4–7	• Shows limited ability to appreciate the factors that influence a modern reader but these points are undeveloped when looking at the texts under consideration • Shows some awareness of contextual influences that have affected how the texts have been received over time • Shows some awareness of the cultural and contextual factors that influenced texts when they were produced, although this is likely to remain at the level of factual knowledge not fully applied to the texts • Makes some reference to the contextual framework within which they as readers can respond, although this may lack specificity.
3	8–11	• Shows some ability to comment on the factors that influence a modern reader and apply this to the reading of the texts under consideration • Shows an appreciation of contextual influences that have affected how the texts have been received over time • Shows an appreciation of the importance of the cultural and contextual factors that influenced texts when they were produced • Makes some comment on the relevance of the contextual overarching framework within which they as readers can respond.
4	12–15	• Demonstrates an ability to analyse the factors that influence a modern reader and reflect on their own reading in the light of this • Demonstrates an ability to analyse the contextual influences that have affected how the texts have been received over time • Demonstrates an ability to analyse the cultural and contextual factors that influenced texts when they were produced and apply this awareness usefully to the texts under consideration • Demonstrates an understanding of the significance of the contextual overarching framework within which they as readers can respond; shows an awareness of how this has worked in practice in the candidate's own response to the texts.
5	16–20	• Demonstrates an ability to analyse, synthesise and evaluate the factors that influence a modern reader, this being reflected in the candidate's own reading and understanding of the texts under consideration • Demonstrates an ability to analyse and evaluate the contextual influences that have affected how the texts have been received over time • Demonstrates an ability to analyse and evaluate the cultural and contextual factors that influenced texts when they were produced and uses this awareness to enrich understanding and response • Evaluates the significance of the contextual overarching framework within which they as readers can respond, therefore showing a mature and developed sense of what it means to read critically.

Structuring your response

Writing your introduction

In your introductory remarks, make it clear what the main focus of your discussion is going to be.

Identify the texts that you are going to discuss and make some response to the proposition.

Developing your argument

Find both comparisons and contrasts between your texts that you can identify, illustrate and comment on. This will address AO3.

Explore these links in detail. Offer your own critical opinion, but be informed by other views too. This will also address AO3.

Relate the links also to the contexts that are essential to full coverage of AO4.

Different aspects of one text may form one part of your argument. Your poetry collection or anthology, or your novel, will enable you to explore a range of ideas that will be relevant to your developing argument.

Develop your argument logically by leading the discussion on from one text to another. Keep making comparisons and connections between your texts linked to specific points.

Remember the sequence 'point, evidence or quotation', and use comment or analysis as a basic method to build up your argument.

If you are writing about two texts it is likely that your discussion will be balanced fairly equally between them. If you are writing about three texts, the third may be dealt with in less detail.

Concluding

In your conclusion, bring together ideas that have dominated your discussion. Sum up ways in which they have illustrated the proposition.

Offer your own informed critical opinion on points that emerge from your discussion.

Sample questions

The remainder of this section provides examples of questions for each of the text groupings in turn, together with some sample responses and examiner comments on how the assessment objectives have been met.

Relationships

Activity 82

1 Read the sample question below:

'Without relationships, novels and poems would be empty vessels.'

Comment on and analyse the connections between at least two texts you have studied in the light of this assertion.

In your response you must ensure that at least one text is a post-1990 text.

In your response you should demonstrate what it means to be considering texts as a modern reader, in a modern context and that other readers at other times may well have had other responses. (60 marks)

2 Using the texts that you have studied, consider how you would address AO3:

   a Note down five points that you think would be relevant.

   b Compare your points to those of other members of your class.

c How many texts did you consider when carrying out this activity?

3 a Read the opening paragraph of the student essay below. Write a brief comment on how you think this opening addresses AO3 and AO4. What you are looking for is a focus on the opening statement of the question (the proposition), an ability to make connections and comparisons, and evidence that the writer is aware of contexts. The last two points are particularly focused on AO3 and AO4.

> In my essay I am going to concentrate on the relationship between Pelagia and Corelli in *Captain Corelli's Mandolin*, that between Marvell and his mistress in 'To His Coy Mistress' and thirdly that between Donne and his dead lover in 'A Nocturnal Upon St Lucy's Day'. What each relationship has in common is that something is not quite right. Corelli and Pelagia cannot consummate their relationship, they are enemies, one being Greek and one being Italian when the two countries are at war. Her father tells her: 'You have renounced the love of a patriotic Greek, in favour of an invader, an oppressor. You will be called a collaborator, a fascist's whore.'

b Read the examiner's comments below. What can you learn from them?

Examiner's comments
AO3

The writer has made some clear links between two of the texts she has studied; one post-1990 novel and two poems from the *Metaphysical Poetry* anthology. There is no mention so far of responses by other readers. So far the writer has not referred to a third text but this is not necessarily a disadvantage; the instruction is to consider 'at least two' texts.

AO4

So far the writer has only demonstrated awareness of contexts through the brief reference to the wartime situation of the Pelagia/Corelli relationship. However, this is only the introduction.

c Repeat the exercise by considering AO1 and AO2.

Examiner's comments
AO1

The writer has expressed herself clearly and accurately. So far there is no use of critical terminology. She seems quite well informed about the issues underlying the question.

AO2

There is so far no awareness of form although there are some implicit references to language in the quotation at the end of this section. The writer is setting out her intentions quite clearly and will develop them in the next part of her essay. The statement of what the writer says she intends to do in the essay's opening sentence would strike an examiner as a somewhat unsubtle approach.

d Can you think of an alternative way of starting this essay?

4 a Read the next section of the student's essay. Comment on how well you think the writer has moved on from the opening paragraph. What comments would you make about the language of these two quotations?

> In Marvell's poem, he is upset about his lover's refusal to go to bed with him. It would be all right 'Had we but world enough, and time' but 'I always hear time's winged chariot' and though 'the grave's a fine and private place,/ But none I think do there embrace.'
>
> Donne's situation is even worse. His lover is dead and on the shortest day of the year he is in mood to almost deny his very existence: 'I, by love's limbeck, am the grave/ Of all that's nothing.'

Examiner's comments

These two comments on the two *Metaphysical Poems* show a good literary sensibility in the writer. A point is both clearly made and precisely illustrated. However, the writer fails to develop either of these points by commenting on the language in the quotations.

5 How would you continue and develop the discussion?

6 How would you develop the argument by introducing a third text to complement the ones already dealt with?

7 If the texts dealt with above are not among those you have studied, plan and write a response to the same essay question using your own choice of texts.

Identifying Self

Activity 83

1 Read the sample question below:

'As readers we are always interested in the diverse ways in which characters' stories are told and their dilemmas resolved.'

Comment on and analyse the connections between at least two texts you have studied in the light of this assertion.

In your response you must ensure that at least one text is a post-1990 text.

In your response you should demonstrate what it means to be considering texts as a modern reader, in a modern context and that other readers at other times may well have had other responses.

(60 marks)

2 Using the texts that you have studied, consider how you would address AO3:

a Note five points that you think might be relevant.

b Compare your points to the other members of your class.

c How many of your texts did you use when carrying out this activity?

3 a Read the opening paragraph of the student essay below. Write a brief comment on how you think this opening addresses AO3 and AO4. What you are looking for is a focus on the opening statement of the question (the proposition), an ability to make connections and comparisons, and evidence that the writer is aware of contexts. The last two points are particularly focused on AO3 and AO4.

In *Great Expectations*, *Life of Pi* and *The Wife of Bath's Prologue and Tale* we have three books that are using a first-person narrator to tell the story. Pip, Pi and the Wife are each telling a kind of autobiography. The diversity lies in the different situations, experiences and worlds that each narrator comes from. The fourteenth century of the wife, the nineteenth century of Pip and the twentieth century of Pi are all very different.

b Read the examiner's comments below. What do you learn from them?

Examiner's comments

AO3

The writer has suggested ways in which the texts can be compared by mentioning their similarities (first-person narrative and fictionalised autobiography) while indicating differences that relate to the times in which they were written. If he is able to develop these ideas and illustrate clearly how other readers have interpreted the texts, both AO3 and AO4 will be dealt with at a high level of achievement.

AO4

He suggests that he is aware of contexts relevant to the times at which the texts were written, and this is something that is likely to be developed later. The writer has declared his intention of writing about all three of the texts he has studied so he is giving himself quite a challenging task, which if successfully achieved could be awarded a mark in the highest band. It should be emphasised, though, that a writer can achieve the highest mark by dealing with only two texts; even if discussing three, they do not all have to be dealt with in the same amount of detail.

c Repeat this exercise by considering AO1 and AO2.

Examiner's comments

AO1

The writer has made a clear statement of his intentions and shows literary awareness through the use of terminology such as *first-person narrator* and *autobiography*. This use of terminology also suggests that the writer has an awareness of form. Because form is addressed here, the point is also relevant to AO2.

AO2

So far language and structure have not been mentioned, although the references to the different times of writing suggest that language is likely to be discussed later.

d Can you think of an alternative way of starting this essay?

4 How would you continue and develop the discussion in this essay?

With a partner, make a list of the points that would develop the argument. Include quotations that would support each point you have made.

5 Consider the conclusion to this student's essay. How effective a conclusion would you say this is?

Therefore we have seen how writers tell stories in different ways and whatever the time of writing they are seen as being in control. Whether their dilemmas are resolved or not is something else again. They are resolved in different ways. In the Wife's prologue it is through her establishing control over Jankyn by destroying his nasty anti-feminist book. In the tale it is through the transformation of the Loathly Lady when she finally establishes her 'maistrie'. At the end of Great Expectations it is through Pip's getting possession of Estella after years of suffering. In Life of Pi it is the conclusion of the italicised narrative when Pi's story, although marginalised 'As an aside', is still recognised as an astounding story of great courage and endurance in the face of extraordinarily difficult and tragic circumstances.

Examiner's comments

Therefore we have seen is not the subtlest way of bringing the essay to a conclusion, although it is a clear signal that it is drawing to a close. The writer is trying to do several things here. The different ways in which stories have been told is likely to have been discussed and we have moved on from the similarities noted in the opening paragraph. The second sentence notes the possibility of different opinions, before the writer's own conclusion is offered. Rather neatly, the resolution of each story is clearly expressed in literary terms, while still dealing with the dilemmas of the central characters, supported by some effective, brief quotations. On this evidence, this essay might achieve Band 5.

6 Plan and write a response to the essay question using your own choice of texts.

Journeys

Activity 84

1 Read the sample question below:

'Life itself is a journey and poems and novels always reflect this in the ways in which they present characters, stories and themes.'

Comment on and analyse the connections between at least two texts you have studied in the light of this assertion.

In your response you must ensure that at least one text is a post-1990 text.

In your response you should demonstrate what it means to be considering texts as a modern reader, in a modern context and that other readers at other times may well have had other responses.

(60 marks)

2 Using the texts that you have studied, consider how you would address AO3:

a Note five points that you think might be relevant.

b Compare your points to the other members of your class.

c How many of your texts did you use when carrying out this activity?

3 a Read the opening paragraph of the student essay below. Write a brief comment on how you think this opening addresses AO3 and AO4. What you are looking for is a focus on the opening statement of the question (the proposition), an ability to make connections and comparisons, and evidence that the writer is aware of contexts. The last two points are particularly focused on AO3 and AO4.

The main journeys in *Reef* seem to be the change of location from Sri Lanka to life in England and how the narrator has travelled from childhood to adulthood and changed his social standing. In the *General Prologue* the journey does seem to be a literal one as the pilgrims make their way from the Tabard Inn in Southwark to Canterbury. It could be argued that the reader undergoes a journey through the different social groupings that the pilgrims represent. In the title poem of *Brunizem* the author is remembering the soil of her native land and perhaps expressing her nostalgia through her impassioned cry 'I don't want English/ To be my middle name.'

b Read the examiner's comments below. What do you learn from them?

Examiner's comments

AO3
So far there are straightforward statements about each of the texts studied. The writer does make some comparisons between different kinds of journeys, so explicit connections have been made from the outset which the writer may well develop later in the essay.

AO4
The contexts are addressed quite specifically. The focuses are on the narrator or writer, seen in the context of the time of writing. How the writing is received by the modern reader may well emerge later in the essay.

c Repeat the exercise by considering AO1 and AO2.

Examiner's comments

A01

There is a straightforward literary awareness and the writing is competent and accurately expressed.

A02

There is some implicit awareness of form in the ways the journeys referred to relate to the texts themselves and how they are written. The quotation from one of the *Brunizem* poems suggests a sensitive response to language. Once again it is to be hoped that the writer will develop this later.

   d Can you think of an alternative way of starting this essay? How would this differ from the one quoted above? Compare your approach and decide which was more appropriate.

4 Read the next section of the student's essay. Comment on how the writer has developed the argument and fulfilled the assessment objectives.

Life as a journey therefore is reflected in Gunesekera's portrayal of Triton's experiences with Mr Salgado (who might be loosely based on the exiled science fiction writer Arthur C. Clarke) framed by the scenes in England at the beginning and end of the novel. The journey is what might be called 'the self-awakening of Triton: he is content in his role as a subservient and becomes accomplished in the crafts he learns.' Tom Paulin called it a 'prose symbolist poem about the art of cooking'.

Bhatt's sense of a journey from one place to another is shown through the ways in which she sometimes uses Gujarati and Sanskrit words in her poems, which reminds us that her first language is not English and that she herself is an exile. The word *Brunizem* itself is a mixture of French and Russian elements, and an anonymous critic has remarked: 'The image of a tri-continental earth is obviously Bhatt's own metaphor for the worlds that nourish her talent.' In an interview with Vicki Bertram, she said that 'my sense of being exiled and an outsider has no doubt affected my writing as well as my need to write.'

In the *General Prologue*, Chaucer is showing a real journey, the pilgrimage to Canterbury, but a number of the pilgrims have made other journeys. The knight has recently returned from his most recent voyage, and may be seen as Terry Jones suggests in *Chaucer's Knight*, a medieval mercenary. The friar, who spends his time wandering around the country begging, Robinson suggests represents 'the corrupt condition of the mendicant orders, which in Chaucer's time had departed from the ideals of their founders' and the Wife of Bath has been on a number of previous pilgrimages demonstrating what Winny calls her 'pent-up energy and physical stamina implicit in Chaucer's account of her many pilgrimages'.

Examiner's comments

The writer is making a sustained attempt to develop the argument that was suggested in her opening remarks. She has also made a very self-conscious attempt to bring in some critical comments from other readers, in this case named critics or academics, to support a number of points in the argument. This addresses the third bullet point of A03 in Band 5. What she now needs to develop is her own critical awareness in appreciating these texts, which would address the second bullet point in Band 4 or 5

5 How would you continue and develop the discussion? Read the opening sentences from some of the paragraphs in the student's essay below, together with the examiner's comments. These will show you some ways in which the writer can develop the argument.

> My own response to *Reef* is that the relationship between Triton and a number of the characters in the novel show his growing awareness of the world around him. This is the metaphorical journey which the character makes in the course of the novel. At first...

The sense of a personal response is obvious, but do look at the raising of the idea of a metaphorical journey.

> In the General Prologue by contrast...

This kind of connecting phrase moves the argument on very clearly.

> My response to *Brunizem* is that Bhatt's journey is a cultural and linguistic one.

The writer tells us she is moving on and developing the idea of different kinds of journey which she will go on to explore.

> Similarly the journey in 'Eurydice Speaks' has taken the classical myth of Orpheus and Eurydice, presented it in a feminist way with the narrative voice of the dramatic monologue...

As well as the reader-friendly discourse marker 'Similarly', references to myth, feminism, narrative voice and dramatic monologue all suggest someone who can use the terminology with some confidence.

> Each writer deals with journeys of different kinds, some literal, some metaphorical.

This sentence leads into a final paragraph that will pull the threads of the essay together with some skill.

6 Read the student's conclusion and assess it against the assessment objectives.

> Each writer deals with journeys of different kinds, some literal, some metaphorical. I enjoyed *Reef's* quite tight prologue/epilogue framework to show us Triton's literal journey from Sri Lanka to England as well as the journey he makes in his developing relationships with characters, where he learns to trust and be trusted (but is also aware of the possibilities of betrayal in the shirt incident mentioned earlier), and his growing skills as a cook and housekeeper to Mr Salgado. As we have seen, Chaucer's pilgrims experience a variety of journeys as well as their common one of the pilgrimage which is what has brought them together in the first place. Perhaps Sujata Bhatt's journey is the most challenging of all, because she has shown in the poetry much of her own journey in terms of language, culture and geography. Perhaps that is best illustrated in the words of her Marie Curie character:
>> while I analysed the progress
>> that has been made in physics...
>> ... at night, I still count in Polish.

7 Plan and write a response to the essay question using your own choice of texts.

War

Activity 85

1 Read the sample question below:

> 'However unpleasant it may be, it is important that writers keep reminding us of the horrors of war.'
>
> Comment on and analyse the connections between at least two texts you have studied in the light of this assertion.
>
> In your response you must ensure that at least one text is a post-1990 text.
>
> In your response you should demonstrate what it means to be considering texts as a modern reader, in a modern context and that other readers at other times may well have had other responses. (60 marks)

2 Using the texts that you have studied, consider how you would address AO3:

  a Note five points that you think might be relevant.

  b Compare your points to those of other members of your class.

  c How many of your texts did you use when carrying out this activity?

3 **a** Read the opening paragraph of the student essay below. Write a brief comment on how you think this opening addresses AO3 and AO4. What you are looking for is a focus on the opening statement of the question (the proposition), an ability to make connections and comparisons, and evidence that the writer is aware of contexts. The last two points are particularly focused on AO3 and AO4.

> In *The Ghost Road* Pat Barker takes the reader back to the First World War and its horrors, in contrast to Khaled Hosseini who is dealing with the much more recent conflict in Afghanistan. In the poems I have read, Wilfred Owen also talks about a dead soldier in 'Futility' and Edwin Muir's 'The Horses' deals with how the world might cope after a nuclear holocaust in an imagined future. Each of them deals with horror in a different way and my essay will focus on the different ways in which writers present these horrors.

  b Read the examiner's comments below. What do you learn from them?

Examiner's comments

AO3

The writer has made an attempt to show where his essay might be heading. He has mentioned three texts, and from his poetry text he has mentioned two poems. The key word in the question, 'horrors', is addressed, so appropriate connections have been established from the outset even if so far there is no mention of other readers.

AO4

The writer has mentioned a range of contexts relating to the various conflicts that provide the settings for the novels and poems he refers to; one would hope that the sense of a modern reader's response would be developed later in the essay.

c Repeat this exercise by considering AO1 and AO2.

Examiner's comments

AO1

The expression is clear, the focus is firmly on the topic of war and, as already mentioned, the key word 'horrors' is picked up.

AO2

So far there is no real reference to structure, form or language, but this will doubtless follow.

---

d Can you think of an alternative way of starting this essay?

4 a Read the next section of the student's essay. Comment on how well you think the writer has moved on from the opening paragraph.

In 'The Horses' not many people have survived, modern technology no longer works and the people are isolated with no means of communicating with the outside world:

> On the second day
> The radios failed.

Examiner's comments

This is a fairly straightforward comment linked to content. There is a useful quotation, but so far no sense of interpretation.

---

5 Develop the student's paragraph above to make the discussion of the situation at the beginning of the poem more analytical. Show that you know you are dealing with a piece of poetry.

6 a Read the next section of the essay. How well does the writer develop his argument? Rewrite the passage to make it more analytical and literary in order to address all the assessment objectives more effectively.

In *The Ghost Road* we are shown what it is like to be in the thick of battle: 'Prompt as ever, hell erupted. Shells whined over, flashes of light, plumes of water from the drainage ditches, tons of mud and earth flung into the air.'

In 'Futility', Owen shows us what has happened to the soldier and how he will never come back to life even though the 'kind old sun... awoke him once'.

The horrors of the situation in Afghanistan in *The Kite Runner* are very different. The war influences Amir and his father when they are obliged to go into exile and have a very unpleasant and dangerous journey before arriving in Pakistan: 'MiGs roaring past overhead; staccatos of gunfire; ... the stench of gasoline, vomit and shit.'

Each of these writers uses language effectively to show the horrors of the wars they describe.

---

b Read the examiner's remarks about the writing and see how far you have addressed the issues raised.

Examiner's comments

So far the writer has drawn some contrasts. There is clear focus on horrors and these are well illustrated. It would have been useful to have had some comments about the language. The writer now needs to make some comparisons between his texts and to offer some considered opinions about how effective he thinks the writing is. If he can do this and offer some different critical opinions, the essay could be developed into something much more promising than appears so far.

He hasn't really differentiated the genres being discussed. For a higher band mark some discussion of how each writer uses form, structure and language is needed. The quotations from each text require detailed analysis of the language used. The writer says that he is about to talk about language and, were he to do so, this would improve the slightly disappointing impression made so far.

---

7 Write a conclusion to this essay.

8 Plan and write a response to the essay using your own choice of texts.

Reviewing your response

When checking through your essay, ask yourself whether you have:

- dealt fully with each aspect of the statement/proposition at the beginning of the question
- compared and contrasted at least two of the texts you have studied
- dealt with at least one post-1990 text
- considered contexts in your answer
- used quotations to support the points made
- structured your argument and reached a valid conclusion
- been fully analytical in your approach
- provided an informed personal response
- considered a range of different possible interpretations of the texts.

If you can honestly say 'Yes' to these questions, the examiner will enjoy reading your answer and it is likely to score highly.

A Choosing your text, topic and approach

This section prepares you for your coursework task. You will learn how one central text can lead to many different topics. You will consider the three possible tasks and select your central text and topic area of study.

Independent research

The canon is the collection of books which are considered to be classically great texts, selected for the moral lessons they teach, for the quality of thought behind the ideas and for the mastery of the ways in which these ideas are expressed. However, you should be aware that there is much debate about the continued value of this hierarchy. Look up 'literary canon' on Google. Begin with www.victorianweb.org and then explore a couple of other sites.

Key term

- literary canon

1 Introduction

Unit 4 is designed to bring together and build upon the skills that you have gained over your whole course of study. You will become empowered as an independent literary critic, and you will enjoy the authority this expertise brings. Whether you respond to a text by writing an extended study, or two shorter studies, or through offering a creative response and commentary, your work will rest upon judgements which you have made for yourself about the texts, and the critical or cultural works which support them.

Prepare for this unit by asking yourself questions about the sort of literature you read, or would like to read. Ask yourself about the issues which are important to you, and why you find them interesting. Remember that you may select texts written in English from around the world. Whether the text is from the literary canon or is contemporary, be bold, take some risks and you will find an enormous excitement as you explore texts and undertake your work for this unit.

The wider skills you will acquire as you carry out your work for this unit will be helpful to you in the future, whether at university, college, the workplace, preparing for a gap year or when you talk about yourself in an interview. You will:

- develop skills in planning and researching
- see the rewards of working hard on an interesting topic
- learn how to argue your case by taking an overview of your material, and selecting and evaluating evidence to justify your views
- strengthen your analytical skills.

2 Literary studies and research

The title of the coursework unit is **Reflections in literary studies**. Literary studies is different in many ways from studying set texts. You will be exploring several areas related to the way texts are written, and how different readers can view a text. In your study or studies you will:

- explore the influences of contexts, such as historical or literary, on the way texts are written
- explore how different contexts can affect the way you and other readers understand a text
- look at your texts through a variety of these contextual frames
- explore different critical perspectives from which texts may be studied
- look at texts from a variety of these critical viewpoints
- make connections between texts but move beyond the straightforward compare/contrast formula.

In other words, you will be exploring exactly why you respond to the text in the ways that you do, bringing into your study a consideration of areas which are outside your text, but related to it. Your final choice of title should reflect this breadth, but the nature of your enquiry is very much up to you. The freedom which this unit offers allows you to work in the way that best suits you.

Undertaking a literary study also requires you to undertake independent research. Research is a way of finding out answers to questions. It is organised and systematic. It requires the collection and analysis of literary textual evidence. Before you begin your research you have to select a general topic area; during the course of your investigations you will be able to narrow down this general area to a precise focus, to formulate a specific task for which you will provide an answer.

You will be working independently, and therefore you need to turn to your friends and fellow students for support and advice on your work. It might be wise to establish working relations with your peer group based upon common needs and not competition. Here are some ideas of how you might do this:

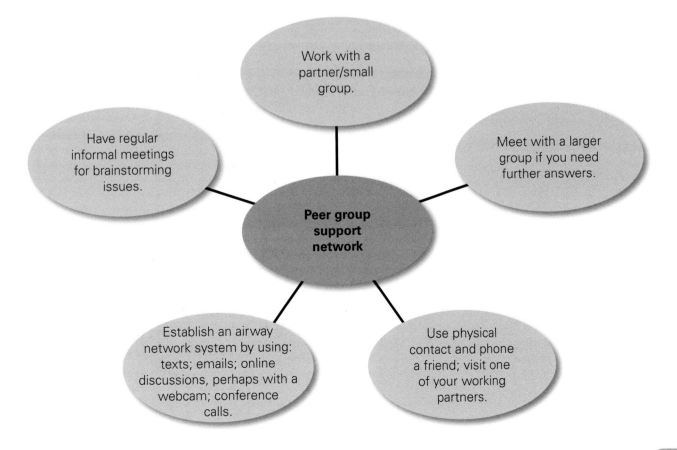

You should plan to hold regular informal meetings for progress checks and formal meetings to present your work for the judgement of peers. Always try to be open-minded, or objective, and fair in your comments; take a balanced view of any criticism or suggestions made about your own work; be cooperative.

To do as well as possible in independent coursework you should be honest in analysing your personal strengths and weaknesses. This will allow you to strengthen areas that seem to require more work.

Activity 1

1 Read Student A's personal profile below. How would you advise him to address his weaknesses?

2 Draw up a personal profile for yourself. Exchange it with a partner's and discuss each of your profiles. How honest have you been, and what changes might you make in your attitudes and behaviour?

Student A

Are you serious in your attitudes and aims for this subject?

Yes, I enjoy English and want to do well.

Are you determined and will you persevere despite difficulties?

I am quite determined, but I can lose my self-confidence sometimes.

Are you organised enough to tackle this stage of the work?

I can waver, so I will make a timetable and try to stick to it.

Do you always give your studies the time they should have?

Weekends can be a bit problematic; I do want to have a life!

Are you always honest with yourself about how hard you are really working?

Mostly, well, mmm ...

Have you got a group of friends to work with?

I can think of two.

Activity 2

1 Now draw up an academic profile, identifying your strengths and weaknesses, to see where you could improve your work. Carry out this exercise with a partner. You should ask yourself:

- Am I trying to build up an appropriate literary vocabulary?
- Do I always try to think about the ideas within a text, and not just the narrative?
- Can I grasp the different ways in which writers express their ideas?
- Can I work out different interpretations of a text?
- Do I understand the idea of different critical perspectives?
- Can I identify and talk about the contexts of a text?
- Do I understand the influences of contextual frames on texts?

2 Exchange your academic profile with that of a partner's and talk about any difference in views your partner may have from yours. Make a 'to do' list for your wall, and work out a study sequence when you can do some extra work on weak spots and revise earlier units. Discuss how you might be able to help each other.

You will be using both of the above profiles later in this section.

3   Choosing your central text

There is freedom in the choice of texts for study in this unit; they may be any text from any time and from any genre – prose, poetry, or drama. There are many ways in which you will arrive at your chosen texts; perhaps your teacher will select the central text for you, and maybe the second as well. On the other hand, you may be free to make an independent choice.

Of the three texts that you have to choose for study, one will be central. You will study your central text in detail. The other two texts may include works of literary criticism and/or critical or cultural context. But the central text is your starting point.

Once you have a copy of your central text you should read it through quickly so that you can think about possible topics as soon as possible. But a quick reading should not be a careless reading. Make some notes as you read, and a summary when you have finished, listing the different themes and issues of the text.

Across AS and A2

Although your three texts cannot include one that you have studied for an earlier unit, your coursework may draw upon interests sparked by other units in the course. In this case, references to texts studied elsewhere are seen as additional to the three studied for this unit.

Activity 3

If you are going to choose your central text on your own, here is a route that you might take. It is a great opportunity for you to develop your own interests.

Write down an action plan in three stages.

1 Think about a text or an area of study which has interested you already. Perhaps you might choose another text by an author whom you have enjoyed? If you can't think of any ideas, the list below (see p132) might help.

OR

If you know that you will write a creative response, think about an author or a genre, such as the dramatic monologue, of interest to you.

2 Talk to your teacher and friends about writers or texts that might be good to choose.

3 Explore this area for yourself through a search engine such as Google by searching for writers on specific topics or styles that interest you.

What is a good central text? It is a text that is appropriate to A level study in nature and of comparable length to the set texts for Unit 3. A 'good' central text will suggest plenty of areas to explore and plenty of areas where connections can be made with other texts.

As an example, take the novel *Atonement* by Ian McEwan (it does not matter if you have not read this). What sort of topics might be based on this text? Here are three groups of topics; the first is based on themes, the second on aspects of style, the third is based on issues that arise from this text:

Theme 1:
doing something 'sinful' to someone else, feeling guilty, so making 'atonement' for this act

Theme 2:
problems caused by class consciousness in society

Theme 3:
war and the effect it has on people's lives

Atonement

Style 1:
use of muddled development of time, of disordered chronology

Style 2:
switching viewpoints at intervals throughout the book

Style 3:
switching locations throughout the book

Issue 1:
how well does a male author 'get into' the female mind?

Issue 2:
how might a Marxist or feminist reader view this text?

Activity 4

1 Select any of the texts which you have studied over the last three years and make a chart of possible topics like the one above.

2 Compare your charts in pairs or small groups. Do the ideas that others have chosen stimulate further ideas of your own?

Remember: you cannot reuse a text that you have already studied as part of your course.

4 Choosing your topic

What is your exploration going to be about? Is there any area you would particularly like to research? One of the most important things about topic choice is to select something that will keep you interested and motivated over the course of several weeks.

Your topic could take one of a number of different forms:

- a study of one writer, or of certain aspects of one writer – for example, Thomas Hardy; Samuel Beckett; Carol Ann Duffy and the use of the dramatic monologue
- a study of one genre – for example, drama; poetry; the short story
- an investigation into one **sub-genre** – for example, Gothic fiction; docu-drama
- an exploration of one particular form – for example, satirical poetry; the sonnet; the beginnings of short stories
- a topic based on a theme – for example, sin and atonement; attitudes to women; the black experience
- an exploration of a literary movement or group of writers – for example, the **theatre of the absurd**; the Romantic poets; **modernist** novels
- an investigation into a literary issue – for example, literature and censorship; whether journalism could be considered as serious literature; whether there should still be a literary canon (see the Independent research box on p128).

Creative response with commentary

Your choice of 'topic' will take the form of a provisional decision about your central text and the choice of literary style for your creative writing.

When deciding on a topic that relates to your central text, think hard about the sort of area that interests you. Always consult your teacher on your choice of topic because they know you well and there might be a list for you to look at. Have a discussion with your friends and share ideas.

Key terms

- sub-genre
- modernist
- theatre of the absurd

Activity 5

1 Share your reactions in class discussion to the topic proposals on the next page. Read through and compare them, discussing:

- how interesting you find them
- how far each of them would stretch *you* if you were to write them
- any ideas they might add to your own coursework plans
- any pitfalls you can see ahead for the students concerned.

2 Discuss as a class how far Proposals A and B seem likely to meet the AOs. Think in particular about:

- how Proposal A might meet the AO3 requirement to consider 'the interpretations of other readers' of the chosen texts
- how Proposal A might meet the AO4 requirement to consider 'the contexts in which literary texts are written and received'
- how Proposal B might meet the AO2 requirement to consider how 'structure, form and language shape meanings' in texts
- how Proposal B might meet the AO3 requirement to 'explore connections and comparisons between different literary texts'
- whether there are any points in Proposal B which you might use in the commentary.

Take it further

Carry out this exercise on the topic that seemed the strongest to you and your partner. Think about it carefully and write a paragraph outlining how you might begin to develop this as a topic. For example, what are the different stages in which the theme became clear to you? Or what are the effects on you of certain aspects of style? Or, if you understand this sort of criticism, what might a Marxist or feminist critic find interesting about this text?

Proposal A

I have become interested in the role and function of 'the outsider' in literature. Using Coleridge's poem *The Ancient Mariner* as my central text I will explore the different ways in which the outsider has been presented. I will go on to consider how readers' reactions to such a figure might change, dependent upon an author's purposes and his and the audience's social contexts. I will also explore what aspects of his contemporary society the outsider might be used to support or criticise.

Proposal B

I am interested in the *theatre of the absurd* and how it has developed. I believe that this theatrical sub-genre has particularly close ties to our own society and is linked very closely to contemporary philosophical thinking. It is a delicate form, and I intend to demonstrate this by writing a third act for Samuel Beckett's *Waiting for Godot*. This extra act can either support or completely overturn what seem to be Beckett's purposes, and I intend to show how this third act could make a significant difference to the ways in which the audience might respond to this play.

Activity 6

Once you have decided upon a topic, write down a brief proposal explaining your choice. Why does this topic interest you, and how does it relate to your chosen central text? Do you have any ideas at this early stage of the other two texts related to this topic that you would like to study?

5 Choosing your approach

There are three different ways in which you can write and present your coursework task:

- One extended study of 2500-3000 words

  OR

- Two shorter studies totalling 2500-3000 words together, or between 1250 and 1500 words each

  OR

- One piece of creative writing plus a commentary on it. The creative writing will be a critical–creative response to your central text. Added together, your writing and your commentary should be about 2500 and no more than 3000 words.

Remember that, whichever approach you take, you can choose your three texts from within or across any genres or periods. They can include a work of literary criticism or of cultural commentary. You will select one of them as your central text.

You will have to make a decision on your chosen approach fairly soon as you have a lot to do in order to complete your coursework on time.

Don't rush your decision, however. You may need to do some research and thinking around your central text before it becomes clearer to you what kind of approach suits you and the texts that you have chosen.

Each approach has different features and implications, outlined below.

One extended study

If you choose to write a single extended study, you have to refer to all three texts. Your choice of topic, therefore, has to be suitable for a long essay. You need to be competent at arguing a case in a piece of sustained writing. You may also need to draw on your reserves of self-motivation and self-control in order to maintain interest and keep on moving forward over a period of many weeks.

The single extended study has the advantage of allowing you to focus on one piece of writing and one central idea, backed up by a single focus of research.

Two shorter studies

If you choose to write two shorter studies, each must refer to more than one text. The central text in each case will be a literary text. Each study must also refer to at least one other text, which may be a work of critical reception or cultural context. You may decide to write two studies around the same central text, but addressing different aspects of the text. Likewise, the same work of critical reception or cultural context may be drawn upon in both studies. Overall, however, at least three texts must be studied and referred to.

For example, you could choose two collections of short stories and a work of commentary. Your first study could be about form, focused on the beginnings of short stories, and the second study might address the use of the Gothic in short stories.

The choice of two shorter studies could mean that you might not have to go into such length or depth in your research and writing. However, if you choose two very different literary texts, you will have to do a lot of reading and thinking. You may prefer to choose a single central text and write two studies on different aspects of it.

You will need to be able to sustain your enthusiasm so that, when you have completed one essay, you can turn to the next.

Creative response with commentary

Here you use at least one of your three texts to stimulate a piece of creative writing. This could take many forms, including:

- a different treatment of a theme in your chosen text(s)
- rewriting material from your chosen text(s) for a different audience.

You might, for example, re-centre *Hamlet* by looking through the eyes of Ophelia, the largely 'invisible' woman of the drama. Or you could change the genre of a poem into prose: for example, focusing on one or two of Carol Ann Duffy's monologues from *The World's Wife* to introduce the thoughts of the silent male 'participants'.

You then produce a commentary on your writing. In this you explain your purposes and how you achieved them. The commentary carries more weight than the writing when your work is assessed, so it is recommended that the creative piece should be between 500 and 1000 words long, and the commentary between 2000 and 2500 words.

Although this option demands similar reading and research to the other options, your response engages creative writing skills as well as your analytical and reflective skills. You will have to focus on both aspects of the task as you research: critical and creative; and you need to make careful choice of an appropriate form for the creative piece.

Don't rule out the creative option because you think that to take it on you have to be a 'gifted writer. On the other hand, don't imagine that this is a 'soft option'. The preparation for this approach is very similar to that for the essay options in learning how to read effectively, understanding how others see a text, and all the other issues to be discussed in Section B. You have to be just as systematic and rigorous in handling this option as students who opt for essay writing. Remember, more marks will be awarded for your commentary than for the creative piece.

Activity 7

Working with a partner, talk through each of the approaches to decide which you think would suit you best. Take into account your chosen central text and topic area. Refer to your personal and academic profiles if it helps you move towards a decision. Look at the extracts from student writing in Sections C and D to help you explore what the different approaches look like in practice.

If your teacher has advised you already on which approach you should undertake, then think about the demands which it will make on you, compare these with your personal and academic profiles and decide where you might need to make any special effort.

6   Assessing ideas for topics and texts

Whatever your approach, and whatever the nature of your texts and topic area, you need to be able to address the assessment objectives (see p127).

Activity 8

1   Read Student A's outline proposal and note the reader's comments on how well it addresses the assessment objectives.

2   Read Student B and C's outline proposals on the facing page and discuss with a partner how well they address the assessment objectives.

Student A

Approach: single extended essay

Central text: Port Elizabeth Plays by Athol Fugard

The television news has often been focused on the response of the African American population to Obama's election campaign for President of the USA. This made me realise that there is still racial prejudice and discrimination. So I have decided to explore the way writers have presented the experience of being black and of being poor. I chose Athol Fugard's Port Elizabeth Plays because they are apparently so simple and so domestic; I then realised that this is a very clever illusion. There are just two or three characters, a simple setting and a home-based plot. The dialogue, too, is simple and colloquial. In fact these four short plays do display a world of deprivation and poverty, yet the vision is not bleak; in each play there is a sense of the importance of family life and the courage and nobility of the human spirit.

Does this proposition address each of the AOs?

AO1: Yes, there is an understanding of the issues of the text and the use of appropriate critical language.

AO2: Yes, the student intends to show how structure, form and language shape the meaning of the text.

AO3: The basis for the response is to experience something through the eyes of other people. The student has also understood that a play written over 30 years ago is still relevant today.

AO4: Yes, the student has concentrated on a social context with a very specific focus.

Student B

Approach: two shorter essays

Central text: *Selected Short Stories* by D. H. Lawrence

If ever a male writer knew what made a woman tick, that writer has to be D. H. Lawrence! He seems to have an instinctive understanding of how easily a woman's heart
5 and soul can be crushed by being married to the wrong man and by living in the wrong environment. To explore this idea I will consider his short stories, but look at them through a Marxist perspective. Of course, this task
10 is made easier by the fact that Lawrence himself had socialist views, but nevertheless, this perspective brings out the ways in which industrialisation has damaged the human spirit. In *Daughters of the Vicar* this is made
15 evident in the poverty-stricken, bleak household. The harshness of the unnatural environment in a small mining town and the effects on another household are evident at the start of *Odour of Chrysanthemums* where Lawrence
20 presents to the reader the noisy, dirty industrial scene where the chrysanthemums are distorted into seeming unnatural. He makes a clear point: Industry kills the spirit; a Marxist reading offers answers as to why this is so.

Student C

Approach: Creative response with commentary

Central text: *Dramatic Monologues* by Robert Browning.

I have chosen to study Robert Browning's *Dramatic Monologues* because of his humour, his use of irony and the way he proceeds in each case by a series of revelations as we move more and more into the mind
5 of each speaker and feel increasingly shocked. *Fra Lippo Lippi* destroyed the idea of Renaissance painting as almost a holy profession; *Bishop Blougram's Apology* revealed a man who was openly ambitious for the wrong reward. But it was *My Last Duchess* which moved me
10 to write. At last there is a woman in the picture: but isn't she being slandered by yet another ruthless male? I thought I would turn the tables a little, and look at one of these brutal males through the eyes of the woman concerned, 'My Last Duchess', and make some
15 of the **inferences** of the poem more concrete.

Her story might have begun:

'I was a very happy child with two loving parents and a nurse who adored me. I spent my happy youth on my
20 father's estate in Tuscany amidst the yellows, pinks and delicate greens of our landscape. Brushing my long hair until it shone, my nurse used to say: "Cara mia, you are beautiful. You'll marry a very rich man one day." If only she knew ...'

Activity 9

1 Write a short proposal like the ones above. List your central text and the approach you have chosen, and explain what your main interest and topic will be.

2 Present your proposal in small groups. Give critical but supportive feedback, especially on whether you think your peers' proposals address the assessment objectives.

3 On the basis of feedback received, do you need to rethink your ideas in any way? How could you refine your ideas so that you end up with a central text and topic that you are happy with?

Remember three points:

- You have not yet refined your topic into an essay title: you will do this in Section B.
- Your study will involve reading and referring to three texts (although texts 2 and 3 do not need to be studied to the same degree of detail as the central text). You will explore how to select these texts in Section B also.
- You may want to change your chosen approach: for example, from one study to two studies, when you begin your research and extend your reading. This is acceptable, but you should decide fairly early on.

Key term

- inferences

Checkpoint

By this stage you should have:

- read your central text
- made some exploration of themes and style
- decided upon a provisional topic area
- chosen a provisional approach for writing.

B Planning and researching your writing

This section will help you to plan your coursework timetable and to start your research. You will explore connections between texts and choose your second and third texts. You will study the skills of reading critically and how to use research material. Finally, you will explore how to move on from a topic to a specific title and focus your material appropriately.

1 Planning your coursework

You must plan your work carefully. Good time management will take the stress out of coursework and will allow you to make the most of your ability. If you manage your time properly you will have a clear idea all the way through the process whether you are keeping up with your work or falling behind. If you are behind with your schedule, catch up at once by doing a little extra work. You should avoid a last-minute rush as this could spoil your chances of doing well. Poor timekeeping is one of the most common causes of students failing to achieve as highly as possible. Good time management could make the difference between an A or a C, a C or an E grade.

When you begin your coursework, you will be given a deadline by which your Unit 4 folder must be handed in. When you have this, you should count the number of weeks you have for your coursework and work out the dates by which each stage of your study should be finished. You may like to plan your timetable using the outline plans below.

These outlines allow 16 weeks to produce the final draft of your study or studies.

One extended study

Stage 1 3 weeks	Stage 2 2 weeks	Stage 3 4 weeks	Stage 4 2 weeks	Stage 5 3 weeks	Stage 6 2 weeks	Submit!

Stage 1: Read the literary text(s) twice; the first time for making sense of the text, and the second time for taking careful notes. Start to address your second and third texts, again making relevant notes on your second reading.

Stage 2: Decide on the topic area, discuss with your peers and begin your research.

Stage 3: Refine your topic to a title and discuss your findings with your peers; target and complete your research, analyse your findings and shape the material into focus.

Stage 4: Write your first draft and present to your peers.

Stage 5: Write your final draft.

Stage 6: Edit, add all the details and do all the revision tasks (see Section E below).

Submit your folder and celebrate!

Two shorter studies

Each of these should take half the time of the extended study, and of course you have to repeat the exercise.

First study:

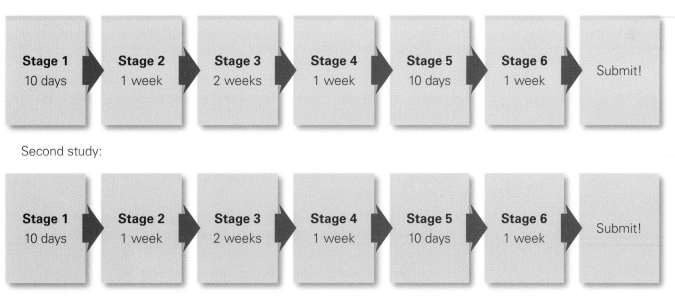

| Stage 1
10 days | Stage 2
1 week | Stage 3
2 weeks | Stage 4
1 week | Stage 5
10 days | Stage 6
1 week | Submit! |

Second study:

| Stage 1
10 days | Stage 2
1 week | Stage 3
2 weeks | Stage 4
1 week | Stage 5
10 days | Stage 6
1 week | Submit! |

Creative response with commentary

The sequence of your preparation for this will be somewhat different from the first two choices.

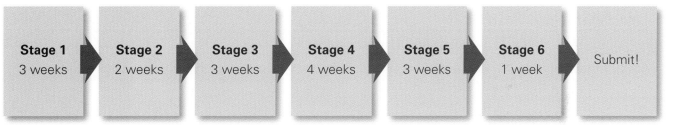

| Stage 1
3 weeks | Stage 2
2 weeks | Stage 3
3 weeks | Stage 4
4 weeks | Stage 5
3 weeks | Stage 6
1 week | Submit! |

Stage 1: Read the central literary text and think about the literary style you will adopt for your creative writing. Choose and begin to read through your second and third texts, annotating/making careful notes. Make notes for your commentary at every stage of your work.

Stage 2: Thinking about genre, form and style, decide on your approach to creative writing. Decide on the aspects of your central text you will focus on, and discuss both of these aspects with your peers. Continue your research.

Stage 3: Experiment with your chosen mode for your creative writing and begin to shape it; target and complete your research, allowing at least two weeks for the commentary; analyse your findings and plot the connections between the four texts.

Stage 4: Write the first drafts of your creative piece and your commentary, spending most of your time on the commentary as that is where the marks lie.

Stage 5: Present them to your peers, and then write the final drafts.

Stage 6: Edit, add the details, do all the revision tasks, then submit and celebrate!

Researching the creative response with commentary

The organisation of your work for this coursework outcome will be a bit different as you are preparing for a literary stylistic response to a text. Your sequence might be:

1 EITHER

- choose the author on whom you will base your study

OR

- select a particular genre, form or style which appeals to you: for example, the dramatic monologue.

2 Regarding this choice as the topic of your research:

- think about the ways in which the second and third texts will be most useful: for example, you might want to read a textbook about literary style to help you plan your own creative writing

- jot down notes for your commentary as soon as you start, tracing each step as you formulate your literary response as well as recording your research route.

3 Regarding your final decision on how you will write as the title of your research. (You might give the creative writing its own internal title later.)

Activity 10

1 Work with a partner and make your own timeline for your coursework.

2 Discuss with your partner how you could best display your coursework timeline: for example, as a wall chart, which could act as a permanent reminder of what to do and how far you have got.

You also need to think about how you are going to fit your coursework into your working week.

Activity 11

Write out a study timetable for one week, showing when you will do your coursework. You should:

- fill in the timetable with all of your classes
- allow for any activities which you have to do such as sport or work
- decide when you will work on your coursework and treat this as unbreakable
- never miss a session you have marked out for yourself
- allow some 'catch-up' time as you will miss some study time for trips or sickness.

2   Starting your research

Research can be interesting and exciting as you develop forensic skills and take your course of study into your own hands. It's a good idea to begin your research once you have decided on your central text and topic, as the process of research will help you to choose your second and third texts and refine your topic area into a precise writing task (see Parts 3 and 5 below).

Before you begin, make sure that you have:

- discussed your topic with your peers to ensure that it is appropriate and will allow you to write to the necessary length
- tested it against the assessment objectives
- checked that there is enough range of enquiry to allow you to do well against the assessment criteria (see p127).

The quality of your research will rest on your attention to detail. When you submit your folder, details of all the texts you refer to must be given in the bibliography, whether they are books, TV/radio programmes or material from the internet. When you come across something in print which you think you might use, write down the title, author, chapter heading, page reference, publisher and date. For internet sources, write down details about the site, author and date. Store your information carefully, making a simple index so that you can retrieve these details quickly if you need to consult your sources again or when you write the bibliography. It is dispiriting and time-consuming to try to retrace your steps.

Your three main resource areas will be books, the media and the internet.

Researching books

When you have decided on your author and general topic area, begin your research at once. On the library computer look up the name of your author, and you will find that relevant books will be listed in a set pattern:

- The works
- Editions of the works
- Biographies
- Critical writing by single authors
- Critical writing printed in collections.

Libraries will stock certain central reference books such as:

The Oxford Companion to English Literature, ed. Margaret Drabble, Oxford 2000
The Cambridge Companion Series, CUP
Cambridge Guide to Fiction in English, ed. Ian Ousby, CUP 1998
The Oxford English Dictionary – you need the concise edition to check written work.

Use a bibliography from a critical book to discover which books are worth reading for your study. The librarian will guide you in this. Make a list, and look at a few pages of the books which seem appropriate.

If you cannot find a copy of a book taken from a bibliography, ask the librarian for help; often books can be requested through an 'inter-library loan' from another library.

Independent research

The *Oxford Companion to English Literature* is a helpful book to search for information on an author or genre. Each entry includes a brief biography and a list of works with some summaries. This text is very helpful when considering genres such as 'Gothic fiction' or 'Romanticism', or the subject of 'metre'. Check the *Oxford Companion* for information about your author, his works and genre, etc.

Researching media resources

Media resources include newspaper reviews, essays (usually printed on Saturdays and Sundays), periodical magazines and journals, often stocked in libraries but sometimes also published on the internet. You can use radio and TV programmes, including interviews with authors and critics, arts programmes, readings and plays related to your area of study. DVDs can be useful, such as *Blackadder Goes Forth*: *Series 4*, which offered an excellent satire on war, and the screenplay is available. Theatre programmes can be helpful.

Films of your selected text may be available, but be cautious as they can deviate from the text, and since you must use the screenplay you are back to the printed word.

Researching the internet

Internet material will be very useful if you are studying a recent text or if you choose works of critical and cultural commentary as one or two of your texts.

You could, for example, use authors' websites, critical websites, blogs, chat rooms, information from reading groups and diaries of people involved in the production of plays/films.

Remember to read websites critically. Unlike books, websites are generally not checked for quality and they could also be out of date or written by an unreliable reader, so be careful what you accept. There are also huge numbers of websites on any topic, which can be time-consuming to sift through.

Nowadays, many authors have their own websites, as they are aware of the importance of reaching out to their readers. Khaled Hosseini, author of *A Thousand Splendid Suns* and *The Kite Runner*, has an excellent website which features an interview, comments on his work and comparisons, and is very much geared to the sort of study you might undertake; similarly, Ian Rankin offers a very informative site related to a specific reading room. Ian McEwan and other authors run blogs and websites which are angled towards students and reading groups.

142

Using research materials: a case study

Here is an example of how a student approached his research. He decided that he would write two short studies, and that the topic for one would be about kitchen sink plays; he selected *Look Back in Anger* by John Osborne (1957) as his central text.

He found it easy to access plenty of research material; the edition he used had a good bibliography to choose from and there were many sites to help him on the internet. There was a range of material from reviews to interviews and information about the reception of the play. So he made a list of what seemed to be the best books to use, from the bibliography, and the best sites, with details of their content.

He then decided to make Osborne's autobiography his second text, *Almost a Gentleman: An Autobiography, 1955–66* (1991), and then faced the task of how to use his research material. To see how he handled his task, read the case study below.

Outline (provisional)

This shorter study is going to be based on Osborne's play 'Look Back in Anger' and his comments about it in his autobiography. The topic I am interested in is *The way kitchen sink plays changed English drama in the 1950s and 1960s*.

I will show why the play caused a great impact when it was first produced. It was a completely different style of play to those of earlier dramatists. George Bernard Shaw's plays were socialist in their sympathies, but were wordy, effectively presenting debates on stage: very much 'drawing-room' drama. Other dramatists like Somerset Maugham, Noel Coward and Terence Rattigan had been popular before and after World War II. This is because they described upper- and middle-class life, whereas 'Look Back in Anger' was about a working-class anti-hero, Jimmy Porter, living an ordinary life in sordid surroundings. Also, Jimmy Porter was the original 'angry young man' who spoke out for the working class against the establishment world of the Conservative government, etc.

I am probably going to use Osborne's autobiography as a context. This shows that he was part of the youth movement in the 1950s which wanted to change society and sweep away old-fashioned attitudes towards politics, religion and morals. I may also refer to the plays of Shelagh Delaney and Arnold Wesker to show that Osborne began a 'kitchen sink' movement in drama that was not just a one-off but went on through the 1960s and beyond.

Note that the student has a clear idea of his central text and general topic. He is already thinking about which other texts he will read and refer to in his essay; further research will clarify these choices. Activity 12 focuses on his research.

With his proposal complete, he selected the following texts for his essay, as they seemed the most relevant to his topic.

Extract A (from Osborne's autobiography, recalling the opening night of *Look Back in Anger* on 8 May 1957 – note that the ironing-board used as a stage prop rapidly became a symbol of 'kitchen sink' drama)

We had one preview night, nearly unknown then when stars would be expected to clean up automatically for weeks in the provinces before descending on the West End. George Fearon [the English Stage Company's press officer] and Tony [the play's director] were baffled by the persistent laughter. When the third act opened to
5 discover Helena draped over Alison's ironing-board, no one could ignore the cheers that applauded the ironing-board's performance. 'But why do you think they're laughing so much?' asked Tony, alarmed. 'Because it's supposed to be funny,' I replied. Neither of them was reassured.

The overnight stardom of the ironing-board was forgotten the following
10 evening, 8 May. The occasion seems to have been confidently documented by the few who were there, but I remember little. I was sitting in the front row of the unfilled dress circle between Oscar Lewenstein and the writer Wolf Mankowitz. Wolf laughed loudly, and alone. Oscar glanced around him like a managing clerk anticipating a disastrous verdict from the jury foreman. By the end of the evening I
15 was very drunk as, for the first time, I went through the playwright's lap of dishonour round the dressing-rooms …

When I arrived at the theatre [on the morning after], still nauseous from the early-hours drinking, George attempted to brace me up but his own disappointment seemed clearer and more stricken than my own. He told me there was a good notice
20 in the *Financial Times*. Tony pretended to be astonished by both of us. 'But what on earth did you *expect*? You didn't expect them to *like* it, did you?' His affected scorn was preferable to anyone's encouraging nod. Meanwhile, a gloomy rearguard action was being rehearsed in the foyer by Fearon. Coining 'Angry Young Man' still pleased him a little, although he could now see no usefulness in it. There was no
25 advance [ticket sales] at the box office. He had spoken to a psychiatrist who had seen *Look Back* and assured him that there were clinical examples of young men who behaved and talked like Jimmy Porter. Expert medical opinion might get us through the week.

Extract B (from a review of the opening night of *Look Back in Anger* by the influential theatre critic Kenneth Tynan)

Look Back in Anger presents post-war youth as it really is, with special emphasis on the non-U intelligentsia, who live in bed-sitters and divide up the Sunday papers into two groups, 'posh' and 'wet'. To have done this at all would be a signal achievement; to have done it in a first play is a minor miracle. All the qualities are there, qualities
5 one had despaired of ever seeing on stage – the drift towards anarchy, the instinctive leftishness, the automatic rejection of 'official' attitudes, the surrealist sense of humour … the casual promiscuity, the sense of lacking a crusade worth fighting for and, underlying all these, the determination that no one who dies shall go unmourned … The Porters of our time deplore the tyranny of 'good taste' and refuse to accept
10 'emotional' as a term of abuse; they are classless and they are also leaderless. Mr Osborne is their first spokesman … I doubt I could love anyone who did not want to see *Look Back in Anger*.

Extract C (from an entry by Noel Coward in his diary for 17 February 1957)

> I have just read *Look Back in Anger* by John Osborne and it is full of talent and
> fairly well constructed, but I wish I knew why the hero is so dreadfully cross and
> what about? I should also like to know how, where and why he and his friend run
> a sweet-stall and if, considering the hero's unparalleled capacity for invective, they
> 5 ever manage to sell any sweets? I expect my bewilderment is because I am very old
> indeed and cannot understand why the younger generation, instead of knocking on
> the door, should bash the fuck out of it … I wonder how long this trend of dreariness
> for dreariness's sake will last. Apparently, in the minds of critics, significance and
> importance can only be achieved by concentrating on unhappiness, psychopathic
> 10 confusion and general dismay. No lightness is permissible.

Extract D (from *State of the Nation: British Theatre since 1945* by
Michael Billington)

> First Osborne's play was seen as a cry of political despair. Then as a social
> document. More recently, as in Gregory Hersov's 1999 National Theatre production,
> it has come to be played as a Strindbergian domestic battle. None of these readings
> is mutually exclusive: indeed the power of the play lies in its ability to frame the sex
> 5 war and the class war against a panorama of England …
>   *Look Back's* most durable impact on the British theatre lay in its freewheeling,
> inclusive and blazingly intemperate language: this is where it really liberated the next
> generation. Osborne talks of his despair, as a young actor, at trying to learn Somerset
> Maugham's dialogue: 'Maugham's language,' he writes, 'was dead, elusively inert,
> 10 wobbly like some synthetic rubber substance.' His own play is a riposte to the
> mechanical glibness of the Maugham school … What Osborne does in *Look Back* is
> forge a distinctive prose style but also one that borrows from sources as diverse as
> Max Miller, Terence Rattigan, Mills and Boon, D. H. Lawrence and Shakespeare.

Activity 12

1 Read the extracts above from the research carried out for this study.

2 Discuss in a small group how the student concerned could make use of these
research items. You might talk about:
  - which of them seem particularly relevant to the topic of the study
  - which of them might provide material to meet the requirements of AO3
  - which of them might provide material to meet the requirements of AO4
  - how *you* would use them if you were writing this study.

3 Read through the research documents and work out one more topic for which this
material could be used. Write down which context(s) apply to it, and compare your
findings with that of a partner.

Reading your texts

Research is important and necessary, but do not neglect the close reading of your texts, especially your central text.

It is important to be able to read critically so that you can stand back from a text and formulate opinions of your own. When an author writes a book he wants to achieve certain purposes and he usually imagines a certain readership who will share his views. To read a text critically you have to remember that you do not have to cooperate in this way.

As you read, try to work out the attitudes and values conveyed; look for 'loaded' words which might lead you to a certain judgement, then make up your own mind. Remember to think about whose interests are being presented. That is how you will come to an interpretation and independent judgement of your own.

Reading strategies can help prepare you to log your material in a systematic way. When you read your texts, make sure that you take careful notes, referring to the ideas and material you will incorporate into your writing, with page numbers. You will need to pause from time to time to collect your thoughts. Reflect upon your title and your research areas; where is the evidence taking you? Is it supporting your title, or are you being led into slightly new areas which may cause you to modify your ideas?

Activity 13

Here is a paragraph from *I Know Why The Caged Bird Sings*, an autobiographical work by the black writer Maya Angelou. Read it through carefully with a partner and try to work out:

- who and what is being criticised
- the author's attitudes and values
- whose interests the author is supporting
- what view the author would like you to take.

> Recently a white woman from Texas, who would quickly describe herself as a liberal, asked me about my home-town. When I told her that in Stamps my grandmother had owned the only Negro general merchandise store since the turn of the century, she exclaimed, 'Why, you were general a debutante.' Ridiculous and even ludicrous. But Negro girls in small Southern towns, whether poverty-stricken or just munching along on a few of life's necessities, were given as extensive and irrelevant preparation for adulthood as rich white girls shown in magazines.

Take it further

Rewrite this paragraph from the viewpoint of the black girl who observes the white lady approaching and responds to her. Change the tone to one of resentment and adjust the attitudes and values conveyed. Your aim is to persuade the reader to accept your viewpoint.

3 Selecting your second and third texts

You have by now chosen a central text and a topic area. You probably already have some ideas about which contexts and aspects of the text interest you or about your creative writing choice. You are reading and researching with these interests and ideas in mind. Choosing your second and third texts is about finding texts that illuminate the central text and help you reflect on it in different ways. You may choose another literary text and a work of critical or cultural commentary, or two non-literary texts.

The texts may connect with your central text in one (or more) of many different ways:

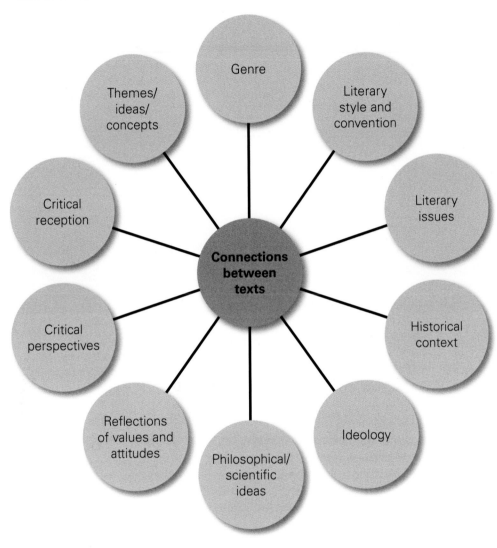

Across AS and A2

You had some experience of exploring contexts in Unit 2, when you studied a central play, a further play and their critical reception. The aim was to foreground a specific text as the focus of a task. At A2 you still have a central text for consideration, but the task is much wider as you explore the factors which influenced both the writing of a text and the ways in which it was received and understood, perhaps by different readers at different times.

Be experimental in your approach to making connections, making sure that you:

- avoid a simple compare and contrast formula
- never handle texts chronologically or sequentially, that is to say, one after the other.

All of these weaknesses would make your arguments and connections rather thin or difficult to achieve. Instead, reflect upon the purposes of a literary study. Your aim is to explore your text embedded in the contexts you have selected so that the particular research you carry out will throw the text up in a new light.

So don't always go for the obvious connections. For example, if you were to explore Keats as a romantic poet, don't feel you have to go for the obvious enquiry into Romanticism; what about looking instead at the fascination the 'outsider' had for Romantic poets? Do you see the difference?

In the case of a shorter essay, imagine your topic area were Gothic literature. Instead of going for the usual enquiry based on *Frankenstein*, you might explore why the Gothic has moved from 'serious literature' to the realms of horror stories, assessing both Gothic and horror short stories against their literary and social backgrounds.

Imagine you wanted to respond creatively about women in society, with E. M. Forster's *A Room with a View* as your central text. Think about the way women were sexually restricted in the 1890s and early into the new century. You may like to draw on Edna Pontellier from *The Awakening* and in your creative response write a dramatic monologue wishing for the freedom that the heroine of Forster's novel finally achieves.

If your central text was Shakespeare's *King Lear*, you might like to focus on the problems of illegitimacy through the ages ('Now, gods, stand up for bastards!'). Your second text could be George Eliot's *Adam Bede*. Your third text could be a film version of *Tess of the d'Urbervilles*, as long as it was treated as a text through the use of a screenplay.

Whatever choices you make, try to place your central text imaginatively with another text, amidst several contexts. Your aim could be to make someone say, 'Well, I never thought of that!'

Activity 14

1 List the different aspects of your topic area that interest you. Try to devise three unusual angles. If you are going to write a creative response, think about different modes.

2 Share your ideas with a partner. Don't rest until you have really interested your partner with a suggestion.

3 Your ideas about different angles and contexts will lead you to make effective choices for your second and third texts.

For example, if you chose as your central text a play, *The Ruling Class*, written by Peter Barnes, produced in 1968, then many different contexts and ideas might occur to you, each of which could spark possible second and third texts to study (see the table below).

Peter O'Toole as the deluded Earl of Gurney in the 1972 film adaption of the black comedy *The Ruling Class*.

Context	Possible texts
Historical/social background at the time – set in a society free of wartime restraints, a time of increased wealth and consumerism and of growing independence for the young	*A Taste of Honey*, Shelagh Delaney: drama, social criticism of a similar period *Blott on the Landscape*, twentieth-century novel, satire of similar social group
Study of the genre of satire – the play satirises attitudes and values of the rich and powerful in society, as well as religion, justice and education	*The Rape of the Lock*, Alexander Pope, eighteenth-century poetry, gentle social satire *Volpone*, Ben Jonson, eighteenth-century drama, vicious social satire
Women in society – the play is critical of the position of women in this society	Feminist criticism: each area of critical theory is discussed in *Learning for a Diverse World: Using Critical Theory to Read and Write about Literature*, Lois Tyson
Problems arising from the distribution of wealth – the play is critical of the distribution of wealth, patriarchy, etc.	Marxist criticism: *Literary Theory*, Terry Eagleton
Study of theatrical genre – the play is theatrically brilliant	*Mid Century Drama*, Laurence Kitchin

Activity 15

1 Reread your list of ideas and think about other texts that you could include in your study. Draw up a table like the one above if that helps.

2 Share your table with a partner. Can you help each other with ideas for second and third texts? Your teacher may have a list to give you, or may offer suggestions. Discuss which context interests you the most and focus on that one.

Remember: you can discover your second and third texts during the process of your research; you do not have to finalise your choices before beginning research.

The influences of culture and contexts

Across AS and A2

In Unit 2 at AS you became familiar with certain critical perspectives on texts. In this unit you might use an *ideological* approach to make connections between texts. Remember, though, that in Unit 4 you are trying to establish critical frames of your own to use in making connections between texts.

Have you thought about how different readers perceive and understand texts differently? For example, a Christian reader in Britain will have a very different experience of Khaled Hosseini's novel *The Kite Runner* from a British Muslim, and more so the besieged reader in Afghanistan. Similarly, responses to Arundhati Roy's book *The God of Small Things* will vary in exactly the same ways for Hindu and Indian readers. Why is this?

When an author writes a book there are contemporary contexts which determine how he or she thinks, feels and writes. For example, Donne's love sonnets are influenced heavily by the scientific theories of the time. You as a reader have a totally different set of contexts: it is the collision between these contexts which allows a variety of meanings and interpretations to arise.

When Charles Dickens wrote the Gothic short story *The Signalman*, he was working within the contexts of his age, which included the following:

- The industrial revolution was at its height.
- Railways were a new invention.
- They were also dangerous and there were many serious accidents.
- In literary terms, the Gothic form was very fashionable.

Activity 16

1 Compare the list of contexts above with your own personal contexts. Make three points which might affect the way you write about railways, and select a style which might suit your writing.

2 Working with a partner, summarise the difference in contexts and in style between you and the original writer over 150 years ago. Can you see how the 'collision' of contexts creates an interesting connection between the texts?

Critical approaches to texts

Assessment objectives

Having a grasp of critical perspectives – interpretations of a text by different readers or groups of readers at different times or periods – is central to attaining AO3 at a good level.

There are broadly two schools of criticism: traditional and modern. Traditional criticism rests on a hierarchy, that is, an ordered list of the great writers, and it is assumed that you will agree. Modern criticism differs in two important ways. It is based on winning you over to a critical perspective – a view which the writer is presenting. Modern critics also think that meanings and readings arise as the result of the influences of contexts not only upon the writer but also upon the reader.

In your work for Unit 4 you may like to read your central text from a particular critical perspective and compare this reading with traditional views. Even if you do not make critical perspective a central part of your study, you need to be aware of different critical approaches to texts that you will come across in your research.

Key terms

- **dialectical**
- **Hegel**
- **ideological**

Take it further

Most modern literary critical theory is a **dialectical** process. Based on **Hegel's** theory, modern critics see literary criticism as an ongoing process. The original text is explored through its connections with its contexts, and what emerges from this exploration changes the significance of the original text, as it has become part of the whole social and cultural history of a society. This significance will develop with each new generation of readers. Try applying one of the newer theories to your text and you will see changes in the ways in which you can assess it.

Critical perspectives are like a set of lenses which allow you to see the text in different ways, and from different viewpoints. They include Marxist, New Historicist, *gender-based*, psychoanalytical, *structuralist* and *deconstructionist* approaches to literary criticism.

Marxist criticism

Karl Marx wrote *Das Kapital* (1867), which inspired the growth of communism and socialism. According to Marxist theory, one class controls the production and sale of goods, reaps all the profit and governs the way society works. Marxist literary critics would claim that literature is generated by this upper class, who establish social values and the literary 'canon'. The interests of the working class are not served. So by viewing a text from a Marxist perspective the reader will find different values and meanings from a traditional reading. It is a political theory.

New Historicism

New Historicists aim to understand a text through its historical context and also to understand society through the cultural and intellectual history revealed in texts. There are some overlaps with Marxism as these critics believe that power controls the social structure.

Gender-based criticism: feminist

Feminist criticism is as political in its views as Marxism and New Historicism. These critics believe that society is determined by *patriarchal* principles: that society is male-dominated, even in the choice of what constitutes 'good' literature. So their judgements on a text will differ again from traditional views.

Psychoanalytical theory

Critics who practise this theory would consider the significance of the unconscious, as perhaps revealed by the writer's memory or dreams. It need not be individual memory; it might be the group memory of society as a whole. For example, these critics suggest that, in Coleridge's poem *The Rime of the Ancient Mariner*, there is a subconscious guilt in the writer's mind which he has inherited as part of English culture, and therefore one of the possible meanings of the poem includes references to the earlier slave trade.

Structuralist criticism

Structuralist critics believe that nothing outside the text is relevant to understanding it. Instead, analysis should focus on structure, where there will be a pattern of opposites balancing each other out, leading towards a resolution. For example, Macbeth and Macduff are opposites. This conflict is resolved through Malcolm. Analyse your text in this way and you will come up with a totally different assessment of it.

Deconstructionism

Deconstructionism is a modernisation of structuralism created by Jacques Derrida. He argues that, because of the nature of language, users cannot truly mean what they intend to mean. This can be demonstrated by showing how the use of certain words or certain passages in a text either don't fit in with or contradict the meaning the author intends for the text as a whole. A 'deconstruction' of a text would probably demonstrate that the text has failed to mean what its author intended. Take any passage of your chosen text and examine it minutely to explore this type of criticism, which offers another way of assessing the 'value' of a text.

Independent research

For a good introduction to Marxist criticism see Terry Eagleton's *Criticism and Ideology* (Verso, 1978). For gender-based (for example, feminist) criticism, see Angela Carter's Introduction to *The Bloody Chamber* (Penguin, 1981). You can see New Historicist criticism at work in collections of critical essays, such as those found in the Norton and Case Book Editions. All areas of critical theory are discussed in *Learning for a Diverse World* by Lois Tyson (Routledge, 2001).

Key terms

- **gender-based**
- **structuralist**
- **deconstructionist**
- **patriarchal**

Take it further

Go to a library and select two editions of a book by a classically great writer: for example, Wordsworth's *Preludes*. Choose one edition that is old, early 1900s, and another that is modern, better still contemporary. Read some of the introduction to each, and explore the differences in the critical approach to each text. Compare the ways they approach and examine the text.

Activity 17

Read through this paragraph from the beginning of the short story *Odour of Chrysanthemums* by D. H. Lawrence (see p151 above).

> The small locomotive engine, Number 4, came clanking, stumbling down from Selston with seven full waggons. It appeared round the corner with loud threats of speed, but the colt that it startled from among the gorse, which still flickered indistinctly in the raw afternoon, outdistanced it at a canter. A woman, walking up
> 5 the railway line to Underwood, drew back into the hedge, held her basket aside, and watched the footplate of the engine advancing. The trucks thumped heavily past, one by one, with slow inevitable movement, as she stood insignificantly trapped between the jolting black waggons and the hedge; then they curved away towards the coppice where the withered oak leaves dropped noiselessly, while the birds, pulling at the
> 10 scarlet hips beside the track, made off into the dusk that had already crept into the spinney… The pit-bank loomed up beyond the pond, flames like red sores licking its ashy sides, in the afternoon's stagnant light. Just beyond rose the tapering chimneys and the clumsy black head-stocks of Brinsley Colliery. The two wheels were spinning fast up against the sky, and the winding-engine rapped out its little spasms. The
> 15 miners were being turned up.

Work with a partner and write a criticism of this scene from three of the different critical approaches.

4   Refining your topic to a writing task

Defining the scope – study/studies

You have seen how to test a topic against the assessment criteria (see p136 above) and chosen or begun to choose your second and third texts in the light of connections between the texts and contexts. During your research, and before you begin to write your study or creative response, you must make sure that you have a title that defines precisely the scope of your task.

One way of refining your topic area to a writing task is to think about the two types of enquiry you undertake in your research: the **closed question** and the **open question**.

Key terms

• **closed question**

• **open question**

• **thesis**

- Closed questions are those to which you already know the answer before the research begins. The purpose of the research is to prove the **thesis** correct. An example of this sort of question might be: 'I am going to explore the reasons why the Revenge Tragedy tradition declined and ended after the great achievement of *Hamlet*.' Here, the outcome of the research is determined by the task: it is there in the title, you are thinking about the end of an era of drama. In a sense, the research is planned for you, although the exact findings are not known.

- In an open question, by contrast, neither the route of the research nor the outcome can be determined. For example, think about the title: 'I intend to explore how and why literary fashions change over time.' This is a totally open question; you will insert your own central and accompanying texts and your selected contexts. So you will establish your own areas; until you get into your research about the periods concerned, you will have no idea of the outcome.

Neither type of question is weaker or better than the other; this is just another step in making your title concrete.

Defining the scope – creative response with commentary

If you select this approach, your first choice will have been to select the author whose writing you want to address in your own creative response. Eventually you must ask yourself questions such as:

- What genre, form or style do I want to end up with?
- What am I going to write?
- How will my creative writing connect with my central text?
- How do I prepare for writing my commentary?

These and other questions will be explored in Section D, but at this stage you should be preparing material for your commentary by:

- beginning with the contexts of genre and literature that relate to your central text
- making notes on each stage of your work to use in your commentary
- organising your research under five headings:
  - > audience
  - > register
  - > tone
  - > genre
  - > literary conventions.

These headings will help you later to connect your creative work with your texts and your commentary.

The distinction between closed and open questions applies equally to the creative option. For example, think of the title 'I intend to subvert Hardy's purposes in his Emma poems by presenting a response to the writer as Emma, written in the speaker's voice from *Color Purple* by Alice Walker.' Here you have a closed question, as you have suggested the nature of your response to Hardy in your choice of topic.

Alternatively, you could take an open route. You might intervene in a text by changing the viewpoint and altering the original values. For example, what might have been the outcome if you were to rewrite parts of *The Color Purple* from Celie's daughter's point of view? Would her response have been as positive and upbeat as her mother's? How might she feel about her abandonment? You won't be sure until you are working through your study.

Activity 18

Prepare for your creative response by experimenting with ways in which you might alter the viewpoint or the values embodied in your central text, then write a brief piece of creative writing. Make some notes about the relationship of the original text to your own, using the five headings above.

Activity 19

1 Write down your topic area, and begin to plan a couple of questions, one closed and one open. Get a feel for what would suit you best.

2 Share your ideas with a larger group for feedback.

Activity 20

1 Read the proposal below for an extended study. The student has identified a topic area and some texts and is trying to refine the ideas to end up with a precise essay title.

2 Remind yourself of the four assessment objectives for this unit (see p127 above). Remember that any coursework folder must meet the requirements of each AO.

Discuss as a class how far this student's proposal seems likely to meet these AOs. Think in particular about how it might consider:

- the 'interpretations of other readers' of the chosen texts (AO3)
- 'the contexts in which literary texts are written and received' (AO4).

Then discuss how AOs 1 and 2 would be met.

3 As a result of talking through this outline, the student refined his topic to this working title:

'Why has the topic of dystopia become so popular among authors in the 20th century?'

Discuss the strengths and weaknesses of this title. Does it seem likely to achieve all the assessment objectives? Will it allow this student access to the higher bands of the marking criteria?

4 What other possible titles might you suggest?

> *Topic:* The way novelists present versions of the future
>
> *Texts:* 'The Handmaid's Tale' by Margaret Atwood – central text
> '1984' by George Orwell
>
> *Research:* J. G. Ballard: Conversations, ed. Vale, E.
>
> *Outline:*
>
> I am planning to connect two novels about the future, exploring why certain writers are fascinated by the idea of dystopia. I will bring out the differences between the way the writers use the idea of dystopia as they present a vision of a wretched society set in decline which exists amidst poverty, illness and oppression. Perhaps they
> 5　both see society as threatened and fragile? Whilst Atwood writes mainly about social change, especially the treatment of women, Orwell writes mainly about political change, but both may be placed within the literary context of dystopia. I became interested in this through reading two of my favourite authors, Ray Bradbury and J. G. Ballard.
>
> 10　I will begin by comparing the narrative technique of the two writers. *The Handmaid's Tale* uses a first person narrative in diary form and has a strong central character's voice; *1984* uses the more conventional third person omniscient viewpoint and voice.
>
> I will then link the writers' ideas with their concerns about contemporary society.
> 15　Finally, I will put the two works within the literary context of dystopia. Throughout I am going to use some of Ballard's comments on *The Handmaid's Tale* and *1984* to establish a critical perspective on my three texts.

Activity 21

1 Write your own proposal. Start from your topic and central text, then include your second and third texts. Refine your topic idea to a list of two or three possible titles. Use the example in Activity 20 as a guide or decide with your teacher on an alternative format.

2 Share your proposal with a partner or a small group. Make constructive comments on each other's work.

3 a) Refer to the four AOs on p127 above. Explain how your coursework is going to meet each of them. Be precise about this. Once your writing is under way, it will be difficult to target any AO you have left out of consideration at this stage.

　b) Add to your proposal a brief explanation of how your writing will meet AO requirements. If you are in doubt about this, make a note for your teacher and discuss it when they have read your outline.

4 Present your proposal to your teacher or peer group and listen to their feedback. Make any changes to your proposal that stem from it.

Checkpoint

By this stage you should have:

- made a timed plan for your coursework research
- selected your second and third texts
- found interesting ways to connect your texts
- selected a title for your essay task
- selected your central author
- made a provisional decision on your creative writing
- made a research plan.

C Writing your study or studies

This section of the book will help you to plan and to write your studies, whether you choose to write one extended essay or two shorter essays. It will also help you to incorporate critical approaches, write appropriate openings and endings and address all the assessment objectives.

1 Planning your study or studies

Across AS and A2

Although you have had experience of organising coursework and your responses to texts earlier in your studies, for example in Unit 2, in Unit 4 you face a much larger enterprise which you have to plan and carry out independently. So you will need to organise your studies in a more effective way.

At this stage in your work for Unit 4 you will have a head full of knowledge and ideas about your central text and your second and third texts. Where do you go from here? How do you turn this chaos into some sort of order? Here is a suggested model to help you organise your research material and shape it ready for your first draft. Read through it first, then prepare your own. It is divided into five stages:

1 Write an outline plan.

2 Identify and index your research material.

3 Read, select and reject.

4 Sequence your ideas.

5 Write your first draft.

Write an outline plan

You will have a working title for your essay. The first step, then, is to draw up an outline plan. This can be very simple, for example:

The central sections are taken up with considerations of three of the central characteristics of your topic. That is all you need for a working plan. (Of course, even at this stage, you may come across something that suggests another heading is needed; that is fine, simply add another one to your plan.)

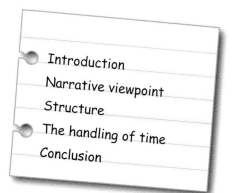

Introduction
Narrative viewpoint
Structure
The handling of time
Conclusion

Identify and index your research material

Your task now is to organise your reading of your texts systematically. Follow these steps:

1 For each text take one clean page of A4 lined paper, and write the three headings down the page, allowing about eight lines for each: narrative viewpoint; structure; the handling of time.

2 Decide upon a colour code and abbreviation for each heading. For example, red for narrative viewpoint, abbreviated to 'N'; yellow for structure, abbreviated to 'S'; green for the handling of time, abbreviated to 'T'.

3 Go through your central text first, scrutinising the notes you have made on the actual book or on paper. Label each reference according to each heading and its related colour.

4 Do the same with the second and third texts.

5 At the same time, as soon as you mark up your book, write down the page number under the appropriate heading on your A4 paper.

At this point you will have a headed index of all the pages related to your topic from your texts.

Read, select and reject

The next stage is to read through your colour-coded lists for each topic, first your central text and then the other texts. This time you should be selective: you will find some repetition and some labelled lines which are really not relevant or perhaps not necessary because you have better examples. Reject these by simply crossing out their page numbers from your list. Here is a model of what your notes will look like when you begin:

```
Central text    Page
Narr. vwpt:    6, 14, 30
Structure:     4, 20, 35
Time:          16, 50, 84
```

```
2nd text
Narr. vwpt:       Page
Structure:     36, 45, 60
Time:          20, 52, 78
               28, 34, 86
```

Next, mark up the actual lines of text you intend to use by highlighting the extract so that it stands out on the page. If you don't want to deface your book in this way, or if you have a library book, simply cut post-it notes into fingers and stick one on each appropriate page with the line references, or perhaps the first and last words of the extract.

Sequence your ideas

You have now, in a sense, emptied your knowledge out of your head and placed it on the three sheets of paper in front of you. You can see exactly what amount of material you have selected for use, so now you have to put the page references in sequence. To do this, first go through the pages with the highlighted text, and decide the running order of the selected material for each heading, writing down this sequence of page numbers. If you are going to use the central text to lead the discussion, read that first and match the other texts to that. If you are going to use the second or third text as the working basis for your sequence, write down those numbers first and match them to your central text.

This is how your final structure looks:

```
Structured plan

Central text              2nd text
Narr.vwpt: 6, 30          Narr.vwpt: 60, 36
Structure: 35, 4, 20      Structure: 78, 20
Time: 50, 84              Time: 34, 28
```

You will notice that the sequence for your essay need not match that of the books.

If you are using the same text for both essays, remember that you will have to use two different sets of colour coding and highlighting so that you can distinguish between the two essays at a glance.

Summary skills will help you when you record your research findings. The guidelines are straightforward:

- Note down only the main ideas; omit examples.
- Take care to distinguish between relevant and irrelevant material.
- Train yourself to distinguish between facts and opinions.
- When you finish a section of work, make sure you arrange the points in a logical sequence.

Practise summarising. Have a pencil beside you as you read and jot down in just a few words the main point of each paragraph, passage of dialogue or poem. Gradually increase the complexity of the texts you analyse, beginning with literary texts and moving on to works of critical and cultural commentary.

Write your first draft

You now have the skeleton of your working plan, but it is a cast-iron structure which takes all the confusion and frustration out of planning your essay. You simply develop your ideas for each area using the pages as you have sequenced them to write your draft. It will be a workmanlike affair since it is the ideas, the evidence and the sequence which matter. When you come to write your final draft, you can embellish your language and polish the presentation of your ideas (see Section E).

Activity 22

1 Discuss with a partner the most efficient way of organising your research material. Decide whether to follow the model outlined above, or to follow your own system, if you have one in place.

2 Draw up a rough outline plan of your essay and get feedback from your partner.

3 Organise your research so that you turn your rough outline plan into a working plan.

As you set out to write your first draft, remember to keep the word limits in mind (see p134 above). If you are writing an extended study, it might help to allocate a number of words to each section of your work. If your choice is two shorter studies, divide the word count into two; don't exceed this in the first essay or the second might suffer. If you opt for the creative writing with commentary, bear in mind that your commentary will gain most of your marks so don't exceed the 500–1000 words recommended; if you write a poem it can be shorter but your commentary will have to compensate so that you attain the word count.

You will, of course, have the chance to add or delete words when you come to revise your draft, but it is helpful to have an idea even at this stage of how close you are to the word limits.

Also remember to refer frequently to your texts in a relevant, focused way. Remind yourself of the mnemonic PEE:

Point

Evidence

Explanation/Exploration

When you have completed your draft, check you are on track by asking yourself these questions:

- Have I kept my focus all the way through?
- Have I made connections between my texts all the way through?
- Have I developed each point and supported them with references?
- Have I fulfilled every aspect of the topic?
- Is my argument clear and coherent?
- Is there anything I could have included to make my case stronger?
- Have I engaged fully with all of the assessment objectives?

Remember to include an introduction and a conclusion.

Introduction

Your introduction should set the scene for your study. In it you should:

- explain your title
- outline the texts you have chosen and why you chose them
- outline the area you have chosen for your study
- explain the way you have structured your research, why it is worth carrying out and what your goals are.

In the introduction you are setting up signposts for your reader which you will follow in the course of your study or commentary. Remember, you are writing for an audience that has a good level of understanding of your field of study.

Remember also that you have to interest your readers, your teacher and the moderator, who will have to read many studies apart from yours. You want to make sure that your introduction:

- is interesting – so that they will enjoy your writing
- is persuasive – so they see you have a clear grasp of your material
- displays a little individuality in the opening line (see the first lines of Proposals A and B on p137).

Activity 23

Draft an introduction to your study or commentary, then check through it with a partner. Does it cover all the relevant areas, and is it interesting?

Conclusion

Keep your conclusion short, simple and, above all, orderly. Never introduce new material. When you are writing your conclusion, you should:

- have your introduction in front of you and remind yourself of it
- summarise your goals
- assess how well your research structure worked
- explain what you discovered or proved
- include difficulties and how you overcame them in the commentary
- evaluate your findings and your success.

Writing your coursework

You should avoid presenting your essay in the first person: for example, using 'I intend to explore …' or 'my'. Formal academic essays should be presented in the third person as it is much more 'professional' for you to reflect upon the text, to stand back and make judgements. Your study should never be presented in a colloquial manner, which is too informal.

Independent research

The term modernism relates to the period between the 1910s and 1930s when authors such as Virginia Woolf and T. S. Eliot were writing. The modernists structured their work in a style that broke away from 19th century literary models to match a new way of viewing human experience. It is an interesting period and the writing and ideas are very accessible. Explore the concept of modernism using a book or the internet.

2 Writing a shorter study

Here is a reminder of the requirements for writing two shorter studies:

- Each study must refer to more than one text.
- The central text will be a literary text.
- Each study must also refer to at least one other text, which may be a work of critical reception or cultural context.
- You may decide to write two studies on the same central text.
- The same work of critical reception or cultural context may be drawn upon in both studies.
- Overall, at least three texts must be studied and referred to.

The following activity offers a case study of how a student approached the first draft of her first shorter study.

Activity 24

1 A student has prepared a title for the first of her two short studies, an outline plan and an introduction and a conclusion. Read these and discuss with a partner how well you think the student has addressed all the assessment objectives (see p127).

2 How effective do you think the introduction and conclusion of the essay are?

Title: Each new age has its own voice. How and why do writers experiment to create a new style for a new period?

Central text: Mrs Dalloway by Virginia Woolf
2nd text: Virginia Woolf's 'Mrs Dalloway': a study in alienation by J. Hawthorne
3rd text: The Modes of Modern Writing by D. Lodge

Outline plan:
Introduction
Narrative viewpoint
Structure
The handling of time
Conclusion

Introduction:

In this essay there will be an exploration of the ways in which Virginia Woolf created a new form for literature to match her contemporary age. Modernist readers rejected the earlier 19th century models of literature and their philosophies. They required a new mode for a new period. Addressing the novel Mrs Dalloway as a modernist novel invites consideration of three key areas. These are: the narrative viewpoint, and the relationship of the author to the protagonist, Clarissa Dalloway; the structure of the novel, which in some ways resembles a contemporary abstract painting; and the handling of time, which in some ways is the most striking of these areas.

Conclusion:

In this essay modernistic elements of Virginia Woolf's writing have been explored to show how she met the new demands of a new readership for a new age. Her innovations in the matters of narrative viewpoint, of structure, and above all in the handling of time are striking and effective. She well deserves her reputation as one of the leading modernist writers and the testimony to her genius lies in the universality of her appeal, that is to say, that her books remain relevant to all readers at all times.

3 Writing one extended study

The following activity offers a case study of how a student approached the first draft of an extended study.

Activity 25

1 Read the title and introduction of a student's extended study with a partner or in a small group.

> *Title:* The dark side of Shakespearean love: the presentation of love in *A Midsummer Night's Dream* and Sonnets 129–152
>
> *Texts:* *A Midsummer Night's Dream*
> Shakespeare's 'Dark Lady' Sonnets
> 'A Waste of Shame' by William Boyd (transcript of a BBC4 documentary)
>
> Towards the end of *A Midsummer Night's Dream,* Theseus says:
> > '*The lunatic, the lover and the poet*
> > *Are of imagination all compact*'.
>
> The focus of exploration in this study will be an exploration of the ways Shakespeare links love, lunacy and poetry in order to show that the experience of being in love can be dangerously deluding, a form of madness in fact, and terrifyingly destructive.
>
> 5 The study will be comparative. First Shakespeare's sequence of sonnets addressed to his 'dark lady' will be analysed and a comparison made between the impressions they give of love and the impressions of love given in the '*Dream*'. These impressions are quite unlike the romantic idea of love as a spiritual or rapturous experience, the highest emotion of which human beings are capable. Both the sonnets and the '*Dream*' present lovers caught up blindly in sexual passion which threatens both their
> 10 sanity and one another. Love, says the speaker in sonnet 129, is:
>
> > '*Past reason hunted, and no sooner had,*
> > *Past reason hated, as troubled bait*
> > *On purpose laid to make the taker mad*'.
>
> The lovers in the '*Dream*' are repeatedly likened to animals, and Bottom is actually
> 15 turned into one by the '*love juice*', leading him to say: '*Reason and love keep little company nowadays*.' This study will examine this theme of love mistaken for unreasoning lust and the feelings of revulsion and self-hate it leads to.
>
> There are two contexts for this study. The first is biographical. William Boyd's 2005
> 20 BBC documentary '*A Waste of Shame*' investigated the links between Shakespeare's life and the '*dark lady*' sonnets. References to this will lead to the suggestion that his presentation of love in the '*Dream*', written about the same time, may have been rooted in personal experience. This will obviously be speculative, but the evidence of the similar language used in both the poems and the play seems to be strong.
>
> The second context is theatrical. Since Peter Brook's landmark production of the
> 25 '*Dream*' for the Royal Shakespeare Company in 1969, theatre directors have often presented it as an anti-romantic play, putting the emphasis less on moonlight and fairies than on the dark passions which being '*wood [mad] within this wood*' brings out. References to the play's production history in the last 40 years will show how the '*Dream*' on stage can be seen to reflect modern life, in which love has
> 30 been devalued by TV and tabloid newspapers to the level of '*Sex in the City*' and '*Desperate Housewives*'.

2 Discuss how well this introduction presents the topic of the study and explains how it might be developed. You might talk about:

- the way the material is organised
- the use of paragraphs
- the balance between general statement and textual reference
- the voice and tone the writer assumes
- the writing style.

3 Share your responses in class discussion. Listen to your partner's views about the quality of this introduction and whether they would recommend it as a model for your own essays.

4 Refer back to the four assessment objectives (see p127). Decide whether:

- the study is already meeting these requirements
- the study seems likely to meet the requirements of each of them.

5 Make sure that your own essay plan incorporates material from the texts and the commentary in an orderly manner.

4 Addressing the assessment objectives

This sub-section will strengthen your skills in achieving the assessment objectives in analysis, comparison and commentary. It does not matter whether you know the texts or not, your skills will be sharpened. You can check how well you have done by measuring your achievements against your assessment criteria sheet.

Activity 26

1 Read the two extracts below carefully. They are from poems by two friends, the American Robert Frost and the English poet Edward Thomas, who died in World War I.

2 Make notes on the following:

- Look at what is common to the poems: a sense of loss, of the finite nature of life and relationships; look at how each ends their poem; decide who expresses the greater loss. (AO1)
- Compare the ways in which the poems are written. (AO2/3) Try to explain the contrast between the informality of Thomas and the formality of Frost.
- Compare the register, tone and use of imagery.
- Think about the viewpoints and the two very different perspectives. (AO3)
- Identify at least three contexts that could be related to this pairing. (AO4) Show where these become evident.

Extract A (from Edward Thomas' poem 'The Sun Used to Shine')

The sun used to shine while we two walked
Slowly together, paused and started
Again, and sometimes mused, sometimes talked
As either pleased, and cheerfully parted

5 Each night. We never disagreed
Which gate to rest on. The to be
And the late past we gave small heed.
We turned from men or poetry

To rumours of the war remote
10 Only till both stood disinclined
For aught but the yellow flaverous coat
Of an apple wasps had undermined;

…

(The poet continues to compare men fallen in war to fallen apples, while others still walk under the same sun and moon through other flowers.)

Extract B (from Robert Frost's poem 'To E.T.')

I slumbered with your poems on my breast,
Spread open as I dropped them half-read through
Like dove wings on a figure on a tomb,
To see if in a dream they brought of you

5 I might not have the chance I missed in life
Through some delay, and call you to your face
First soldier, and then poet, and then both,
Who died a soldier-poet of your race …

10 …

How over, though, for even me who knew
The foe thrust back unsafe beyond the Rhine,
If I was not to speak of it to you
And see you pleased once more with words of mine?

Key terms

• temporal

Take it further

Try to conceptualise the themes of Thomas' poem. To do this, view the text in abstract terms rather like a painting, perhaps through examining patterning, a sequence of images or overall meanings. This will allow you to assess abstract areas of thought which form the deeper themes of this poem: time and eternity, the frailty of human existence, the value of friendship in our brief lives. Try to work at this level of abstract thought alongside focusing on concrete details.

Checkpoint

By this stage you should have:

• developed a strategy for handling your research material

• planned your essay to include all your material

• become familiar with writing introductions and endings

• begun to write your first draft in readiness for presenting it to your peers.

Activity 27

1 Read through Extract C below at least twice. Relate the commentary to the two poems, using Thomas' poem as the central text. Follow these steps:

• Connect the comments to the poem by Thomas but, at every paragraph, also make a connection with the Frost poem, so that you are writing about all three texts at once: the two poems and the commentary.

• Go on to consider the difference in perspective of the two men, then the difference in your perspective, that of a modern reader.

• Decide which of the poems you find a) the most moving, and b) the most relevant to today. Give reasons for your choice.

2 Write an introduction to the two connected poems as if you had to introduce them to another group of students, and also write a conclusion. You should make it clear how you are going to interpret the themes, explain why they might still appeal to modern readers and outline ways in which they might relate to society as a whole.

3 Working as a group, read out your writing and discuss the strengths and weaknesses of individual cases.

Extract C (an extract from a work of critical commentary on Edward Thomas' poem 'The Sun Used to Shine')

This poem commemorates Edward Thomas' friendship with Robert Frost when the American was living in England between 1912 and 1914. Thomas skilfully unites formal rhymed stanzas with flexible rhythm. The poem consists of only seven sentences, all of them enjambed across
5 stanzas, and the balance of short and long sentences creates the sense of a voice speaking, pausing for reflection then developing an idea in an apparently improvised way. You can see this through hesitations and repetition at the start of the poem. The tone is relaxed and intimate, but never slack or loose in its expression.
10

The imagery draws on light and darkness, sun and moon establishing a *temporal* perspective with WW1 seeming far away, but which would soon become very real to Thomas. Time and space are bridged by friends' talk which ranges from minute observations on the natural world to ideas of life, death and eternity. The human mind can hold so
15 many things in solution.

There is a dark ending to the poem as, with hindsight, the poem becomes a dark prophecy of the sad events that would bring the friendship of these two poets to an end rather than a pause; yet thanks to the poem, the friendship still survives.

Activity 28

1 Write the first draft of your own essay, whether it is a shorter or an extended study.

2 Check it against all of the points made in this section, and against the assessment criteria.

3 Work with a partner exploring your responses to each of the assessment objectives. What level do you think you have achieved?

4 If you have fallen short of your target level, then try to develop your response so that it moves higher.

D Writing your creative response and commentary

This section will help you to plan and write your creative response and commentary.

Your Advanced Level coursework tests how you respond critically to the texts you have selected. Instead of presenting your findings in the form of a literary study or studies (see Section C), you could decide to write a creative critical response which will illuminate your central text and illustrate your ideas. Your commentary will make connections between your creative piece, your texts and your research.

The total word count should be between 2500 and 3000 words. Your commentary will carry most of the marks.

Remember to refer to the assessment objectives grid on page 127.

You will now have a head full of knowledge and ideas about your central text and your other two texts. You will also have a working focus for your creative response and commentary. Where do you go from here? How do you turn this chaos into some sort of order?

Both your creative response and your commentary need to show evidence of your exploration of, and reflection on, the central text and the connections between texts. It makes sense, therefore, to organise your reading and research notes under the following headings:

- Audience
- Tone
- Contexts, including reception
- Register
- Genre and literary conventions
- Connections between texts.

These headings will be useful when you come to write your commentary. However, it is also important to focus your research findings in this way as a preparation for writing your creative response.

Your next task is to write a first draft of your creative response; then you will discuss how and why you have written it in your commentary.

Activity 29

Organise your reading and research notes under the key headings as described above.

Across AS and A2

In all of your earlier units you have studied how to respond critically to texts. In Unit 2, for example, you explored how to write a creative critical response to a selected play. In Unit 4 the task is more complex because you will actively involve yourself in reworking a text to demonstrate your critical findings.

Assessment objectives

Your creative response and commentary are marked against all four assessment objectives. Most of the AOs relate to your critical understanding; as a guide to the marking, the commentary will be awarded about 75% of the marks and your creative response about 25%. Use this as a guide to the number of words you produce for each piece of work.

1   Writing your creative response

In Section B you explored how to read a text critically. This will provide a foundation for your exploration or exploitation of your central text. You do not have to agree with the author's reading of their own text, their purposes in writing it and the readership they have assumed for it.

Textual intervention

To begin, it is helpful to distance yourself from your text, to stand back and ask a series of questions, such as:

- Why has the author made the decisions which determined the outcomes?
- What would have happened if different choices had been made?
- What sort of sequences might have followed certain changes?
- How might such changes affect the reader's or audience's response?

The point of this exercise is to help you to get into the mind of an author. You will find that you have a fresh understanding of their purposes and means, so you will be well placed to offer a creative response to the writing.

In other words, you are examining the text to see where you might intervene to explore the author's decisions. The following diagram will make this point clear.

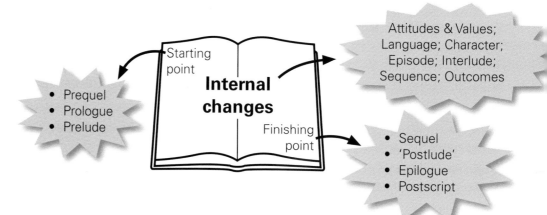

Key term

- textual intervention

Textual intervention means altering the text by making additions or changes to the original. Just as essay writers explore a text through analysis, you can explore a text by actually getting inside it. You will find that this process gives you some understanding of the challenges the writer faced and the issues of the text will become clearer to you.

As you can see from the diagram above, you can intervene before the author's actual starting point, or after their finishing point, as well as during the development of the text. By intervening, you are aiming to throw the text off-balance in some way and altering the ways in which a reader might respond; for example, a prequel or sequel (or the equivalents in drama and poetry) creates additional contexts which could influence this response. Earlier in your studies you may have looked at *The Wide Sargasso Sea* by Jean Rhys, which creates some sympathy for Rochester's wife, who is presented as mad in *Jane Eyre*. Rhys changes the reader's reception of the novel by redistributing sympathy towards this woman.

In Ian McEwan's novel *Enduring Love* the central character, Joe, tells a disturbing story about the desperate effects on his life of being stalked by a madman, Jed Parry. Jed is convicted for his pursuit of Joe and the novel apparently ends. But McEwan offers a series of documents after the plot has concluded. These 'postscripts' include a technical definition of de Clérambault's syndrome (a psychological condition or obsession caused by unrequited love), a psychiatrist's report and love letters Jed has written to Joe.

Activity 30

Discuss these questions:

- How would you feel if you were to come across documents like these when you think that the text is finished?
- What effects might they have on the way you respond to the manic Jed?
- Do you think that your perspectives on characters and events would have been altered in some way? If so, how?

Take it further

Take a familiar myth or Bible story which will inevitably be presented from the male viewpoint. Rewrite it in just 200 words to change the critical perspective to a feminist or maybe a Marxist reading (see p151).

There are many ways in which our responses to texts may be modified. Many of Keats's odes are derived from Greek myth as are some of Carol Ann Duffy's monologues in *The World's Wife*, which draws upon biblical characters as well. The reader is forced to rethink and re-evaluate the originals and the more modern versions enlarge and adjust our responses to these mythical characters. They become more relevant and more complex to a modern reader. For example, everybody who knows the biblical story thinks of Delilah as the evil woman who destroyed noble Samson. By giving the account a feminist twist, Duffy forces the reader to stand back and think about other perspectives which have never been considered. But, more than this, the reader begins to wonder whether, as Duffy suggests, the whole collection is male-dominated in every way.

Always read beyond and outside your text as you prepare for this work and remember the many choices made by the author (and other readers). When you open your text there have already been interventions: the writer and editors will have made changes; reviewers will have created certain new contexts for it. You are only the most recent reader to intervene.

Here are some possible routes for textual intervention:

- Look for holes and gaps in texts.
- Think about silent or invisible participants.
- Re-centre the text by changing the point of view, outcomes or sequences of events.
- Shift power balances.
- Transform the genre.
- Write an imitation by responding to one author through the voice of another.
- Write a **pastiche** through imitation of one or of a combination of different authors.
- Write a parody on style or content.
- Write a satire based on the original.
- Bring together different genres such as in Stephen King's *Duma Key* and Ian McEwan's *Enduring Love* or create a collage around a text.
- Change perspectives: retell for a different audience or different period.
- Use one of the critical approaches to transform your text; you may rewrite an extract as a Marxist or feminist, which will alter the values and viewpoints of a text.

Key terms

- pastiche

Textual intervention can be immensely enjoyable. Remember, though, that your purpose is serious: to understand more about your chosen writer(s) and so make more informed judgements. Your purpose is also to illuminate connections and comparisons between texts, so from the very start you need to have all your chosen texts in mind (see Part 2 below).

Independent research

Read this introduction for yourself, as it will generate ideas for you. Make notes on the way Angela Carter worked.

Practising textual intervention

One way of practising this is to choose a fairytale, as Angela Carter did in *The Bloody Chamber*. In the introduction to this text she explained how she worked:

1 She took the narrative base from western European fairytales, and told them afresh.

2 She changed the targeted readership for these texts by writing for a different audience. Since submerged meanings are usually violently sexual, what once were bedtime stories for children became adult tales of sex and violence.

3 She created dialogue and action which were neither naturalistic nor realistic so the reader was distanced from the text.

4 She used emblems: raven's feathers; bloodstains; moonlight; snow. Many were Gothic elements which she combined with a striking pattern of strong colours such as red and white, black and green.

Activity 31

1 Choose a fairytale of your own and write a short version of it, about 200–300 words.

2 Compare your results with a partner's. How have you each intervened in the text?

Activity 32

You can intervene effectively in any genre; here is an example using poetry.

1 Read the poem below carefully. It is 'In Church', one of Thomas Hardy's *Satires of Circumstance*. As a class discuss your first response to the poem.

> 'And now to God the Father,' he ends,
> And his voice thrills up to the topmost tiles:
> Each listener chokes as he bows and bends,
> And emotion pervades the crowded aisles.
> 5 Then the preacher glides to the vestry-door,
> And shuts it, and thinks he is seen no more.
>
> The door swings softly ajar meanwhile,
> And a pupil of his in the Bible class,
> Who adores him as one without gloss or guile,
> 10 Sees her idol stand with a satisfied smile
> And re-enact at the vestry-glass
> Each pulpit gesture in deft dumb-show
> That had moved the congregation so.

2 Now consider how you might bring about changes in one of the five ways outlined below. Divide into five small groups and each work up one of these changed perspectives on Hardy's poem.

3 Share your responses and talk about the effectiveness of each. What light do the changes throw on the original text?

A
Change your response to the central character by changing some of the words. What are the value words which help to determine your response; for example, what might be the effect of changing 'satisfied' to 'saddened'? There are many similarly loaded words in this poem; can you identify them and suggest changes?

B
Change the perspective on the clergyman. Who is speaking? Is it a reliable observer, or someone with a grudge? What might happen if one of the 'listeners', the silent participants, were to present a portrait? What might happen if the pupil were to describe this incident? Or a devoted member of the congregation?

C
Change the viewpoint by giving other non-visible characters a voice, such as the organist, who knows the man well, or perhaps his wife, or his bishop?

D
Change the genre of this poem. You might write an experimental play or a short story.

E
Change the starting point or ending point of the poem. What if the clergyman had been accused of failing to make his listeners respond? What if he were preparing to introduce a younger cleric to the art of making a sermon?

Independent research

If you are studying a drama text, work up a short piece including yourself as one of the characters. What interactions might be created?

Sometimes you can intervene by entering a 'hole' in the text. Think about Emily Bronte's *Wuthering Heights*. In the middle of the novel Heathcliff disappears and makes his fortune. The reader is not informed of where he goes or how he does it; this is a 'gap' or 'hole' in the text which you might use for a creative response.

In drama similarly there are silent characters; think of the young grooms who were drugged and killed by Lady Macbeth or Macduff's young children, who were murdered. What effects might be created if they were to be given voices? How would you respond to the character Macbeth if you were to overhear a triumphant conversation among the witches?

Activity 33

Think carefully about your central text to see if there are similar holes or silent or invisible characters or speakers: is there an opportunity for intervention there?

You could also change the hierarchy of power among the characters. What if you were to shift the power from, say, Hamlet to Ophelia? In the TV drama *Lost in Austen* Amanda Price, a fan of Jane Austen's writing, was transported back in time and had a glorious experience interacting with the characters of *Pride and Prejudice*. This almost wrecked the original plot, but some serious questions were asked about the comparison between attitudes and values in contemporary 21st century society and those of the early 19th century.

Independent research

You might include a **humument** in your creative response. Go to http://humument. com and explore this modem form a poetry.

Key terms

• courtly love

• humument

Activity 34

Work with a partner to manipulate the structure of your central text. Take the key points of your text: the beginning, middle and end. What would happen if you were to change the situations at any of these important stages? What sort of sequence would develop? Take 15 minutes and chart a new route for your text as a result of such a change.

You can alter the whole scheme of values in a text by some modification. What might be the effects of suggesting that Iago's actions in *Othello* were triggered by Venetian suspicion of a powerful and popular black man in their midst? Or if the Wife of Bath were actually a serial killer who enriched herself at the expense of her dim-but-wealthy husbands?

The use of parody can create entertaining effects by presenting a collision between two different writers' voices.

Activity 35

Imagine that one student paired *The Big Sleep* by Raymond Chandler, the great detective fiction writer of the 'New Wave' writers of the American late 1930s and 40s, with Sir Philip Sidney's 16th century lyrical poetry.

1 Read the proposal and extract from the creative response below.

2 Discuss these questions in groups:

- How well does the creative response achieve the aims set out in the student's proposal?
- How are the concerns of the texts both different and similar?
- How does this collision of styles heighten your awareness of the ways each writer creates effects?

Central text: *The Big Sleep* by Raymond Chandler
2ⁿᵈ text: *Astrophil and Stella*, a sonnets sequence by Sir Philip Sidney
3ʳᵈ text: *The Critical Response to Raymond Chandler*, ed. J. K. Van Dover

Proposal:

I chose *The Big Sleep* as my central text as I am interested in the way Raymond Chandler uses the detective fiction genre. Although there are crimes to be solved, Chandler's submerged theme is far more profound than this.

5 On the first page of the text Private Investigator Philip Marlowe describes a stained glass panel depicting a knight trying to save a damsel in distress. As there are more references to a knight later, I realised that Chandler was presenting the idea that a chivalrous code of conduct was out-of-date in his contemporary American society.

Through a computer search I discovered the concept of **courtly love** and learned that there were still remnants of this tradition in English lyrical poetry of the 16th century.

10 I decided to read Sir Philip Sidney's sonnets *Astrophil and Stella* as my second text.

The focus of my study will centre on the contrasts of attitudes and values in American society of the 20th century and English society of the 16th century. I intend to present a collision between the two historical periods which is bound to create some sparks.

15 Therefore I decided to adopt a 'sparky' style as well. Writing in the form of parody I will imagine that the two 'knights' have been able to communicate with each other across time and space. Philip Marlowe, hard-bitten and worldly wise, will offer advice on the topic of love to Sir Philip Sidney.

Sidney's sonnets will form an ongoing exchange with Marlowe, who will reply in his typical manner.

The materials below represent an extract from the student's folder of work.

Creative writing

Brothers-in-Arms: How to Handle Love
To Sire Philip Marlowe

Astrophil and Stella: XXI

Your words, my friend, right healthful caustics, blame
        My young mind marred, whom love doth windlass so
        That mine own writings like bad servants show,
My wits, quick in vain thoughts, in virtue lame;
5   That Plato I read for nought, but if he tame
        Such coltish gyres; that to my birth I owe
        Nobler desires, lest else that friendly foe,
Great expectation, wear a train of shame.
        For since mad March great promise made of me,
10 If now the May of my years much decline,
What can be hoped my harvest time will be?
Sure you say well: your wisdom's golden mine
        Dig deep with learning's spade; now tell me this,
        Hath this world aught so fair as Stella is?

To Sir Philip Sidney

Hey, brother, sure can help you here; I do lotsa research – specially in the apartments of tall blondes. You Brits, you're not the best writers in the world but you're sure the best dull writers! That ole knightly thing's ok, but when you need to do something you just gotta do it, and to hell with all the fine words.

5   What's all this fuss about? Is she a classy broad? From thirty feet away does she look like class, or at ten feet do you wish it was thirty? So this is your chat-up style? You won't draw her to tears, buddy, you'll bore her to tears. On and on you go and everyone knows, pal, that when a man talks all technique he's clean out of ideas. Love's like alcohol. The first kiss is magic, by the third it's routine! After
10 that – get the dame's clothes off!

Get yourself some great gear – not that frill round your neck, a pair of roly-poly pants and those … those … gal's tights. Downtown in a bar you'd look as outa place as a tarantula on a slice of angel cake.

You gotta get some action goin'. This courtly love game, pal, is just like chess. The
15 most damned waste of intelligence outside an advertising agency. Think god invented it on a wet Sunday night. Take a slug or six; cut to her room; have a guy with a gun tear through the door. She'll grab you then.

Wouldya believe me? Well, you gotta! A poet's like a P.I. – don't get married – get a life instead! Remember, pal, a dead man weighs heavier than a broken heart and
20 you ain't got that much time left before the Big Sleep!   Marlowe

---

Activity 36

Write a first draft of your own creative response. As you do this, you will be thinking about how your writing connects to the texts you have read. Jot down your notes and ideas, as it will be important to include these in your commentary.

2 Writing your commentary

Assessment objectives

You will be assessed for all of the assessment objectives in your commentary. As you write, keep checking your work to make sure that you have addressed all the AOs with appropriate emphasis on each.

The purpose of the commentary is to explore the links between your reading and research and the creative response you have written. Since you began your research you will have been making notes to be incorporated into your commentary. You will need your plan and notes in front of you when you begin to write up the first draft of your commentary.

Here is one model which might help when you begin to write.

---

1 **Start with a statement about your own research area**
Your opening statement should set the scene for your commentary by:

- introducing your subject area
- explaining how you arrived at this choice
- introducing the texts you studied and why you chose them
- describing briefly the different areas of research you have undertaken (critical reading and contextual studies)
- explaining why you carried out this research and what you hoped to discover.

2 **Discuss your creative response**
Explain the preparations you made and what you tried to do, for example:

- how you prepared yourself to write creatively
- how you chose to formulate your creative response
- what you hoped to achieve in your writing.

Remember to show your awareness of audience, register, tone, genre and literary conventions and contexts (including reception).

Explain the web of connections between your four texts: the central text, the second and third texts and your creative writing.

3 **Evaluate your outcomes**
Think about what you have discovered from this research, including:

- how successful your research was
- how successful your creative writing was
- the challenges you faced along the way.

Activity 37

1 Read the extract from the commentary on the Sidney/Marlowe proposal below.

2 Working as a class, assess how well the commentary below and on the next page explores the links between the student's reading and research and the creative piece. How well does it show awareness of:

- audience
- register
- tone
- genre and literary conventions
- contexts
- connections between the three texts and the creative piece?

Key term

• sestet

Commentary

I realised as I read *The Big Sleep* that this was more than a straightforward detective novel; on the opening page Chandler presents an image which is surely intended to stay on the reader's mind. A stained glass panel depicts a knight trying to help a damsel in distress, and Marlowe comments 'I would sooner or later have
5 to climb up there and help him'. (p9) To emphasise his point, Chandler presents the reader with a second set of images when Marlowe returns to his apartment later on. His chessboard shows a 'knight's problem' to solve. (p150/1) When this motif is combined with Marlowe's first and last interviews with the General, it becomes clear that the knight was a sort of forerunner of the hard-boiled private investigator,
10 but Marlowe's ironical tone suggests that the chivalric code is hopelessly out of date in this seedy, greedy, lawless contemporary society. I included a reference to the chess game in my own piece. I thought that this reading made a good link between my two correspondents who were indeed 'brothers in arms'.

This clarified my route to the second text; after discovering the concept of courtly
15 love during a computer search, and reading that English lyricists of the 16th century represented the remnants of this tradition, I opted for Sir Philip Sidney's *Astrophil and Stella* sonnets. Amused by the contrast in tone in the literature of two hugely different historical periods, I decided to capitalise on this and play on this collision of contexts, with their different attitudes and values. Wanting an
20 equally startling style, I decided to write a parody based on exchanges between the two knights on the topic of love.

Courtly love conventions were evident in the sonnet; the almost religious worship of the woman ('has this world aught ... '), the hopelessness of the quest in the **sestet** and the ritualistic complaining all the way through. Against this I pitched Marlowe's cynical
25 tone and apparently cynical attitudes, as in the second paragraph of my writing. The contrast in attitudes and values is apparent in the clash between Sidney's idealisation of the woman, whilst Marlowe's views are not exactly misogynistic, but are definitely anti-Romance.

Aiming to emulate Chandler's style, my Marlowe echoes the witty comments he makes
30 throughout *The Big Sleep*: the references to the classy broad, to love and to alcohol, and the use of wildly oddly structured similes, 'you'd look as outa place as a tarantula on a slice of angel cake'.

Take it further

The 'submerged' theme which addresses knightly behaviour lies deep in the heart of the text. It is far below the level of plot and the literary conventions of detective fiction. To explore a text in this way is to work conceptually, to winkle out the root concept behind the text. You would find a variety of firm links based on this. Check your own notes. Have you managed to find the conceptual level? When you have, write some additional notes for your study.

35 My third text opened up many interesting ideas about the different interpretations of *The Big Sleep*. After studying this text I realised that it was the gap between the idealistic, perhaps knightly code that Marlowe holds and the tawdry reality he confronts that results in his amazing metaphors. Carmen has 'teeth ... as shiny as porcelain'. (p 4)

However, images like this are not there as decoration for they serve a serious purpose.

40 P. I. Philip Marlowe is at heart a principled man, evident in his concern over the four females in the text. A man-to-man respect for heroism is also obvious when he tells the reader that he respects Harry Jones for taking poison rather than putting his woman's life in danger, 'you died like a rat but you're no rat to me.' (p 173)

I wanted to emphasise the different audiences for whom these texts were written.
45 Sidney's sonnet is obviously very learned and refers to his reading Plato; he obviously expects his readers to be on the same wavelength. Chandler, on the other hand, wrote for his contemporary audience in the L.A. of the 1930s. But strangely enough his way of writing is very complicated. He doesn't offer a straight detective story, but hides the purpose of his writing at a fairly submerged level. He refers to
50 classical and to contemporary authors, expects his readers to be able to play chess and pick up the medieval references. In fact he writes for an equally educated and intelligent readership as Sidney; I did not expect to discover that.

If I were to sum up my findings I would say that whilst I have hugely enjoyed this exercise, I have started to think about how attitudes and values change; I
55 now realise that it is up to each one of us, just like P. I. Marlowe, to make sure that our principles remain intact. I will stress the point that both Sir Philip Sidney and Marlowe make: we should all do our best because we don't have that much time left before our own *Big Sleep*.

Activity 38

1 Write the first draft of your own commentary.

2 Check it against all of the points made in this section and against the assessment criteria.

3 Working with a partner, exploring your responses to each of the assessment objectives. What level do you think you have achieved?

4 If you have fallen short of your target level, try to develop your work so that it moves higher.

5 Remember your running word total. Never make a cut without checking that it would not weaken your address of an assessment objective. Similarly, if you are running short, add the extra words to areas where you think the address of an assessment objective might be thin.

Checkpoint

By this stage you should have:

- organised your research material
- chosen your approach to the creative response
- written the first draft of your creative response and commentary to present to your peers.

E   Revising and editing your work

In this section you will explore how to revise and edit your coursework. You will consider the areas that should be checked and how to present your work for submission.

Resist the temptation to 'down tools' when you have completed your first draft. The revision process is extremely important, as it allows you the opportunity to make changes and corrections, and therefore to improve your work. All writers make changes to their work; this process of revision is hidden by the fact that the reader usually only sees the final, polished version.

Before you submit your first draft to the peer review process, do a final check:

All three options

- Check that you really have addressed all of the assessment objectives and that you have paid equal attention to each.
- Check your word count. Remember the moderator will stop reading your study once you reach 3000 words and you will be marked on what you have written up to that point. So don't go over the limit. If you have not reached the minimum limit, your work will be weaker than it might be. (Quotations are included in the word count, but the references, bibliography and appendix are not.)

The study or studies

- If you are writing two shorter studies, you should have allowed half of the total words for each study. You should also have divided the assessment objectives between the two essays.
- Make sure that you have maintained focus all the way through, and that the quality of your argument remains constant.

The creative response with commentary

- The commentary gains you more marks. Check that you have addressed all of the assessment objectives in your commentary and that you have linked your creative response to your reading and research.
- Remember that the word limit of 3000 words is for both the creative writing and the commentary.

Key term

• plagiarism

Activity 39

When you have finished the first full draft of your study or creative response and commentary, you should present it to your peer group for serious and helpful criticism. During the discussion that follows, be ready to listen and to respond when necessary.

1 Approach this experience in a positive frame of mind; your friends and colleagues are there to support you in your efforts. Therefore, whilst being pleased by praise, do not be unwilling to listen to and to act upon advice, and do not deny points made if it is just criticism.

2 Hear what is being said in an objective, academic way.

3 Listen carefully to the points being made. What is the general view of your study and your standard?

4 Where strengths are noted, is there anything which you could improve on?

5 Are any negative responses valid? Can you refute them or do you need to make some changes?

Now read through your draft and ask yourself your own review questions:

• Have I covered all the assessment objectives?

• Can I rephrase arguments here and there to make them more crisp?

• Is my study or commentary fully on focus? Where are there areas of irrelevance? Can I pull it back into focus?

• Can I add a little crispness to my language? For example, can my introduction be a little livelier? Or my conclusion a little more impressive? (Take this opportunity to embellish your language a little.)

• Is the register always appropriate to A2 study?

• Can I improve the quality of my language? For example, can I delete any unnecessary words which often include adjectives, adverbs and connectives? (Your language needs to be taut and on target, and to avoid sloppiness or uncertainty.)

• Have I used quotations to support my points, and supported each quotation with a comment?

• Have I acknowledged the work of other writers when I quote them directly or refer to them? (If you do not, then you could be open to a charge of *plagiarism*.)

• Are all my quotations correct in every detail and presented correctly?

Activity 40

As you read your draft and answer these questions, make the necessary changes to your work. Incorporate any changes that you have decided to make as a result of the peer review. Take pride in this process. You are polishing your coursework so that it can shine in its final form.

It is also important to go through the sources you have named in your study or commentary. Make sure that these are genuine and that the details which you have given about them are accurate. If you think that any source is unreliable because you cannot trace the author or a particular publication, do not use it. It is possible that the moderator will check these.

How to make references to the work of others

There are three main methods of making reference to the work of others in the body of your investigation, depending on the circumstances. If you are referring to the author by name, put the date of the publication in brackets after the name, for example:

> Willmott (1990) says that Blake was a man of his times.

Where the author is not named, put the author's name and date at a suitable point in the section, for example:

> In *Songs of Innocence* Blake attacks the abuses which oppress the human spirit (Willmott 1990).

If you are including something from published work in your report, you must put the quoted section in speech marks and, if it is several lines long, separate it from your own text by indentation. Acknowledge the quotation and give a page number so that a reader of your work can trace the quote directly.

> Discussing Blake's use of imagery, Willmott (1990) says:
>
> 'The sparkling of the *stars* perhaps links them with spears and then tears (17–18), which can also sparkle in the light.'

Your bibliography should contain the main texts you read in the course of your research. It doesn't need to be very long: two or three books may be sufficient in many cases.

Include in your list any books or articles you have referred to in the course of your research which have given you ideas or influenced your opinions. All items should be listed in alphabetical order by the author's surname.

The lists below outline the information required for references to books, chapters in books and journals, and some styling conventions.

Books
Author(s) surname(s) and initials
Year of publication of the edition used
Full title of the book in italics
Edition of the book
Place of publication
Publisher

Example with one author:
Hall D, 1992, *To Read Literature*, 3rd edition, London: Cengage Learning, Thomson Learning

Example with two authors:
Lakof G and Turner M, 1989, *More Than Cool Reason: A Field Guide to Poetic Metaphor* (1), Chicago: University of Chicago
Example with more than two authors:
Grabber G, et al, 1998, *The Emily Dickinson Handbook* (1), Amherst: University of Massachusetts

Chapters of edited books

Chapter author(s) surname(s) and initials
Year of publication of the chapter
Title of the chapter in quotation marks
'in' + first initial and surname of editor + 'ed.'
Title of the book in italics
Edition of the book
Page numbers of chapter
Place and date of publication
Publisher

Example:

Edwards G, 1982, 'Repeating the Same Dull Round' in D Punter, ed. *William Blake, New Casebooks* (1), pp 108–123, London, 1996: Macmillan

Journals

Article author(s) surname(s) and initials
Year of publication of the article
Title of the article in quotation marks
'in' + first initial and surname of editor + 'ed.'
Name of the journal in italics
Volume number in bold
Issue number in brackets
First and last page numbers
Place of publication
Publisher

Example:

Davidson A E, 1981, 'The Concluding Moral in Coleridge's *The Rime of the Ancient Mariner*' in B Snider, ed. *Philological* Quarterly **60** (2) pp 90–99, Iowa State: University of Iowa

Remember to number the pages and include a running word count at the bottom of each page. Your study should also include a contents page and a title page, including the word count, such as the one below:

An exploration into how the advent of Marxist criticism has altered the definition of what may be considered as 'good' literature

By

James Foxwell

2950 words

The final step is to proofread your work. It is easier to proofread when the work is printed out in front of you on a desk or table than on a screen. Ask a friend or family member to carry out the proofing with you, because you know your own work and might skim. It is also helpful to place a ruler or sheet of paper below each line to ensure that you are reading each word on every line.

Proofreading is a mechanical process but an important one. It would be annoying and disappointing to lose marks for something relatively straightforward.

There are some common errors that would spoil the presentation of your work so it is worth checking these points. They include:

Common misspellings, such as 'there'/'their'

Beginning sentences with 'And'

Failing to include a verb in each sentence

Repeating similar points and similar words

Using the 'and then' sequence

Muddling the numbering

Failing to use a dictionary to check awkward, difficult or technical words

Misspelling the names of authors or books

Inaccuracy in using quotations or in the bibliographical details

Activity 41

Proofread your study. Make sure that you have presented your work accurately and that the technical details are all correct.

Checkpoint

By this stage you should have:

- completed all the editorial processes
- satisfied yourself that you cannot make any further improvements
- handed in your coursework
- congratulated yourself on a job well done!

Glossary of key terms

Alliteration [page 16]
a sequence of repeating consonantal sounds in a stretch of text

Assonance [page 11]
the correspondence, or near correspondence, in two words of the stressed vowel and sometimes those that follow

Authorial comment [page 25]
an opinion addressed directly by a writer to the reader, intended to guide the reader's response

Autobiographical fiction [page 45]
a narrative which takes the form of a character's life-story, told in the 1st person

Ballad [page 17]
a poem that tells a story or describes a series of events, originally sung by a strolling minstrel

Bathos [page 39]
anti-climax used for effect in a text, e.g. 'Shadwell alone of all my sons is he / Who stands confirmed in full stupidity' (John Dryden) – a device typically used to satirise a character

Broad comedy [page 85]
a type of comedy which is down-to-earth, involving elements of farce such as physical humour and bawdy jokes

Characterisation [page 30]
the description of the distinctive qualities that a character possesses

Clichéd language [page 105]
language which has become so familiar by use that it has lost its original impact, e.g. 'as white as a sheet', 'an awesome achievement'

Closed question [page 153]
a form of question which allows for a limited number of answers, often just Yes or No

Colloquial language [page 25]
the kinds of expressions and grammar associated with ordinary, everyday language

Conceit [page 70]
an elaborate comparison in which disparate ideas are related together, typically found in metaphysical poetry

Connotation [page 11]
the ideas, feelings or associations that a word suggests in addition to its primary, literal meaning

Consonance [page 11]
the repetition of similar consonant sounds for effect in a sequence of words

Context of production [page 87]
the factors that influence the writing of a text, e.g. social, historical, literary, biographical

Context of reception [page 87]
the factors that influence the way a text is responded to and interpreted by readers

Courtly love [page 170]
a conception of love developed in France in the 12th century and modelled on the relationship between a feudal lord and his follower. Such ever-increasing love, which is never marital, has the quality of a religious passion

Deconstructionist [page 151]
approach to literary criticism which seeks to demonstrate that a text has failed to reflect the author's intentions due to the nature of language

Dialectical [page 150]
the method of reasoning developed by the 19th-century German philosopher G.W.F. Hegel in which thesis combined with antithesis to form a new synthesis

Dialogue [page 24]
a conversation between two or more people

Diction [page 7]
the language a writer gives to a character; the choice of words in a literary text, also sometimes called lexis or vocabulary

Direct speech [page 7]
the exact words uttered by a speaker, presented within quotation marks

Dramatic monologue [page 20]
a poem in which a fictional character addresses the reader directly in his/her own voice, without authorial comment

Enjambement [page 12]
an effect in poetry caused when a line is not end-stopped, but the sentence continues to the next line without a grammatical pause or stop.

Extended metaphor [page 12]
a comparison or image which is developed over several lines in a poem or over several sentences in a narrative

Feminist criticism [page 102]
literary criticism from a feminist viewpoint, focusing on female experience and showing how literature from the past foregrounded male attitudes

Figurative language [page 26]
words that are not being used literally in the text, such as in metaphors or similes, often suggesting a comparison between two things

First-person voice / first-person viewpoint [page 33]
a device for telling a story which uses the 'I' and 'we' form of address to the reader; a story told from the standpoint of a character in the text

Focaliser [page 110]
a character through whose eyes events in the narrative are predominantly viewed. There can be different focalisers at different points, or the same throughout

Form [page 7]
the shape of the poem on the page

Free indirect style [page 33]
the term used when the text mixes elements of the third person report of indirect speech with first person direct speech, allowing the author to be free with the phrasing and to create ambiguity or a colloquial feel for literary effect

Free verse [page 17]
poetry that does not use traditional rhyme schemes or metrical arrangements

Gender-based (feminist) [page 151]
approach to literary criticism based on the belief that society is determined by patriarchal (i.e. male) principles

Genre [page 19]
a type of writing with its own characteristic form and style

Genre convention [page 46]
a literary device typical of a particular genre, e.g. the use of suspense in a crime thriller, the death of the hero in tragedy

Graphology [page 46]
The study of the visual aspects of a text

Hegel [page 150]
an influential German philosopher who formulated the idea of the dialectic as a means of historical progress. In this dialectic, factor A combines with factor B to formulate the new condition of C. His most famous work is probably The Phenomonolgy of the Spirit

Humument [page 170]
a humument is a form of poetry derived from Tom Phillip's work in art. Students take individual lines from a text and place them together to create a fresh text which somehow illuminates the original

Hyperbole [page 39]
exaggeration used for effect in a text, e.g. 'A man so various that he seemed to be / Not one, but all mankind's epitome' (John Dryden) – a device typically used to satirise a character

Iambic pentameter [page 18]
a poetic rhythm with five strong and five weak beats to the line: di Dum/ di Dum/ di Dum/ di Dum/ di Dum

Ideological [page 150]
resting upon or referring to a political theory or system

Idiolect [page 32]
the term for an individual's language or speech pattern

Idiom [page 25]
a colloquial or slang expression

Idiomatic language [page 25]
language characterised by colloquial or slang expressions

Imagery [page 7]
the use of descriptive language, including figures of speech, that draws a mental picture or conveys a sensation; a comparison to describe something through simile, metaphor or personification

Incongruity [page 39]
a deliberate mismatch between two ideas, typically used by writers to amuse or shock the reader

Inferences [page 137]
conclusions derived from observations

Irony [page 38]
language that says one thing but means another

Jargon [page 20]
words or expressions specific to particular subjects, often precise, complex and difficult to understand

Juxtaposed [page 112]
set next to each other, for literary effect

Legend [page 99]
a story from the past which has developed proverbial status through re-telling

Literary canon [page 128]
a body of approved works which consists of the works of a given author and/or the best examples of a specific literary tradition

Lyric [page 17]
a short poem or song written in the first person expressing a particular emotion or sentiment

Magic realism [page 105]
a narrative technique where non-realistic events are described in a realistic way

Marxist criticism [page 102]
literary criticism from a Marxist viewpoint, based on the idea that all human behaviour is shaped by social and historical forces and can be interpreted by reference to them

Metaphor [page 7]
a figure of speech in which an object, person or thing is described in terms of another, without using 'as' or 'like', to suggest a comparison or relationship between the two

Metonymy [page 112]
the use of one particular attribute to describe something in general, e.g. 'the crown' to describe royalty; the use of one attribute as shorthand to describe a character in general, e.g. 'he was all mouth and no action'

Metre [page 17]
the dominant pattern of stressed and unstressed syllables that give rhythm to a poem

Middle English [page 80]
English language and literature from medieval times, i.e. between the 5th and the 15th centuries

Modality [page 112]
the manner of a piece of writing; the use of a literary technique or convention in a text

Modernist (modernism) [page 133]
originally the works of authors writing between 1910 and 1930 in reaction to the conventions of 19th-century literature. The category has been extended to include works of their followers

Mood [page 19]
a predominant emotion, atmosphere or frame of mind in a composition created through a writer's use of tone

Moral fable [page 105]
a story told in order to convey a message, typically concerning the differences between virtue and vice

Myth [page 98]
an ancient story based on supernatural or imagined characters and events, designed to convey a message about human life in general

Narrative perspective / narrative point of view [page 21, 82]
point of view or opinion of the narrator

Narrator [page 23]
the person telling the story, either the writer or a character in the story

New Historical criticism [page 102]
a 20th century school of literary criticism which interprets a text through relating it closely to the historical context in which it was written

Omniscient point of view [page 33]
a third-person narrator, telling a story from the outside and knowing both everything that occurs and the internal workings of all the characters

Open question [page 153]
a form of question which allows the responder to give as much explanation as they choose

Paradox [page 70]
an idea or statement that sounds contradictory but which expresses a truth as the writer sees it, e.g. a moment of happiness which seems never-ending, the idea of a woman as a goddess

Parallel stories [page 90]
two or more narratives in the same text which deepen meaning by mirroring one another

Parody [page 40]
a humorous mockery of a literary text through the use of incongruity

Pastiche [page 167]
an imitation of the style of another author or a collage of a number of different authors' writings

Pathos [page 85]
the pity or deep sympathy a reader is made to feel for a character

Patriarchal [page 151]
originally a system of society governed by wise, older men; it has come to mean a system of society governed by men for the benefit of men

Persona [page 8]
an individual's social façade that reflects a role the person is playing; the characters in a fictional work

Personification [page 12]
the representation of a quality or idea as a human figure or having human characteristics

Perspective (point of view) [page 8]
the way that a writer views something; his/her point of view

Plagiarism [page 176]
to take or use another person's thoughts or writing as one's own

Poetic sequence [page 71]
a succession of poems in a collection which are linked in subject-matter or by a common theme

Psychoanalytical criticism [page 102]
literary criticism based on the theories of the psychologist Sigmund Freud, interpreting human behaviour in terms of the workings of the unconscious mind

Quatrain [page 17]
a stanza comprising of four lines

Realism [page 70]
a type of writing which seems to be true to life, emphasising the external appearance of things

Register [page 19]
a form of language suited to a particular situation or context

Religious allegory [page 105]
a story intended to be interpreted symbolically in theological, usually Christian terms

Rhyming couplets [page 12]
two consecutive lines of poetry which rhyme, typically written in iambic pentametre

Rhythm [page 11]
the pace and pattern of words and sounds in a piece of writing

Satire [page 20]
a literary composition in which contemporary vices or follies are ridiculed

Second-person voice [page 70]
a device for telling a story which uses the 'you' form of address to the reader

Sestet [page 173]
a group of six lines; in Petrarchan sonnet form, the final lines rhyming cdcd

Setting [page 21]
the time, location and circumstances where a narrative or drama occurs

Shakespearean sonnet [page 18]
a type of sonnet (14-line poem) made up of three quatrains and a couplet, rhyming abab/cdcd/efef/gg

Sibilance [page 13]
repetition of 's' sounds

Simile [page 12]
a comparison between two things that are not usually compared, using the words 'as' or 'like'

Slang [page 20]
informal language, usually spoken, often short-lived

Stereotype [page 105]
a character who fits into a conventional, social mould and who represents a particular human trait, e.g. the nosy neighbour, the likeable rogue

Structural pattern [page 16]
the shape given to a text by the way the writer constructs it; the use of genre conventions to create the form of a poem or a narrative

Structuralist [page 151]
approach to literary criticism which does not accept that anything outside of the text is relevant to understanding it – instead focusing on the text's structure

Structure [page 7]
the way that language is put together and given shape

Sub-genre [page 133]
a category which falls under the general heading of a genre

Subject matter [page 7]
the surface meaning of a text, as opposed to its theme

Subordinate clause [page 37]
clauses which function as nouns, adjectives or adverbs in complex sentences

Syntax [page 21]
the arrangement of words in their appropriate form and in the proper order to achieve phrases, clauses or sentences

Temporal [page 164]
relating to time

Textual intervention [page 166]
the process of using a base text as a springboard for creative writing. Intervention may take place before, during or after the development of the base text, or it may involve the use of a base text to develop an original, although related, text

Theatre of the Absurd [page 133]
drama which gives expression to the philosophical notion of the 'absurd', a view of the world which emphasises its mysterious and indecipherable nature

Theme [page 7]
the ideas or issues raised by the story in a narrative or drama

Thesis [page 153]
a proposition to be maintained during the course of a dissertation

Third-person narration [page 24]
a story that relates the events using 'he', 'she' and 'they' to refer to all the characters, though the story can still be told from the point of view of one character only

Tone [page 7]
the character of a voice, the way it expresses feeling

Unreliable narrator [page 44]
a narrator who has a partial or biased view of the events s/he reports and therefore cannot be trusted by the reader to be objective

Villanelle [page 18]
a 19-line poem with an aba rhyme scheme and five three-lined and one four-lined stanzas, in which lines from the first stanza are picked up and repeated in the rest of the poem

Voice [page 21]
an opinion or attitude uttered by someone that reflects that person's identity

Published by Pearson Education Limited, a company incorporated in England and Wales, having its registered office at Edinburgh Gate, Harlow, Essex, CM20 2JE. Registered company number: 872828

Edexcel is a registered trademark of Edexcel Limited

Text © Pearson Education Limited 2009

First published 2009

12 11 10 09

10 9 8 7 6 5 4 3 2 1

British Library Cataloguing in Publication Data

A catalogue record for this book is available from the British Library

ISBN 978 1 84690 250 5

Typeset by H L Studios, Long Hanborough, Oxford

Picture research by Ann Thomson

Cover photo/illustration © Edexcel

Printed in Great Britain by Henry Ling Ltd., at the Dorset Press, Dorchester, Dorset

Acknowledgements

The author wishes to extend grateful thanks to Paul Dean and Mike Ferguson for their consultancy in respect of Unit 4: Reflections in literary studies

We are grateful to the following for permission to reproduce copyright material:

Alan Brodie Representation Ltd for an extract from The Noel Coward Diaries edited by Graham Payne and Sheridan Morley, 1982 copyright © Alan Brodie Representation Ltd; The Arvon Foundation for an extract from Almost a Gentleman: An autobiography, Vol II by John Osborne, from Looking Back by John Osborne published Faber & Faber, reproduced with permission the Arvon Foundation; Barbara Levy Literary Agency for the poems "Base Details" by Siegfried Sassoon from Collected Poems of Siegfried Sassoon, "The Rear-Guard" by Siegfried Sassoon from Here to Eternity: An Anthology of Poetry edited by Andrew Motion 2002 and an extract from Sherston's Progress by Siegfried Sassoon 2004 copyright © Siegfried Sassoon by kind permission of the Estate of George Sassoon; Bloodaxe Books Ltd for the poems "To Virgil" from Out of the Blue: Poems 1975-2000 by Helen Dunmore, Bloodaxe Books, 2001; and "Close" by Imtiaz Dharker from The Terrorist at my Table, Bloodaxe Books, 2006, reproduced by permission of Imtiaz Dharker and Bloodaxe Books Ltd; Bloomsbury Publishing plc for an extract from Down the Clinical Disco, Angel, All Innocence and other Stories by Fay Weldon, 1995; Brooks Permissions for the poem "Sadie and Maud" by Gwendolyn Brooks, reprinted by consent of Brooks Permissions; Canongate Books for extracts from The Life of Pi by Yann Martel published by Canongate Books, reproduced with permission; Curtis Brown Group Ltd for the poems "Invitation" and "Loveact" by Grace Nichols published in Fat Black Woman's Poems copyright © Grace Nichols 1984, reproduced with permission of Curtis Brown Group Ltd; David Higham Associates Limited for the poems "Jigsaws II" by Louis MacNeice, from Collected Poems of Louis MacNeice, Faber and Faber; and "Fern Hill" by Dylan Thomas, from The Poems of Dylan Thomas, Dent, reproduced with permission of David Higham Associates Limited; Faber & Faber Limited for the poems "Harp Strings" by David Harsent published in Legain, 2005; "The Horses" by Ted Hughes published in Collected Poems of Ted Hughes, 2005; "Les Grands Seigneurs" by Dorothy Molloy published in Hare Soup 2004; "The Horses" by Edwin Muir published in Collected Poems of Edwin Muir, 1984; "This Dead Relationship" by Katherine Pierpoint published in Truffle Beds, 1995; "Words" by Sylvia Plath published in Collected Poems of Sylvia Plath, 2002; and extracts from Spies by Michael Frayn, 2003; and The Spire by William Golding, 2005 copyright © Faber & Faber Limited; Granta Books for an extract from Reef by Romesh Gunesekera, 1998 copyright © Granta Books; Guardian News & Media Ltd for extracts from "An afghan hounded by his past" by Amelia Hill, The Observer 7 September 2003 and The Final Passage Book review by Alan Sinclair The Guardian 1985 copyright © Guardian News & Media Ltd 1985, 2003; HarperCollins for an extract from The Dice Man by Luke Rhinehart, reprinted by permission of HarperCollins Publishers Ltd copyright © Luke Rhinehart 1999; Tony Harrison for the poem "Long Distance II" by Tony Harrison published in Tony Harrison Collected Poems by Penguin Books, 2007 copyright © Tony Harrison; Headline for an extract from Small Island by Andrea Levy, 2004 copyright © Headline; Henry Holt, LLC and The Random House Group Ltd for the poem "To E.T." from The Poetry of Robert Frost edited by Edward Connery Lathem, published by Jonathan Cape, copyright © 1923, 1969 by Henry Holt and Company. Copyright 1951 by Robert Frost. Reprinted by permission of The Random House Group Ltd and by arrangement with Henry Holt and Company, LLC; John Murray (Publishers) for the poem "Executive" from Collected Poems by John Betjeman copyright © John Murray (Publishers); Little, Brown Book Group for an extract from Quite Ugly One Morning by Christopher Brookmyre published by Abacus, an imprint of Little, Brown Book Group 1998, reproduced with permission; Nick Hern Books Ltd for the review of Look Back in Anger from Theatre Writings by Kenneth Tynan, edited by Dominic Shellard copyright © Nick Hern Books Ltd 2008; Penguin Books (UK) Ltd for an extract from The Ghost Road by Pat Barker copyright © Penguin Books, 1996; Penrose Literary Agency for the poem 'First Love' by Mick Gowar copyright © Mick Gowar; Pollinger Limited for the poem "The Horse" by William Carlos Williams, reproduced by permission of Pollinger Limited and the Estate of Carlos Williams; The Random House Group Ltd for extracts from Captain Corelli's Mandolin by Louis de Bernieres, published by Vintage; The First Casualty by Ben Elton, published by Bantam Press 2006; and Birdsong by Sebastian Faulks published by Hutchinson. Reprinted by permission of The Random House Group Ltd; Rogers, Coleridge & White Ltd for an extract from 'The Snow Child' from The Bloody Chamber by Angela Carter copyright © 1980 Angela Carter. Reproduced by permission of the author c/o Rogers, Coleridge & White Ltd., 20 Powis Mews, London W11 1JN; Simon & Schuster, Inc and David Higham Associates Limited for an extract from The Great Gatsby by F. Scott Fitzgerald copyright © 1925 by Charles Scribner's Sons. Copyright renewed 1953 by Frances Scott

Picture Credits

Websites
The websites used in this book were correct and up to date at the time of publication. It is essential for tutors to preview each website before using it in class so as to ensure that the URL is still accurate, relevant and appropriate. We suggest that tutors bookmark useful websites and consider enabling students to access them through the school/college intranet.

Disclaimer